More Praise for *The Secrets of Happily Married Men*

"Once in a generation a book is published that changes the discourse about men and marriage. *The Secrets of Happily Married Men* is that book. Dr. Haltzman weaves a compelling yet humorous argument for a man's ability to master the skills necessary for understanding his wife and developing a marriage he can be proud of. Haltzman obviously relishes controversy and has several provocative discussions about traditional feminist-based marriage therapy being unfair to men, as well as the brain- and hormone-based differences between women and men."

—Barry McCarthy, Ph.D., professor of psychology,
American University; author, *Getting
It Right the First Time* and *Rekindling Desire*

"This terrific book is full of stuff you can do (yes, you!). It will guide you in how to connect with your wife in ways that count. She may have bought it, but you need to read it. Get busy. By the way, my wife grabbed this book and read it before I did and she thinks it's wonderful. Maybe you could read it before your wife does! Big points, fella."

—Scott Stanley, marital researcher; author,
The Power of Commitment: A Guide to Active, Lifelong Love,
and co-author, *Fighting for Your Marriage*

"Written in the language of men, this brave, take-no-prisoners, highly practical, pro-marriage book is a must-read for men and women alike. I read it from cover to cover."

—Pat Love, Ed.D., author, *The Truth About Love*

"This book will reach married men (and women) in their minds and hearts. Rather than portraying men as deficient in relationships, Scott Haltzman shows men how to bring their unique strengths to their marriage and how to manage their unique challenges. He blends neuroscience, clinical experience, and everyday stories of men in marriage in a compelling way. A gift to the married men of the world."

—William J. Doherty, Ph.D., professor of family social science,
University of Minnesota; author, *Take Back Your Marriage:
Sticking Together in a World That Pulls Us Apart*

"In a culture that too often blames men and their alleged 'lack of relationship skills' for failing marriages, *Secrets* tells it like it is—men can and often do take successful action to help their marriages. It helps point men in the right direction and tells the truth about how traditional marriage counseling is often an inhospitable environment for men."

—Glenn Sacks, columnist and host of radio
talk show *His Side with Glenn Sacks*

"We live in a world that has largely given up on the idea that men might be fit for family life and cooperative, communicative equality with women. Psychiatrist and marriage therapist Scott Haltzman now comes to the rescue. Scott spends his life listening to men, to the pain and confusion of guys trying to answer Freud's immortal question, 'What does a woman want?' or, more germane, 'What does a woman's therapist or self-help guru want?' Scott has written an invaluable book, crammed with good advice for men on marriage and with cues for women to understand what it feels like to be a man and how men might be useful if everyone would stop trying to fix the fact that they are men. (Scott is well aware that being a man is no excuse for being a pig.) This book should be on the bedside table of any marriage with a man in it."

—Frank S. Pittman III, M.D., author, *Man Enough* and *Grow Up!*

"My wife and I have been married for forty-one years, with never any doubts, and yet, somehow, reading Haltzman's *Secrets* was rewarding. It revealed new things about me, us, and her."

—Gary Sutton, business-turnaround expert; author,
Corporate Canaries

"Finally, the book that every man needs to read and every woman will want her special guy to memorize. This book destroys the myth that men know nothing and care little about how to have a successful relationship. In fact, most men want to be good husbands more than anything else in life. Not only that, but given half a chance we're actually quite good at it. Dr. Haltzman gives us the tools we need to make marriage work. But I warn you, this book is not for the politically correct or for those who think that men need to be fixed. This book celebrates our differences and recognizes that there is nothing more important in life than learning to have a successful marriage. Get a copy for him and for her and for everyone else you care about."

—Jed Diamond, author, *Male Menopause* and
The Irritable Male Syndrome

"Every decade or so, a book about marriage comes along whose perspective is unique, essential, and marriage changing. *The Secrets of Happily Married Men* is that kind of book. Like *Men Are from Mars, Women Are from Venus* and *The Seven Principles for Making Marriage Work*, this book is hard to put down whether you are a woman or a man. It grips you from the first page and challenges you to tell the kinds of secrets that lead to real happier marriages and human love."

—Michael Gurian, author, *What Could He Be Thinking?*,
The Wonder of Boys, and *The Minds of Boys*

The Secrets of Happily Married Men

Eight Ways to Win Your Wife's Heart Forever

Scott Haltzman, M.D.
with Theresa Foy DiGeronimo

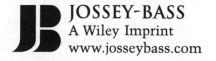

JOSSEY-BASS
A Wiley Imprint
www.josseybass.com

Published by Jossey-Bass
A Wiley Imprint
989 Market Street, San Francisco, CA 94103-1741 www.josseybass.com

The anecdotes in this book are based on Dr. Haltzman's life experience, clinical work, and research. In cases involving client information, names and identifying characteristics have been changed to protect confidentiality.

Jossey-Bass books and products are available through most bookstores. To contact Jossey-Bass directly call our Customer Care Department within the U.S. at 800-956-7739, outside the U.S. at 317-572-3986, or fax 317-572-4002.

Jossey-Bass also publishes its books in a variety of electronic formats. Some content that appears in print may not be available in electronic books.

Library of Congress Cataloging-in-Publication Data
Haltzman, Scott, date.
   The secrets of happily married men : eight ways to win your wife's heart forever / Scott Haltzman with Theresa Foy DiGeronimo.
      p. cm.
   Includes bibliographical references.
   ISBN-13: 978-0-7879-7959-1 (alk. paper)
   ISBN-10: 0-7879-7959-7 (alk. paper)
   1. Husbands—Psychology. 2. Husbands—Conduct of life. 3. Wives—Psychology. 4. Marriage. I. DiGeronimo, Theresa Foy. II. Title.
   HQ756.H34 2005
   646.7'8—dc22
                                              2005013191

Printed in the United States of America
FIRST EDITION
HB Printing   10 9 8 7 6 5 4 3 2

Contents

Acknowledgments   vii

Introduction   1

1. You've Got Male   9

2. Beware of Marriage Counseling   29

3. The First Way: Make Your Marriage Your Job   55

4. The Second Way: Know Your Wife   79

5. The Third Way: Be Home Now   97

6. The Fourth Way: Expect Conflict
   and Deal with It   125

7. The Fifth Way: Learn to Listen   163

8. The Sixth Way: Aim to Please   187

9. The Seventh Way: Understand the Truth
   About Sex   205

10. The Eighth Way: Introduce Yourself   229

Epilogue: Celebrate Your Love   257

Notes   265

About the Authors   275

In memory of my mother, Dolly,
who always told me that
no goal was beyond my reach
and
In honor of my father, Jay,
who taught me more than any textbook could
about what it means to be a great husband

Acknowledgments

I make marriage my job. In the process, I also have made writing about marriage my job. And, as is true of every worthwhile task, many individuals have participated in my success.

My wife, Susan, has been my principal source of inspiration. I thank her for her edits, large and small, of both my writing and my behavior. She has helped me learn how to be a better husband and a better author.

My family is a web of support and a model for how marriages can work against all odds. Thanks to Dad, Matt, Alena, Jonathan, Mark, Jennifer, Bonnie, Shelly, Cliff, Walter, Jane, Amy and Richie, Andy and Karen, Brian and Patricia.

Alan Rinzler is an editor's editor. Alan never accepted the premise that men don't think much about relationships; he pushed me to answer tough questions about who we are as men, and what to do about it. I am forever appreciative of his foresight and wisdom.

Theresa Foy DiGeronimo, my coauthor, displayed a brilliant capacity for keeping me focused and grounded. I am indebted to her for her patient collaboration.

John Martin—journalist, marketer, and tennis partner—deserves special recognition for his writing help. Early on in this endeavor, John helped me find my voice; his influence can still be found throughout the pages of this book.

My secretary, Jennifer Correia, has supported my passion for saving marriages by fielding calls, arranging travel, and handling all the details that escape my attention. As I tell her at the end of each day, "Thanks for all your help."

Betty Galligan, of Newberry PR, helped me spread the word that husbands matter. She worked hard for me, and I appreciate that.

I want to extend thanks to Nancy Ellis, literary agent. Nancy made sure that editors saw my work. She never wavered in her belief that the world needed this book.

Many of my friends have offered me opinions along the way, from "Uggh" to "Bingo!" Special thanks to Michael and Jane Mizrahi, Michael Meyerheim and Judy Nathanson, Bill and Sarah Donohue, Marshall and Therese Sonenshine, John and Abigail Carr, Howard and Nancy Feinglass, Scott Triedman and Mary Jo Kaplan, Mark and Sherra Rego.

Therapists Peter Kramer, Andrew Slaby, John Wincze, Diana Lidofsky, and Russell Pet read early versions of my book. I took every word they said seriously. Their help meant a great deal to me.

Others in my community pitched in to support me, including Rabbi James Rosenberg, Christian Stephens, Nancy Paull, and Pat Emsellem. Thank you.

When I began research into husbands, I discovered a phenomenon called "the Men's Movement." I wish to acknowledge the brotherly support of Bert Hoff, Steve Inman, Mark Hoover, Jed Diamond, Michael Gurian, Glenn Sacks, Scott Garman, and Warren Farrell.

As the book progressed, there were many experts in the marriage movement who were generous with their time. I want to express special appreciation to Julie Baumgardner, Bill Doherty, John Gottman, John Gray, Roger Harms, Janice Levine, Pat Love, Barry McCarthy, Cheryl McClary, Mike McManus, Frank Pittman, Tom and Beverly Rodgers, Rozario Slack, Scott Stanley, John Van Epp, Peggy Vaughan, Michelle Weiner-Davis, and the late Shirley Glass.

None of this would have been possible if a woman named Diane Sollee, founder and director of Smart Marriages, didn't exist. Diane's passion for marriage education inspires so many. "Thanks" doesn't come close to being the right word to express how much her support has meant to me.

In the end, it was all the married folks out there who helped me write this book. My clients, and the thousands of participants in the SecretsofMarriedMen.com community, have been kind enough to share their marital wisdom. What they have taught me has strengthened my marriage. I thank them for giving me the secrets that I can pass on to others.

And did I mention my wife? She's my first, my last, my everything.

The Secrets of Happily Married Men

Introduction

Slam!

That's the sound that one million American men hear each year as their wives push them out the doors of their homes and into the divorce courts. In three generations, the divorce rate has escalated from 14 percent to nearly half of all marriages. But although this "national epidemic" is widely reported, you rarely hear about the fact that it's *women*, at rates much higher than men, who are the ones telling researchers that they are not happy in their marriages.[1] In fact, wives initiate more than two-thirds of the splits.[2]

How can this be? Shouldn't women be fixing relationships rather than declaring them dead? Women are supposed to be the relationship experts. They go to therapists, watch relationship gurus on TV, read magazine articles, or seek answers in self-help books. But still their marriages crumble beneath their feet. Why can't women stem the tide of divorce and make their marriages work? It is because in the vast majority of cases, it's the men that the women are complaining about, so the problems in a marriage won't be solved until *men* do something about improving the relationship.

Husbands must accept this challenge. If they don't, the doors to their homes will irreversibly slam shut behind them. And with the closing of these doors come the devastating consequences of divorce:

broken families, financial devastation, spiritual and physical decline, and damaged children.

DEFEAT IS NOT AN OPTION

Prior to the 1960s, religion and culture prevented most marriages from falling apart. Now attitudes are more liberal. Our culture says, "If you're not happy, get out." And so for many couples, divorce lurks just around the corner every time an argument tears apart the sense of personal bliss.

But divorce is not pretty. It represents the transformation of love, affection, sharing, patience, understanding, and commitment into frustration, anger, distrust, emotional abuse, trauma, grief, and feelings of failure. No one should have to witness marital joy reduced to bitter abandonment of hope.

You don't want to go there. So it's time to reject the idea that marital unhappiness automatically means the relationship is over. When the marriage falters, it's our job as guys, who innately hate to admit defeat, to revive it. We have no other option. Strengthening, improving, and saving a marriage is not something we can do at our leisure. It must be done right, and it must be attended to on a daily—make that an hourly—basis.

But . . . let's face it, when it comes to securing a better relationship, many men don't know where to start. These men may know how to smash a backhand, teach their daughters how to ride a bike or drive a car, pursue advanced educational degrees, and have dynamic careers. Many know how to build their own businesses, navigate a narrow channel through a stormy inlet, negotiate a complicated contract, lead a team of doctors delivering health care in a developing country, or defend a friend from unfounded accusations in a community of peers. However, when they face the biggest challenge of their lives—a collapsing marriage and a complaining wife—the most action many of them can muster is a shrug of their shoulders, which just makes their wives complain more.

Men Can Save Their Marriages

Men don't have to feel so helpless—they can save their marriages. I know. I've worked with hundreds of husbands and surveyed thousands more on the Internet. I've spoken to them in seminars and in support groups. I've interviewed World War I veterans and men just out of college. Each has described times when his marriage was strained. Each has struggled with his place in marriage, questioned his identity as a husband and father, and faced serious challenges to his commitment. Yet through a persistent commitment to fix the problems, these men have saved and improved their marriages.

Unfortunately, far too many men do not have this attitude. They have been conditioned to believe that they can't fix a broken marriage because they lack the necessary skills—and that they lack those skills *simply because they are men*. This book hopes to explode that notion. You possess the means to save your marriage *because you are a man*.

EQUAL BUT VERY DIFFERENT

Men and women are different. In recent years, it's become politically incorrect to utter such a thought out loud. But it's true. Women have tremendous strengths, capacities, skills, and resources that men don't have. And the same is true of men. They are intrinsically, basically, fundamentally different from women in so many ways: their bodies, their hard-wiring, their hormonal and biochemical makeup, their brains—all different. Everyone knows this instinctively, from the gut and the heart. Boys are different to begin with: they develop differently, and they mature with certain strengths and weaknesses that are different from those of women.

Yet, oddly enough, for several decades now, husbands have been encouraged to read books and articles and to listen to "experts" who say that in order to have a good marriage, men have to reason, react, and talk more like women. They tell men they should be softer, kinder, gentler, less intimidating, more sensitive—*and* do more laundry. I've read hundreds of these books and articles and have concluded that it's all bunk.

The reason men avoid self-help marriage experts and make no progress toward improving their relationships is that they get the clear but misguided message that they have to reinvent themselves in order to understand their wives. Most men don't want to do that, and I don't blame them.

I take a different approach. Like most marriage counselors, I certainly will ask you to take stock of the instincts, attitudes, behaviors, and especially the words you use that influence your marriage. But I won't ask you to change anything about yourself.

Let me repeat that: I won't ask you to change anything about yourself. You are okay. Men are okay. You do not have to discover your feminine side in order to become a better husband. You do not have to abandon, dampen, or camouflage any aspect of your personality or way of viewing the world that is commonly described as "male thinking" or "male behavior." You can even remain bullheaded, as long as you are bullheaded about making your marriage better and your life happier.

Evolve or Die?

I honestly believe that men innately possess the skills necessary to succeed at marriage. Being a man is an advantage, not an obstacle. I know this goes against what you read in newspapers and magazines, not to mention the images of husbands depicted in popular culture, and it is an opinion that I guarantee will be met with raised eyebrows in mixed company. In some situations, saying that you are fine just the way you are will be thrown in your face as evidence that men are arrogant, insensitive, and uninterested in understanding women. Indeed, there are some who, upon hearing such a statement, will suddenly see you as shorter and hairier, and wearing a loincloth while carrying a club.

Current thinking is that men need to evolve. We are told constantly that it doesn't count anymore if we're strong and silent, because women expect something different. But I don't believe that women's expectations have really shifted all that much. I'll devote more time to this subject early in this book because it's key to understanding why you really don't need to stop being "a typical guy" to have a good marriage. This evolve-or-die mentality presents a trap for men who attempt to change the tenor of their marriage by living up to some politically correct definition of the New Age husband—in other words, trying to be something they are not.

After more than sixteen years in private practice, I have come to believe that men are born with the ability to make their marriages last for the rest of their lives. They don't necessarily need to unlearn anything. They don't have to stop thinking like a man. They don't need feminizing. They are not, by virtue of their gender, incomplete, incompetent, or incapable of satisfying their spouse's emotional needs. In fact, in one way or another, I tell couples I counsel that if we begin the work of repairing a marriage by assuming that the husband needs fixing, the odds of success are greatly diminished, if not doomed.

I start by reminding couples that men who marry usually do so because of an overwhelming desire to be domesticated. They want to be happily ensconced in an exclusive relationship with a person they chose as more special and deserving of their love than anyone else. During courtship, men are inclined to be romantic, thoughtful, and considerate; they enjoy the challenge of pleasing their chosen mate. They say "I love you" with abandon, and take immense pleasure in connecting with their wives in intimate ways. Most married men—even those whose marriages lay in ruins—demonstrated at one time or another that they have these feelings and can do these things. That's why most women want their marriages to be more like their days of courtship.

So why not give your wife what she wants—and at the same time get from your marriage exactly what you had hoped for the day you said "I do"? This book will give you eight ways to make that happen.

MAN TO MAN

Since becoming a psychiatrist, I've met with thousands of individuals and encouraged them to tell their stories. As they sit across from me, my clients share their fears, joys, and disappointments, but right from the beginning, I noticed that the men I counsel hold back—they struggle to be honest and forthright when talking about their feelings and fears.

This isn't surprising. After all, current American culture provides few opportunities for men to talk about relationships with each other. After the frat house days, a code of silence binds men to secrecy about their intimate lives. We might talk about investment portfolios or last night's game, but marriage-building strategies are almost never shared man to man.

That's why my search for information about relationships led me to the Internet. When I launched my Web site, SecretsofMarriedMen.com, early in 2001, I expected that there would be dozens of Web sites devoted to married men. In fact, mine was the only noncommercial site dedicated to researching and supporting husbands' marriage skills. Slowly over time, people found SecretsofMarriedMen.com through surfing the Web, by word of mouth, or on referral from therapists or marriage educators.

The results were amazing. Through this site I was able to tap into a level of intimacy not found even in the privacy of my psychotherapy practice. I took advantage of computer technology to ask specific questions about men's marriages. I solicited information in the areas of gender roles, sex, infidelity, work, therapy, and gifts. I asked men about their experiences sharing with other men. I inquired about how problems are resolved in the household. I asked how they would define a successful marriage. I wanted to know if most married men considered themselves to be happy.

BREAKING THE BARRIER OF SILENCE

Men wrote openly about the richness of married life—the intensity, the fury, the deceptions, the connectedness, the separateness, and the ecstasy. I got what I was looking for—the answers to my many questions that men would never tell me in face-to-face therapy sessions.

For months, I sorted through the hundreds of posts to my site. Deciding how to compile the contributions amounted to a tremendous challenge. Is this comment about sex or about infidelity? Is that one a confession about past sins or a pre-wedding warning to others? Pro-marriage or antiwoman? Contented or complacent? Not surprisingly, categorizing each comment eluded any simple formula. In the end, I chose to group the contributions into eight different ways that men have found helpful in building and keeping strong, loving marriages. This collection eventually evolved into this book.

The thousands of men who have contributed to Secretsof MarriedMen.com have broken the silence barrier. I am indebted to all of them for sharing themselves with me and for allowing me to share their lives with you. In loud, clear messages, they have told me that men do have the skills necessary to build strong and loving relationships. And through their discussions and comments, they have revealed to me a remarkable phenomenon: when these men worked hard to improve their marriages by using their inborn manly skills to put their wives' needs above their own, not only did their marriages improve, but they were happier and more fulfilled than at any other point in their lives.

This is the secret of happily married men.

1

You've Got Male

I jumped into the cab, hoping to catch a quick ride from one side of Rhode Island to the other. During the thirty-minute trip, I fell into an easy conversation with the cabbie and soon learned that he was typical of so many men I know—great at managing and negotiating the complexities of life in general, but insecure and frustrated in his marriage.

At first he told me, with great pride, about his car. He planned to replace the horns because of water buildup. He talked about needing to get the transmission rebuilt and how he was able to strike a good deal. Did you know he paid $1,500 for the job on a Buick that had almost 300,000 thousand miles on it?!

Soon, the banter shifted to family (probably because I can't help asking people, "So, are you married?"). My cab driver told me that he had two sons and that he had been married for twenty years. Losing the bravado of our earlier conversation, he quietly admitted that he'd been separated from his wife for the last two years.

"My wife and I just can't agree on the right way to raise the kids," he said with a sigh that gave away his frustration and resignation. "I didn't want to separate, because I think it's the coward's way out," he was quick to add. "But I just couldn't figure out how to make things better."

Usually, as a psychiatrist, I'm the one with the meter running. But during this impromptu session, I was paying for *his* time, and before we arrived on the other side of Rhode Island, I had something important to say to this man. Here's the short version:

> You're a creative man who has a marvelous knack for fixing things. If something's not working in your car, you figure out a way to fix it. If you can't, you find someone who can. You've stuck with your car when most owners would have sent it to the trash heap. You have a real sense of commitment and a knack for getting things to work. What makes you think you can't use those same wonderful qualities to save your marriage?

When my trip was over ($60!) and my little speech done, my driver look startled, but also relieved, as he said, "No one's ever told me that before, Doc. Thanks."

For a long while, I thought about this conversation and about many similar discussions I've had with my patients and colleagues. It's obvious to anyone who studies male behavior that men demonstrate extraordinary skill in sales, mechanics, politics, medicine, finance, construction, and many other areas. So why is it, I have to wonder, that when it comes to problems in relationships, men resign themselves to their fate, act helpless, and give up? After long thought and study, I think I know.

For too long, men have been told that they are relationship-incompetent. Maybe that's what you've heard, and maybe that's what you believe. I'm telling you now, loud and clear, it's not true. *You are competent.* I've got a little more time with you than I did with my driver, so let's talk about *you* for a while.

It's a sure bet that if I were to ask her, your wife would say that you do not contribute as much as she does to the success of your marriage. Find two women talking to each other, and you're likely to hear them joke about how their guys are so useless. You know it's true. Most women are quite vocal about the "fact" that men do not uphold their end of the matrimonial bargain because they simply do not meet the women's standards.

Just one question: Who determined what these standards should be? I have a strong feeling that the finger of blame for unhappy and crumbling marriages most often points to the male because of unrealistic and unattainable expectations. I'm the first to admit that men bear at least an equal share in the blame department, and I've got some ideas about how we men can better contribute to the job of building strong relationships. But first we have to get past the idea that to have a good marriage, men have to be something they are not. Yes, you can have a happy marriage and still be a man.

> **Psst!** ———————————————————————
>
> ## SecretsofMarriedMen.com
>
> I think men and women truly see different things in the same experiences. And the more intimate we are, the more important those different ways of interacting become. Unfortunately, I've found that the differences in perception cause the interactions to go so badly so much of the time.
>
> —Ned, age 45, married 11 years

THE MEDIA MAN

Where does the image of a "typical" man come from? Turn on your TV and there he is. On any night of the week, on any channel, you'll see sitcom husbands who are clueless when it comes to marriage. Generally they are out of shape and uncouth, and can't match a shirt to a tie, but, hey, they have gorgeous wives! These television caricatures get their comeuppance every episode because they are men—inflexible, selfish, shortsighted, overbearing men who have to be humbled before they can behave appropriately. Most sitcom wives have little role beyond providing a means of measuring a man's gender-determined marital inadequacies.

It is fashionable in today's culture to poke fun at the hapless man who is more enamored of his remote control than his spouse. Homer

Simpson, Ray Romano, Jim Belushi, and a host of other sitcom husbands and fathers are consistently redeemed by their more clever and sensitive wives, thus keeping the marriage on track. Even a blowhard tyrant like Ralph Kramden can be easily tamed by Alice, a woman who knows the exact moment to give him his just deserts and still earn the heartfelt declaration that she is the greatest. The message is clear: Ralph never contributes to the good of the relationship on his own because he so totally lacks Alice's relationship skills.

Hollywood movies are equally unrealistic, but from the other extreme viewpoint. They mold their leading men to get the girl by being sensitive, intuitive, romantic, and well . . . more like a woman than a man. (This image was not found in most movies of the mid-twentieth century, when the likes of John Wayne and Clark Gable were allowed to be manly men.)

Now, I happen to like Tom Hanks as an actor and humanitarian. But when I think about the character he plays opposite Meg Ryan in *You've Got Mail*, I'm reminded of the typically skewed image of men and the feminine ideal of marriage that our society embraces. Hanks plays an arrogant businessman whose bookstore chain threatens to put Ryan's quaint shop out of business. Unknown to either, they are already anonymous email pen pals. He is unbearably pompous and obnoxious, until love turns him into a sensitive, attentive, and selfless gentleman—in short, the perfect catch. This film, like many in the chick-flick genre, projects a classic example of how Hollywood perpetuates a standard for men's behavior in a relationship that is drawn wholly from the woman's point of view.

When couples have finished watching that movie, you can almost see the mental bubble captions over their heads. Hers reads, "God, I loved that movie and the way falling in love made Tom Hanks's character become so much more 'human.'" His says, "Hmm. If we hurry, I can catch the fourth quarter of the Knicks-Celtics game."

But somewhere also resonating in the guy's mind is the message, "Gee, if I were just more like Tom Hanks, I would have a happier marriage." But we men aren't all like Tom Hanks. It's a ridiculous standard. I'll bet even Tom Hanks isn't like Tom Hanks.

Psst!

SecretsofMarriedMen.com

Men and women do not communicate on the same level. There have been so many times in the past five years that I have tried to talk about important things when my husband is sitting quietly thinking, or drinking coffee, or anything. I get no response. That makes me think he's ignoring me and that I am just talking to a brick wall. I have learned, though, that our brains do not work the same. Our makeups are so different. That's why patience is such an important key in marriage.

—Natalie, age 23, married 5 years

NO WONDER WE FAIL

When we examine Hollywood's portrayal of romance, whose reality are we talking about? Tinsel Town and the media in general convey feminine standards of romance that are tailor-made and marketed to the sensitivities and expectations of women. In other words, they perpetuate expectations that are nearly impossible for men to meet. No wonder we fail.

And when we do, where does the finger of blame point? Common wisdom says that when couples fall apart, men are to blame, as author Jack Kammer confirmed in a survey of his university students. When the class was confronted with the statistic that 75 percent of women precipitate divorce, his students concluded that the man must be at fault. When given the opposite (false) statistic that 75 percent of divorces are precipitated by men, the class still voted that it must be the man's fault.[1]

Obviously, we can't win. When emotions are involved, males rarely get the benefit of the doubt—even as young kids. A classic study tried an interesting experiment to note the way babies were viewed by adults based on their gender alone. In this study, parents watched a videotape of a nine-month-old child reacting to a startling jack-in-the-box. Some were told they were watching "Dana," whereas others were told they were watching "David," although it was the same baby in both cases. The majority interpreted the baby's startled reaction to the jack-in-the-box as "anger" when they thought the child was a boy, and as "fear" when they thought it was a girl. Even when it comes to babies of nine months, people assume that females need to be protected and nurtured and males need to be tamed and lassoed in.[2]

With so much going against us, it's easy to react the way my taxi driver did: throw our hands in the air and say, "Fine, you win. I just can't be the kind of husband you want." But wait. Maybe if we stop trying to meet impossible expectations, we'd be better able to be true to ourselves and still be good husbands.

Psst!

SecretsofMarriedMen.com

Wives shouldn't expect lots of emotive displays from their husbands. Testosterone gets in the way of how a man feels. Unless it's a feeling of aggression (which men can, and do, feel), men usually don't want to talk about feelings even if the marriage is good, alive and thoughtful. That's just the way they're made.

—Christine, married 28 years

MEN AND WOMEN *ARE* DIFFERENT

In the 1960s and 1970s, the woman's liberation movement in America opened our eyes to the cultural biases against women. No longer would females be content to be nothing more than adoring eye candy at the side of their husbands. The message was trumpeted throughout the land: men and women are equal.

Although the lasting positive gains of this movement are undeniable in the workplace, in civil rights, in the courts, and in our homes, militant feminists were, and still are, working from a false platform. Women should certainly be considered equals to men, but women are not the same as men. There are biological differences in our mental and physical makeup that cannot be denied or ignored in our quest to understand each other.

To make your marriage great without giving up who you are, it's important to recognize that some of your so-called failings as a husband are very often not failings at all, but simply the result of the fact that you and your wife do not think and feel the same way.

To dissect the ways in which males and females are biologically different, we'll start with the seat of personality, the brain. The brain comprises two sides, the left and right hemispheres. Most folks, even left-handers, are left-brain dominant. The left brain is associated with linear and sequential thought; it's the part of the brain that puts things together piece by piece by piece. The left brain is also the part of the brain that controls the comprehension and expression of speech. When a person dissects speech word for word to determine its meaning, he uses his left brain.

In contrast, the right brain is more intuitive and holistic. It ignores the parts and sees the whole. When you solve problems through hunches or impulse, you are using your right brain. It's also the side of the brain that houses such skills as reading maps and reading expressions.

All brains contain both hemispheres and the connecting fibers between them. But not all brains are alike in all ways; otherwise we'd all think and act like one another. Recent scientific studies have shown not only that brains differ from one individual to another but also that there are profound differences in the development of the male and female brain.

Here are some of the most interesting findings:

- Before a child is even born, there are noticeable brain differences between the sexes. At six weeks in utero, the male brain gets a large dose of the male hormone testosterone, which changes the brain permanently and determines sexual identity.

- Some scientists believe that our early understanding of male and female gender roles is inborn, caused by the fact that in the womb males are exposed to higher levels of androgens, and females to higher levels of estrogens. The belief that this influences gender roles is based on research done with opposite-sex twins who naturally share both the androgen and estrogen hormones. In these cases, the male tends to have more feminine attributes (lower levels of activity, loudness, confidence, intensity, and selfishness) than his male peers, and the female twin exhibits more masculine attributes (better spatial and mathematical abilities and increased dominance and sensation-seeking behavior) than her female peers. Researchers believe that these results are caused by the transfer of androgen and estrogen hormones from one fetus to another. This finding supports those who believe that at least some male-female differences are the result of hormone exposure in the womb and not the result of social conditioning alone.

- The male brain is 10 percent larger in mass than the female brain. Much of that larger mass is white

matter—the stuff that surrounds the nerve cells.
In contrast to men, women have a higher percentage of
gray matter—the actual source of brain activity.

- The cerebral cortex contains neurons that influence
  intelligence and memory and that interpret sensory
  input. This region is thicker in males on one specific
  part of the right side of the brain: the area associated
  with spatial skills, such as measuring, mechanical
  design, perceiving direction, map reading, and working
  with blocks or other objects. These are skills that males
  usually excel in throughout life.

- In contrast, women enjoy a broad range of verbal
  brain processes. Brain scan images that reveal how
  we use our brains show that women use multiple areas
  of their brain, on the left and right side, to process
  speech. Men, on the other hand, are limited to only
  two areas, both located in the left brain. In tests of
  verbal ability, study after study shows superiority in
  women.

- Parts of the connecting band of fibers, the corpus
  callosum, are larger in women. As we will see in
  later chapters, better developed pathways between the
  two hemispheres may enhance the female's ability to
  integrate information from the logical (left) brain
  with the intuitive (right) brain and allow women
  to use both parts of the brain when processing
  information.[3]

There certainly are still many who claim that the superior male
abilities coming out of the right brain are nurtured by teachers and
parents who give males more attention and praise when they
practice these skills, but we just can't ignore the strong evidence
that the male's advanced spatial skills are inborn. When men work

REMEMBER THIS
Not Everyone Agrees

There is biological evidence that women and men are different. There is no debate that men have penises and women don't. Men are generally taller and have deeper voices than women. Men have hair on their chest and face; women do not. Agreed? But dare to suggest that the brains of males and females may be different, and the world will condemn you as a brutish fool. Just ask Lawrence H. Summers, president of Harvard. In January 2005, Summers offended women at an academic conference of the National Bureau of Economic Research by suggesting that innate differences between the sexes may explain why fewer women succeed in science and math careers. He further noted that such differences might stem from biological roots. Female academics were furious—as demonstrated by Nancy Hopkins, a biology professor at MIT who walked out of in the middle of Summer's speech saying, "I felt I was going to be sick."[4] Front-page news stories threw rocks, and intellectuals around the country wondered aloud why Summers felt women were so inferior. All the man did was note that there is research supporting the idea that the brain of a male is different from that of a female. Many people are not yet ready to accept this idea.

on visual-spatial tasks, their testosterone levels surge—and they get better results, on average, than females. Perhaps that's why men are more inclined to seek work that involves visual-spatial excellence, such as jobs as pilots or carpenters.[5] And perhaps football coaches . . . Talking about Bill Belichick (the man who led the Patriots to three Super Bowls in four years), a news article notes that his friend Rob Ingraham points directly to his perception and insight. "Perhaps his most unheralded virtue," says Ingraham, "but one that explains plenty to me, is his innate curiosity. Bill wants to know what makes things tick, and when applied to his passion for football, this extends to every facet of the game: 'What makes this blitz work? How do you counter this blitz? How can you disguise this blitz? How can we vary this blitz? Who can I call tonight to talk blitzes with?' . . . No stone goes unturned because his curiosity drives him to learn everything he can."[6] This drive to know what makes things tick, common to so many of us men with our strong right brains, says more about our innate abilities than all the research out there.

As Dr. Summers of Harvard pointed out in his controversial comments, the preponderance of the evidence does show that men are endowed with a larger right frontal lobe[7] and more innate mechanical competence. But this doesn't mean women don't have their own special right-brained skills. Earlier, I spoke about how the ability to express speech was housed in the left brain. In contrast, the ability to interpret emotion and comprehend nonverbal messages is housed in a right-brain area (apart from the visual-spatial centers) where women reign supreme. To study these differences, researchers expose subjects to photographs of the classic expressions of fear, happiness, surprise, anger, and sadness, and monitor their brains as they describe what they see. Males are at their worst when they are in adolescence; study participants were consistently unable to recognize when someone expressed fear. (That's why social scientists think that boys are more inclined to rowdiness; boys don't realize when they have gone too far because they can't read the fear in people's faces.) But even into adulthood, it is harder for men to discern facial expressions. In almost all cases, women dominate interpretation.[8] I know this myself because my wife will recognize emotions in me long before I even know I am having them.

Some say that we're failing to socialize females to be more right-brain dominant. Maybe, but I don't think that socialization is

responsible for the greater brain mass in the right hemisphere seen
in almost all male primates. Anthropologists and social researchers
have proposed that some of these differences are the product of
prehistoric gender-role differences, still seen in the few remaining
hunter-gatherer cultures. Greater spatial ability among males was
necessary for long hunting expeditions away from home (talking
would just scare away the prey). Women benefited from their better
capacity to use words to coordinate their search for edible plants and
roots; details of the immediate area that surrounded her living space,
including the emotional states of her children, were paramount.

I'm convinced that biology is destiny (Freud said that first, not
me), and we have to pay attention to these differences. To me, the
right upper cortex of the brain endows me with the perfect way to
understand the world through its physical form. The problem is, my
less developed verbal centers and my smaller corpus callosum make
it tough for me to talk about it!

GUILTY AS CHARGED

Some of the complaints that wives lodge against their husbands are
based in truth. We are, indeed, not like them, and these differences
can drive some women crazy.

The nature-versus-nurture debate will not be resolved any time
soon. But when it comes to how husbands and wives live together,
I believe that it doesn't make much difference whether the preference of the man of the house for tinkering with household objects
over buying shoes is caused by the way he was raised or by the hormone he was exposed to in utero. Either way, the fact is that there
are typical "male" ways of acting.

Of course, not all men have all the characteristics of this stereotype, but what follows is my understanding of what researchers of
social behavior have learned about why we men are the way we are.
Consider this information not as the gospel truth but as a way of
observing human behavior to better understand who we are as men.

And because of who we are, women too often complain that we're not more like them.

Women Say: Men Don't Reach Out and Form Close Social Relationships

Men's social roles do not focus on relationship development as a primary objective; improving a relationship is a means to an end. When two men get together, they establish a hierarchy of interaction based on one-upping the other. Maybe it's the call of the wild. We've all seen on the Animal Channel how the rams fight each other for dominance. Some of that instinct is alive and well in the human male.

Barbara Tannen, author of *You Just Don't Understand*, says, "The essential element of status [among men] is asymmetry: People are not the same; they are differently placed in a hierarchy." She contrasts this with the woman's mind-set, in which "the essential element of connection is symmetry: People are the same, feeling equally close to each other."[9] This difference in mind-set explains why it less likely that a man would build a close relationship for the sheer joy of doing so. If a woman doesn't understand this, she's likely to see her man as fatally flawed, rather than as in need of her help to learn how establishing closeness with her would benefit him.

Women Say: Men Just Aren't as Emotional as Women

Up to this point, we've discussed the cerebral cortex—the part of the brain associated with thinking and acting. But much of the human brain runs on autopilot. This inner core of the brain doesn't differ much from mammal to mammal; it contains the centers that control respiration, temperature, balance, and those activities that are thought of as "instinctual." Deep within this core is an almond-size section of the brain called the amygdala. The amygdala is in charge of making emotional connections to life events.

Although the amygdala is larger in men than in women, this is a case where bigger isn't necessarily better. The amygdala scans the signals that enter the brain and stands sentry, ready to light up in recognition of a friendly smile, or send out an alarm if it perceives any threats. When triggered, the amygdala releases a flood of stress hormones into the bloodstream. This flooding shuts down the "thinking" part of the brain, freezes the body to prepare for assault, and prepares the memory centers to retain any necessary information for future reference.

Up to this point in the process, guys and dolls have the same physiological processes, but our brains differ in several important ways. Studies suggest that females are more sensitive and responsive to social cues, including threat signals, than are males. That's why she's more likely to have a visceral response to upsetting signals, especially if they come from your angry face.

REMEMBER THIS
The Brain Is the Largest Sex Organ

Researchers find that men's amygdalas are much more reactive than women's when exposed to sexual stimuli. Remember that when this brain center gets activated, it shuts down the normal operating procedure of the thinking part of the brain, the cortex!

This difference between men's less responsive reaction to threat signals and a women's more sensitive alarm system may be one reason why women don't think we are as emotional.

Another reason is that even when our emotional reactions are equally strong, men tend to be better able to shut down their amygdala and redirect their brain activity back to the cortex— the place where logical thought takes over. This may seem like emotional coldness to women, but to men it may be a way of making sure our emotions don't get in the way of getting the job done.

Men may also have internal mechanisms to dampen the seriousness of frightening thoughts. MRI scans have shown that when given two sets of words, one neutral and the other designed to stimulate intense negative emotion, men relied on their left brains and didn't discern a difference between the two sets of words. In contrast, women's right and left brains were involved in recalling both sets of words, and emotional centers were activated when the intense words were recalled. Moreover, women (not men) had an increase in blood flow to the area of the brain that stores memory when negative emotions were triggered. Apparently, women are not only deeply hurt by words, but they implant those slights in their memory for . . . who knows how long?

That's not to say that men can't, or don't, experience negative emotions. In fact, studies show his amygdala is much more responsive to sadness than his wife's. But unlike women, men will shut down the amygdala to keep the cortex in control and thus appear ever confident and emotionally stable.[10]

Women Say: Men Are Not Good Housewives

Lots of men are very good at lots of things. Most can competently care for their kids. Many do the family laundry. And many men can maintain strict organization of their CD collection, *and* recite all the songs in order on *Abbey Road*. So why is it that so many of us fall apart when we're left alone to keep house and watch the kids for the day?

If you're one of those guys who burns dinner while the baby is screaming to be changed, and then loses it all when the doorbell rings and your neighbor wants a rundown on the big game, you'll be glad to hear that once again the reason for this chaotic state may lie in the way your brain is structured.

Keep in mind that every brain in every person is different, but as we noted before, women on average have more gray matter in their brain than men. Gray matter is composed of nerve cells that make connections between other cells to move information around in the brain. Scientists have found that besides having more of these important cells, women also have a greater number of connections between these cells than men do. No, there's not a direct correlation between the number of nerve connections and how easily a person can attend to many demands at one time, but scientists do theorize that one reason a woman can manage better is because there are many more areas of her brain that process information at once. A woman's brain is more like a shotgun, a man's more like a rifle. She sends so many nerve messages with each impulse that she's more likely to hit several targets at once.

Another reason some men do not multitask as well as their wives do may have to do with that brain bridge I spoke about earlier: the corpus callosum. When the man's well-endowed right hemisphere—the visual-spatial area—is hard at work, you'll notice he's not talking. That's because the right side of the brain is slow

REMEMBER THIS
We Are Not Slaves to Biology

The function and structure of the brain partly explains why you and your wife think differently about so many things. However, it's important to remember that the biological foundation of human differences accounts for only a portion of who we are and how we act. Women can train themselves to love math; men can learn to be adept at interpreting emotion. We are affected by our biology, yes, but we are not slaves to it.

in moving information over to the left side of the brain, where the verbal centers are nestled. One of the reasons men have to turn off the car radio when they are lost is to cut down on interference between the (right) side of the brain that says, "If I turn left here, will I be able to detour around the construction?" and the (left) side of the brain that is trying to decipher the lyrics to "Bennie and the Jets."

Women Say: All Men Think About Is Sex

Without a doubt, men and women are biologically different in the sex department. These distinctions stem from gender-based differences in hormone levels. Hormones are the chemicals that are produced in one part of the body and race through our blood to other organs, causing changes in the delicate balance of our behavior—and our desire for sex. For men, it's testosterone that fuels the drive.

Testosterone is produced in the testes and flows through the blood to affect the functioning of nearly every other organ system, from cholesterol levels to muscle strength to brain function. This hormone is the reason why your wife is right: you do think about sex far more often than she does—because you have ten to twenty times more testosterone flowing through your system than she does, causing you to have more thoughts of sex and a greater desire for sex (most of the time) than your wife.

Although testosterone also contributes to an increased tendency to be competitive and even aggressive, and affects energy levels, motivation, and drive, evolutionary endocrinologists think that its influence on the sex drive is the most pronounced. They speculate that this has something to do with why married men, and other men in committed relationships, have a 20 percent drop in their testosterone—to help keep them from straying.[11]

There are a great many ways in which the brain and certain body chemicals influence the way men act and the way they see the world. In later chapters you'll see how higher testosterone levels make men more aggressive than women and less able to hold eye-to-eye contact. You'll learn that levels of other hormones are responsible for our strong need to bravely protect our homes and our mates (as well as our occasional desire to wander away from home). You'll learn about oxytocin, a bonding hormone that surges when a man has an orgasm (dispelling the myth that men aren't looking for emotional connection in the sex department). You'll come to understand that men are different from women but that this does not make them incompetent husbands or lovers.

SecretsofMarriedMen.com

After twelve months of counseling with a psychologist and after reasonably extensive reading, I am coming to suspect that men do think, feel, react and perceive a lot of things very differently than women. Especially related to emotions and sexual interactions! It is probably a particularly accurate partial explanation of some of the "challenges" experienced by my husband and me these last couple years. I believe that females can most assuredly learn a lot about their other half by paying attention to biologic differences. And I also think that husbands (specifically mine) can better deal with the problems in their relationships by recognizing these differences.

—Barbara, age 44, married 20 years

TIME FOR A CHANGE

I've described to you a small portion of the reams of research that make it very clear that we men differ from women and have been unfairly judged in our marriages. Ready to do something about that? Good. Because although this book challenges some of the unrealistic and unfair standards that I believe can be unattainable, that doesn't mean you can just stand there and do nothing.

No, men are not blameless here. And I'm not simply "making excuses" for bad or wrong behavior. When I say that the definitions of romance and marriage are one-sided, I am not necessarily saying that men have a more reasonable grasp of the subject. The truth is that the average husband, unless pressed for answers, does not actively think much about relationships.

In his *Complete Guide to Guys,* humorist Dave Barry compares men's relationship savvy to an ant's view while standing on top of a big truck tire. The ant knows he is sitting on a tire, but he can't fully comprehend it. "And if the truck starts moving, and the tire starts to roll, the ant will sense that something important is happening, but right up until he rolls around to the bottom and is squashed into a small black dot, the only distinct thought that will form in his tiny brain may be, and I quote, '*Huh?*'"[12]

Barry is wildly popular because there is logic behind his humor. He says that men act this way because they have "guy brains." Guy brains, he says, are basically analytical, problem-solving organs. Barry didn't make this up—his ideas could have come out of a neuropsychology text. Men like things that are definite, measurable, and specific. Accordingly, they don't automatically think about romance, relationships, and marriage nearly as much as they think about earned-run averages, gigabytes of memory, mortgage refinancing rates, and the advantages of leasing over buying a car. But just because they don't think about romance doesn't mean they can't be romantic.

What I am offering in this book is permission, if you will, for husbands and wives to consider the advantages of redefining their relationship in new and different ways. I'm suggesting that you identify differences between you and your spouse—some of which I believe are determined by gender—and get past feminized and idealized notions of the "perfect" marriage. Once you do this you can stop feeling inadequate, apply your "guy brain," and begin improve your marriage.

Here are some words of wisdom that I'll impart as I end this chapter about being male, words I didn't get a chance to pass on to my cabbie friend: you don't have to measure up to someone else's standards, especially when they're almost impossible to reach. Hollywood, TV, and women's magazines set the bar for what men ought to be at such an intimidating height, it's no wonder we buy into the notion that men are duds when it comes marriage. But contrary to media images, husbands bring extraordinarily positive qualities to a relationship. Although these manly strengths may not be easy to find in movies at your local Blockbuster Video, I know they exist. I see them all the time in the men who come into my practice looking for ways to improve their marriages, and I hear about them from the thousands of men who have shared their thoughts on my Web site, SecretsofMarriedMen.com.

Unfortunately, one of the most time-honored means of breaking down the barriers that keep men and women from understanding each other—couple's therapy—too often encourages that negative view of men as incompetent bumblers. In the next chapter, we'll take a look at the reasons why couple's therapy can sometimes be the worst thing for a marriage.

2

Beware of Marriage Counseling

Sure, things in Jack's marriage aren't perfect. Yes, they could be a lot better. Of course he loves his wife and wants to learn how to improve their relationship. Okay, he'll go to a marriage counselor if that's what his wife thinks is the best thing for their marriage.

So thirty-four-year-old Jack and his wife attend therapy together. For Jack, it's a rewarding experience. He writes to my Web site, "Couples therapy forces me (and us) to be intentional about expressing my (our) internal state. It has been quite fruitful to see how we do this differently, how we process our experiences, and how we make decisions. It is in our differences that we deepen our sensitivity to one another. No other person has seen the depths of my goodness and the depths of my depravity more than my wife has. Marital counseling is the place where that dichotomy is accepted and loved."

What a great way to feel about the benefits of therapy.

Jack's friend Bob lives across the country. He's not really all that keen on therapy, but he has talked to Jack every once in a while about life since their fraternity days. He hears about Jack's satisfaction with therapy and decides that's just what his marriage needs also. And so with blind faith and optimism, Bob and his wife walk into the therapist's office and begin an exploration of their relationship. They start to explore their inner feelings, their hurts, and their expectations of the other. But, as the treatment progresses, Bob finds that his marriage isn't improving. He gets more frustrated as the counseling just seems to stir up bad feelings between him and his wife. Session after session, he leaves feeling unappreciated; she leaves feeling unloved. Bob knows therapy is supposed to help, but he begins to dread the usual Tuesday night meeting. He gets more anxious, feels less in control, and argues more than ever. Now, in addition to the other conflicts he and his wife were dealing with, they argue about therapy as well!

How can this be? Bob's a good guy. He went with the best of intentions—it was even his idea. Isn't marriage therapy supposed to help? Supposed to, yes. But it doesn't always. In this chapter we'll take a close look at counseling. We'll talk about how it can help your marriage. But we'll also take a good, hard look at the reasons why therapy often lets men down when it comes to marriage. We'll see why it sometimes asks them to become something they are not and reinforces their wives' expectation that if the guy doesn't change for her, he just doesn't care enough. We'll also explore how therapists must change their approach in order to bring about positive changes in marriage.

THE WONDERS OF THERAPY

For about eight hours each day I see clients—individuals and couples—in my office for therapy. As a psychiatrist, I sometimes use medications to treat major mental illnesses. But even when pharmacological management is called for, my treatment almost always includes talk therapy. The clients and I talk about things that are going on in their lives. We talk about how their past experiences affect the way they look at life. And we focus on what their strengths are and how to use these strengths to feel better about their situations and themselves.

There's a lot to be said for the power of talk therapy. Sometimes, as we'll see in Chapter Seven, having someone in your life to listen to you can have amazingly powerful healing properties. Some people benefit greatly from insight-oriented therapy, which helps them clear out the ghosts from their emotional closets and find new ways to see old problems.

Cognitive-behavioral therapy is also frequently helpful. It differs from insight-oriented therapy in that it helps people improve their coping skills, not through gaining awareness into why they are the way they are (for example, this form of therapy doesn't pay much attention to how you developed a fear of elevators), but through specific techniques that will help people gain back a sense of control (by having you gradually, step-by-step, begin to get on elevators again). This therapy has been proven helpful to many individuals who are paralyzed by their anxiety or negative moods.

I've spoken to many people who have expressed appreciation for how these strategies have helped them either individually or as a couple. But too often that potential is never realized, and, as in Bob's case, marriage problems continue or worsen.

REMEMBER THIS
There's Nothing Wrong with Going to Therapy Because "My Wife Sent Me"

Many men enter my office for individual therapy, not because of any perceived internal conflicts; they come because, they say, "My wife sent me. She thinks I need help." I welcome these men with enthusiasm. I let them know that if their wife thinks they need help, then they do—at least insofar as it shows the wife that her husband cares enough about the relationship to give therapy a try. I don't usually leave it at that, though. At some point, I invite the wife to come in so that I can hear in her words how she sees the problem.

THE PROBLEM WITH COUPLES THERAPISTS

It's tough to get two people in a room together to talk. It's hard for two people to work on painful issues. It's difficult for two individuals to understand the other's pain, or the histories of how and why they are the way they are. There are many reasons why couples therapy is challenging. But the problem on the top of my list is the therapists themselves.

I know this statement won't make me very popular with the many social workers, family therapists, psychologists, or psychiatrists in my community. But I'm not interested in being popular; I'm interested in making sure that if you (or your wife, or both of you) seek therapy for your marriage, you know what you are getting yourself into. All psychotherapists are taught some form of family or couples therapy. I myself partook of several seminars on the subject and had a social work supervisor during my fellowship in psychiatry. I thought it was good training. But was it enough for me to know how to counsel couples? I used to think so, but I was wrong.

The Problem with Licensing

The American Psychological Association allows any licensed therapist to hang out a shingle advertising himself or herself as a "marriage counselor" or "couples therapist." The most current statistics show that 81 percent of all private practice therapists in the United States say they do marital therapy. But only about 12 percent of them are certified marriage and family therapists who were required to take course work in this field or have had supervised clinical experience in marital or couples therapy.[1] In other words, most "marriage counselors" are operating on a combination of old textbooks and life experience to guide them in their therapeutic techniques. In the words of Dr. William Doherty, a psychologist who researches this aspect of therapy, "From a consumer point of view, coming in for couples therapy is like having your broken leg set by a doctor who skipped ortho-pedics in medical school."[2]

The Problem with Emphasizing Personal Rights

A second problem with marriage counseling is the emphasis on per-sonal rights and happiness. In individual psychotherapy (the type in which the majority of couples therapists are trained), the emphasis often is on shedding those things that are obstacles to personal peace and growth. For many clients, such an exploration into the "self" can be enlightening and liberating. Unfortunately, the therapist who uses this model for counseling a troubled marriage operates on the wrong premise.

Marriage isn't just about you and your self-actualization as a separate individual. Marriage isn't all about resolving your conflicts from childhood or providing support for your needs solely. That kind of self-centered, selfish, and immature approach too often pushes one or both partners to view their mate as an impediment to their personal growth. When spouses think "me" and "mine" instead of "us" and "ours," they end up choosing the short-term route to personal happiness through divorce rather than the longer and often more difficult road to saving the marriage.

Marriage can contribute to your happiness; intact partnerships are associated with longer life and better mental health. It is in negotiating the hills and valleys of living your life with one indi-vidual, and in enduring the challenges of raising your family with that person, that you develop a deeper and fuller sense of the self.

Marriage is a crucible for character building. It tests one's self-lessness, interaction, learning, devotion, and commitment. I know it's tempting to look at yourself, as you do in one-on-one therapy, and aim like the dickens to get what you want out of your marriage by ironing out all your faults and your mate's faults as well. But you will learn, as you proceed through this book, that setting your sights on nurturing the marriage, not yourself, is the surest way to attain happiness.

Consider the thoughts of Thorton Wilder in his play *The Skin of Our Teeth:* "I didn't marry you because you were perfect. I didn't even marry you because I loved you. I married you because you gave me a promise. That promise made up for your faults. And the promise I gave you made up for mine. Two imperfect people got married and it was the promise that made the marriage. And when our children were growing up, it wasn't a house that protected them; and it wasn't our love that protected them—it was that promise."[3]

I recently gave a presentation at a public seminar called Marriage CPR. In advance of the talk, I tried to drum up an audience by asking therapists for referrals. "I have one couple," said a clinician I work with, "but they're too far gone. They have no hope for reconciliation." Ouch! No couple willing to attend therapy to save their marriage should be labeled "dead on arrival."

The Problem with Commitment

Another flaw in marriage therapy is that it is often lumped together with couples therapy—therapy for two people who are not married and not sure they ever will be. It seems logical, I know. But you'd be surprised at the statistics which demonstrate that marriage and cohabitation are horses of different colors. The level of expressed and implied commitment is dramatically stronger in marriage, particularly on the part of men. To treat these two entities as though they were the same robs the married couple of the chance to use the greatest tool at their disposal, their devotion to each other.

For most people, the active decision to get married signaled an agreement to move past the "significant other" stage. And standing in front of their family and closest friends and promising to stay together "'til death do us part" meant something. A good therapist understands and respects this couple's vows. This understanding makes the difference between meeting with a couple and saying, "Let's see if you're compatible," and saying, "I know you two were compatible; that's why you decided to marry. Now let's find out more about the special qualities of your relationship."

The "Problem" with Men

Last on the top of the list of reasons why marriage counseling can let you down is the fact that too many couples therapists still believe the false premise that men have weak relationship skills. Those who follow this school of thinking insist that we must abandon our "typical" male attitudes and traits in order to get in touch with our feminine side so that we can be more "sensitive," "empathic," and "expressive" like our wives.

In principle, there's nothing wrong with asking men to be more warm and fuzzy. We men do need to learn to be good listeners and to communicate our feelings well. Some men are naturally good at this; others have struggled with these skills since childhood. The problem with these rules of engagement for therapy is that, for a man, progress is measured by how well he can successfully become something he is not. That robs the man, and the couple, of the chance to take advantage of the intrinsic skills that a husband brings to the table.

As you'll see throughout each chapter of this book, men have relationship abilities that are different from their wives' but equally effective in creating a strong marital relationship. Yet many therapists still sit back and watch men squirm. As the men struggle to get in touch with the woman within, their frustration mounts—they ask themselves, "What's wrong with me that I can't do this?" The men leave these sessions feeling that they aren't good at relationships—hey, that's what they're told by their wives and then by the therapist.

Remember that men tend to be competitive; they may not want to be in therapy, but, gosh darn it, if they're going to go, they want to come out a winner. And when therapy fails, many husbands believe it's their fault—kind of like when your football team loses, you take responsibility if you're on the squad. In these circumstances, there's no way men can come out ahead feeling good about themselves or their marriage.

REMEMBER THIS
The Therapeutic Environment Is Created for Females

You can tell as soon as you walk in the door of a therapist's office if the female point of view is likely to dominate your session. The suite will be decorated to appeal to the female esthetic—not the male. Typically, the waiting area is painted in muted pastels. Impressionist prints hang on the wall noting the dates of recent or remote museum exhibits. More than likely, either New Age or light rock music pipes through the waiting area speakers. It's a good bet there won't be a TV tuned to CNN or ESPN. And there won't be any guy magazines lying around. Once inside the counselor's office, you'll find a damask couch, some throw pillows, and perhaps a vase of silk flowers. The overhead fixtures are kept off, as floor lamps and desk lamps provide the oh-so-soothing indirect lighting (even though, compared to women, men have more trouble seeing in dim light). Your needs are not going to be catered to here.

THERAPEUTIC FALLACIES

My clinical experience has taught me the critical truth that men and women recognize signs of trouble in their marriage in different ways. They also tend to respond to these signs in typically male or female ways. Therapists who are not attuned to these differences make critical mistakes that make men feel like losers. Here are a few of the most common therapeutic beliefs that result in therapy failure.

Fallacy 1: Men Need to Get in Touch with Their Feelings

Of course it's a good idea to reach deep and try to access our feelings, but when we have trouble doing that, it's not necessarily because we don't want to or because we're too stubborn to try. We often struggle with this part of our psyche because we're not hard-wired to do this easily—blame it on the limbic system, the amygdala, and the hippocampus:

The Limbic System

Current research has found that females often have a larger deep-limbic system than males. The male brain possesses fewer neural pathways to and from the emotion centers in the limbic system. Bingo! Reason number 1 that females may indeed be more in touch with their feelings than males.[4]

The Amygdala

This section of the brain handles aggression and the emotional connection to events. Interesting studies of the amygdala have found that when men and women are exposed to pictures of sad or frightened people and asked to imagine what they are thinking, their amygdalas light up. But then the researchers note that the men's amygdalas shut down in a few minutes, and higher cortical functions light up; men simply don't hold on to emotional responses very long before searching for a rational response to process the emotion. The female brain lingers longer on the negative feelings.[5]

Let's say, for example, that your Aunt Josie dies unexpectedly. You and your wife will both feel the emotions typically associated with grief, but *you* may be quicker to move to the practical side of things: "When will the wake and funeral be? I have that important meeting on Tuesday." Your wife will probably say hateful things about your insensitivity and wonder how you can be so cold. But the fact is, after processing the feelings of grief, your brain shifted your thoughts into the rational realm. That's not wrong—it's just different from the way your wife will deal with Aunt Josie's death.

The Hippocampus

When an emotional event passes, females tend to hold on to the memory, whereas males tend to let it go. That particular difference can be traced to the brain's hippocampus (the memory center). It is larger in women and has more neural pathways from it to emotive centers. That's why women remember emotional events more than men.

How many times has your wife asked in exasperation something along the lines of, "How can you *not* remember how upset you were when your foreman made you rebuild that deck last summer? I had to console you for days!" Well, here's your answer. A man will remember less of his emotional experiences than a woman will. He can remember the dimensions of the deck he rebuilt, but unless the conflict with his boss was a major issue with him (like something that led to being fired), he hasn't held on to the emotional meaning of the event. That's also why it's so hard for husbands to follow a therapist's dictate to dig deep and recover those feelings. Sometimes they're just not there to remember!

SecretsofMarriedMen.com

My "thought life" seems to be the area that is the most complicated to deal with. The thoughts I have are not the thoughts that I want to spend my time dwelling on.

—Bradley, age 54, married 32 years

Fallacy 2: Men Need to Talk More About Their Feelings

I'm sure that you've been told that learning how to talk about your feelings will increase the quality of your marital relationship. But this therapeutic tactic favors women. Biologically speaking, many men do not have the cerebral ability to put emotional feelings into words as easily as women. It is the female whose left hemisphere of the brain—the verbal expression center—links better with her right hemisphere—the touchy-feely part of the brain—making her far better than her husband at listening and at communicating feelings.

Men, in contrast, can't simultaneously activate both parts of the brain as readily as females. To talk about their feelings, they need time alone to think and *not* talk. Because they aren't wired to access their feelings as easily as women, it is more difficult for them to put experiences into words, and they take longer to express emotional thoughts. This fact isn't honored in therapy sessions that push men to be more open with feelings. Many men simply can't—not necessarily because their fathers never said "I love you," but because their brains aren't wired to hold on to emotions, never mind verbalize them.

Despite this evidence demonstrating that men can't communicate like their women, therapists urge men to do so and set them up to fail. By trying to generate equality where there is a relative lack of brain ability, therapists increase a man's sense of incompetence, leaving the wife even more disappointed.

For what it's worth, I believe that this whole idea of talking about feelings may be overrated to begin with for both males *and* females. A number of fascinating research findings call into question the long-held assumption among therapists that it's unhealthy to keep your feelings to yourself. In studies involving traumatic events (such as the 9/11 terrorist attack, death of a spouse, or sexual abuse), people who process problems by *not* thinking or talking about them did better in many cases (with less emotional distress) than those who felt the need to replay the negative or traumatic event.

For example, in Tel Aviv, researchers studied people who had had heart attacks to track the long-term outcomes for those who minimized or denied the traumatic effect of this medical event. They found that those who tended to think about, worry about, and talk about their heart attacks had a poorer outcome than those who chose to ignore or deny. Only 7 percent of the more stoic group developed posttraumatic stress disorder seven months after the heart attack, compared with 19 percent of the more reactive group.

Other studies of different traumatic events have had similar outcomes. Research findings like these suggest that in some cases repression and avoidance are healthy coping tactics—and that overly processing negative events can actually *increase* emotional stress in many people.[6]

Although the studies didn't address gender differences, I believe this finding may be especially true for men. Therapists' push to "dig down deep and get in touch with your feelings" may make things worse for many guys who, by nature, feel more empowered and in control when they manage intense emotions by repressing them.

> ### Psst!
> ## SecretsofMarriedMen.com
>
> My wife has said numerous times that she wants me to share my feelings, to open up, not to clam up or shut down. But on the occasions when I do express my angry feelings, she gets very upset. I guess I'm allowed only to have happy feelings.
>
> —Greg, age 26, married 2 years

Fallacy 3: Men Must Learn to Empathize in Order to Understand Their Wives' Feelings

On average, women are better at empathizing. They are better at understanding how another person feels because they are born with a superior ability to decode nonverbal communication and to pick up subtle nuances from tone of voice or facial expression.

The evidence for an inborn advantage in this area shows itself at a very early age. At birth, female babies look longer at a human face than do males—males prefer to look longer at a suspended mechanical mobile. By twelve months, girls make more eye contact than boys—giving them more opportunity and greater ability to "read" the feelings of others. This greater eye contact by girls at one year is accompanied by a show of more empathic response to the distress of others, showing greater concern through more sad looks, sympathetic vocalizations, and comforting.[7] Have females been socialized by age one to care more about the feelings of others? In part, yes. But there's more to the story. Some studies have found differences in perception from the first hours of birth. And researchers have found that how much eye contact children make is in part determined by a biological factor even *before* birth. Here's one startling research finding: the more prenatal testosterone measured in amniotic fluid, the less eye contact a boy will have with his mother at one year of age![8]

As children grow, this gender difference in overt empathy continues. For example, studies show that when children play together with a little movie player that has only one eyepiece, boys tend to get more of their fair share of looking through the eyepiece by shouldering the girls out of the way. Less empathy, more self-centeredness. Or, if you leave out a bunch of those big plastic cars that kids can ride on, you'll see that more little boys play the "ramming" game. They deliberately drive the vehicle into another child. The little girls ride around more carefully, avoiding the other children more often.[9]

I don't know if most therapists know about these studies in empathy and the inborn tendencies of men and women. But if they do, they ignore them each time they insist, "Bob, whenever you answer your wife's question without turning to look into her eyes, you show her you don't love her," or " When you take the last piece of cake without asking her if she would like it first, you demonstrate that you don't respect her." To impute some sinister intent on the husband's part is uncalled for and simply not true. But it is often the case that therapists who use such strategies are attempting to shame men into behaving differently. It doesn't work.

No, I don't think Bob has the right to be rude, even if he is a guy. But here's what the therapist should be saying: "Bob, when you eat that cake, it may feel like a lack of respect to your wife. I think you ought to offer to share because, for her, that's how you let her know you're her friend." Now *that's* useful advice.

Psst!

SecretsofMarriedMen.com

My first experience with therapy was after a severe anxiety attack. I had no idea what had happened to me. A talented LCSW [licensed clinical social worker] helped quite a bit. When my wife and I had come to an impasse we decided to go back to this woman for marital counseling. I would do anything to get out of sitting down and discussing emotions in such a stilted, contrived way. My wife became frustrated with me and blamed me for not wanting work on our problems. Our relationship continued to deteriorate because of it. I've become so frustrated with my inability to get my feelings voiced accurately that I've taken to writing them in an email or letter to her. I have much respect for the counselor, but I couldn't feel like we were going to resolve anything when the method left me at a huge disadvantage.

—Ben, age 45, married 18 years

Fallacy 4: Men Should Show Their Vulnerable Side

The ambiance is soft and friendly. The therapist really appears to understand Bob and assures him that all that is said in the office is fodder for growth and will strengthen the marriage. "It's okay, Bob," he says. "Let it all hang out." Now, at last, a man is free to talk about his pent-up emotions.

Hold on a minute, Buckaroo. Men aren't "safe" in therapy, despite the assurances of therapists. In the early phases of therapy, when a man opens up and shows his vulnerable side, there is an ever-so-slight chance that his wife will say, "Ah!" and comfortably accept his view of things. But that's the exception, not the rule.

In my experience, such revelations most often face three possible reactions from his wife—all negative. Let's say that during a counseling session Bob breaks down and cries, saying that he feels his wife doesn't really love him (or, alternatively, that he no longer is sure of his love for his wife). Here's what's likely to happen:

1. She loses respect for him: "I thought you were more mature (manly, secure, and so on) than that. How could you embarrass me and yourself by saying such a stupid thing?"

2. She panics over his loss of emotional control: "Oh no. He's starting to lose it. What if he has a breakdown? I need him to be strong. I need him to support my children and me. My God, if he can't handle all his responsibilities, what will I do?"

3. She responds as if she feels attacked: "How can you say that about me? That just isn't true! You have a lot of nerve to make a personal attack on me when you're the one who doesn't know how to show love."

It's hard for a man to talk about his pain. Vulnerability runs counter to the primitive role of man as "cave protector," which is rooted deeply in the psyche of wives—even in this modern day. I've had women tell me that they lose respect for their husbands when they admit to feeling vulnerable—being scared at the prospect of losing a job, feeling inadequate when standing up to his brothers in a fight over the estate of their deceased father, or feeling uncertain about how to diaper a baby. Some women in my office have taunted their husbands because they have discussed feelings about being physically abused by their wives.

Here's the key point: a man's vulnerability is often taken as a signal by the woman that he might not be strong enough to support her. When therapists insist that such revelations are a requisite for therapy, couples often grow further apart—not closer together.

Many men have learned to put up their shields—in life, yes, but also in their marriage. I do believe that at some point in a relationship, men have to express their needs. I said *at some point*, but I've got news for you: the time is *not* in the first months of therapy.

When, early in treatment, the therapist encourages the man to talk about his feelings and allow his wife to see his vulnerable side, and the hapless fellow lets down his guard and takes the therapist up on his or her offer . . . wham! This is not good for the relationship. The competent therapist first establishes trust in the wife that her husband will be strong and by her side no matter what he's feeling. Once she knows this to be true—and it doesn't happen

Psst! SecretsofMarriedMen.com

Couples therapy definitely puts men at a disadvantage. My husband and I have been to joint counseling several times, at my request, to help us become "more communicative." Looking back, I realize it didn't do much more than give me an opportunity to gripe in front of an "unbiased" therapist and resulted in a lot of buried, unarticulated anger on my husband's part. Counseling was never proactive; it was always oriented toward airing our anger, which was not ultimately productive for the marriage. Finding a skilled, pro-active, *trained,* and *experienced* marriage counselor is like finding a grain of salt in a mound of sand. Most therapists call themselves skilled in the realm of joint counseling but they are almost universally oriented toward leading a couple toward acknowledging their resentments, which, by the way, only leads toward more resentment, pain, and possible dissolution of the marriage.

—Rita, age 43, married 20 years

overnight—she then has a better perspective with which to see his emotional viewpoint.

Fallacy 5: Men Have All the Power in the Relationship

Too often the therapist buys the feminist position that men have all the power in the relationship because in the majority of marriages they produce more money and are physically stronger. Do these advantages give husbands power? Not if you ask men.

Ask most men who was the one who decided where the children would go to school, what kind or color of car the family would use, or what furniture to buy for the living room. Ask men who holds the veto power over whether they do or do not have sex. Moreover, ask men who decided that they had to attend therapy. In some of these cases, guys have all the control, but in my clinical experience, most men don't feel that they have the majority of the power in the household. Yet many men feel unnecessarily labeled as abusive because of their perceived physical advantages.

When men are upset, it's natural for them to raise their voice, pace the floor, and show physical aggression. Of course, if they strike their wives, they are guilty of abuse, no questions asked. But because of their tendency to resort to physical action (for example, pacing, slamming their fists on the table, hitting the wall) to smooth out inner turmoil, many men get unfairly labeled as "unsafe at any speed." (There is more information about how men handle the emotion of anger and frustration in Chapter Six.)

Such an attitude on the part of the therapist only reinforces what a man may be feeling inside: shame at his lack of self-control, guilt about the pain his wife feels when he acts that way, and powerlessness regarding his inability to find a positive resolution to the problems in his marriage.

REMEMBER THIS
Marriage Education Is an Alternative
to Marriage Counseling

Every couple seeking to improve their marriage should consider marriage education as an alternative to marriage counseling. This book, *The Secrets of Happily Married Men,* is a form of marriage education: you didn't need to hire me as a therapist in order to have me help your marriage. Working with a marriage educator differs from attending therapy because appointments are typically scheduled for groups and because the group leaders don't really ask couples to address their individual problems during the session. Instead, these classes teach strategies and exercises for husbands and wives to improve communication and problem-solving skills. Couples come from different backgrounds and go to the classes for different reasons, yet they are frequently surprised to find that they share similar issues in their marriages. One useful resource for learning more about these education classes is a Web site called SmartMarriages.com. I regularly refer couples from all over the world to this site to find out about marriage education classes in their communities.

Fallacy 6: Couples Should Avoid Sex While Working Out Their Problems

Many therapists tell sex-starved men that while they're working to improve their marriage, they must not have sex with their wives unless their wives initiate it. In Chapter Nine, you'll see how studies show that couples who fail to work on improving intimacy—even when their other communication problems are not ironed out—have a greater chance of never getting back on the sexual bandwagon. Nonetheless, therapists advise this questionable practice; maybe they don't know that during sex, men produce an increased level of the hormone oxytocin, which actually causes them to feel closer to their wives.

Encouraging couples to intentionally avoid opportunities for sex sets up a pattern of chronic avoidance. When therapists fail to integrate this knowledge into their clinical practice, couples suffer an increase in hostility and a decrease in sexual satisfaction. I just don't get it.

I recall speaking to a presenter at an annual conference of the American Psychiatric Association. I was enthralled by his insights into sex as adult play and how play can reengage a de-energized couple. I asked if he finds this approach a useful adjunct to couples therapy. He responded, "Oh, I never use this in marriage therapy. There's too much conflict in these couples already. This is only for partners who are looking for sexual therapy." I don't see how it's possible *not* to bring sex into marriage therapy. There's just no way around the fact that sexual encounters are just as valuable as talk encounters.

I was interviewed about husbands by the *Providence Journal* soon after the launch of SecretsofMarriedMen.com. In this interview, I discussed the irony of how recommending a therapy that men would avoid (such as setting aside time each day to talk) was preferred over one that men would relish. I suggested that an equally good piece of advice would be to propose setting aside a half-hour each day for couples to have sex. Of course, this was the part of the article that got put in bold headlines, and I was severely criticized for this advice. (You can probably guess the gender of those most upset by this idea.) But the point remains: verbal communication is overvalued in marriage therapy. Nonverbal communication is equally important, and couples (and therapists) should not ignore the powerfully positive effects of lovemaking.

SecretsofMarriedMen.com

I would love to go on and on about how absolutely despicable couples therapy is for men. I am a master's level social worker, whose wife is in medical school. We have gone to several therapists over the past few years and the result of all of them is just more pain. I would most strongly advise men to not go to therapy, but instead go to marriage education workshops (recommended on a forum like SmartMarriages.com). I believe this most strongly. None of the couples therapy that I have attended has ever had any written goals or exercises. It is the equivalent of having weekly discussions about the flat tire. Show me the tools and we can solve this together— without therapy! I'm not sick, OK?

—Roger, age 57, married 30 years

Fallacy 7: Happy Couples Resolve All Problems

Put on your accountant's hat and wrap your mind around the following data: (1) studies show that wives bring up more than 80 percent of household and relationship problems; (2) in happily married couples, 69 percent of all major conflicts in the household are never resolved even after working on them for five years.[10]

Armed with these statistics, you don't need to be an Einstein to figure that most of the problems that are not resolved in marriage are problems that the wife has noticed . . . and wants fixed. There's a paradox then for the man who simultaneously wishes to avoid emotional confrontation and also desires to resolve his marriage problems.

Enter the therapists, who see their specialty as settling conflict, rather than educating couples that being happily married doesn't mean resolving all your major problems (not even half your problems, actually). The two of you may never agree about whether the kids should go to religious school, whether you should have Christmas Eve with your parents or hers, or whether the piano should be in the parlor or the studio. (You'd think that the families who were fortunate enough to have a piano, a parlor, and a studio would realize how lucky they were and not argue about such nonsense, but they do.)

Poorly informed therapists try to steer couples toward behavior that doesn't work in even the best marriages—fixing problems. And because women are the ones who tend to raise these problems, guess who's supposed to make them better? That leaves men with an unrealistic task, one that is likely to fail in most cases. After the attempt falls short, the therapist will insist on revisiting the danger zone again and again in hopes of defusing all the land mines. That strategy is not so good for improving marriage—you have to wonder who ever thought of it.

Don't get me wrong; I'm not suggesting that couples shouldn't discuss problems or attempt to resolve them. But many couples who can't find solutions find a way to live with the problems and work around them. No, it's not a perfect system. Brushing problems under the rug may be a strategy that men have perfected, but for many couples, that's what works, and that's what therapists should allow to happen. It gives the question "Can we agree to disagree?" new life. (And as my wife would answer, "Sure . . . but I win, right?")

Psst!

SecretsofMarriedMen.com

My wife and I are at present having a very difficult time in our marriage. We have attended counseling and from my point of view it has accomplished nothing! I am a faithful, loving husband. I work hard. I am a good father. I don't cheat, gamble, drink, or otherwise do anything bad to my wife or family. What more do they want?

—Ben, age 37, married 7 years

IF YOU ARE IN THERAPY

I'm not suggesting that all marriage counseling is bad and beyond redemption. But I feel strongly that if the sessions are skewed to favor the female mind and the woman's needs, there is always the potential that therapy will do the marriage (and the psyche of the man) more harm than good.

If you and your wife are now involved in, or are considering, couples therapy, here is my list of suggestions that you should use as a measuring stick to decide if the therapist is capable of acknowledging your skills, strengths, and needs as a husband who is perfectly capable of contributing to the improvement of your marriage:

- The therapist should emphasize the strengths of each spouse rather than the varied ways in which each drags the other down. He or she should at least occasionally focus on your strong points. When your wife begins, "He's a great father, a loving son, and a good business-man, but . . . ," does the therapist intervene to ask, "If he's so good at all those things, why do you assume he can't be good at being a husband too?" The therapist should acknowledge that you do *not* have an inherent lack of character that precludes you from succeeding at marriage.

- The therapist should show an understanding of the natural inclination of men toward action over talk. If you hear a complaint by your wife, it's natural for you to want to find a way to fix it, rather than continue to talk about it. Is that okay with the therapist? Does the therapist expect you to sit silently and wait your turn while you are being torn apart? Does he or she realize that your strength is in action, not in sitting still and listening?

- The therapist should allow you to meet with him or her without your wife if that makes you feel more comfortable. Why not? If you were seeing a job coach because you were looking for ways to get ahead at work, would the coach say, "I can't help you unless you bring your boss in too"? Of course not. Although it helps to have both members of a marriage at counseling sessions, it's also understandable that it can be difficult for men to talk about their vulnerabilities or their intimacy problems with their wives present. Although it helps to have two people committed to improve a relationship, *one person alone has incredible power to change a marriage for the better.*

- The therapist should honor the male need to have a structured session. For the male whose brain mass is greater in the visual-spatial areas, having a clear, organized structure to the session is very comforting. One husband, Jonathan, told me about his former sessions with a very competent male psychologist in our community. Jonathan said that the sessions were very frustrating because he never knew exactly when they would be over. "I would avoid getting into a really big issue, like sex," he said, "when I thought there was only three minutes left, only to find that we ended up staying another twenty minutes. It was like playing a football game in which the refs arbitrarily decided to throw in a couple overtime periods." Establishing time limits, clear guidelines, and a general overview of the objectives for the therapy session goes a long way toward helping men arrive at a positive outcome.

- The therapist should not assume that you are open to a trial separation or divorce as a solution to your marital problems. Whether or not it's scientifically or

statistically true, it seems to me that men perceive
themselves as having a greater sense of honor than
women, and this translates into the belief that if they
gave their word to be married "for better or for worse,"
they mean it. Their word is their bond, and they take
their obligation to protect and honor their wives and
children very seriously. If you feel this way, your therapist should respect your sense of commitment, not
try to talk you into being apart from each other.

If you find yourself in a marriage counselor's office, speak up and
ask whether the therapist feels there's hope for the marriage. If the
answer is no, turn around and go to the nearest restaurant, order a
light meal, and get out the Yellow Pages. Then find a therapist who
believes in your marriage—and is willing to help you fight to make
it work.

Therapists Help Those Who Help Themselves

When the phone rings in my office, there's a good chance it's a
couple looking for help in their marriage. Across America, there are
thousands of therapists who are getting the same calls. And in many
of these situations, the man drags his feet, dreading the encounter
because of fears—reasonable fears sometimes—that he will feel
uncomfortable, unappreciated, and unhelpful. But husband and wife
go together for therapy because, at their core, they believe it can
improve the quality of their marriage. And it can.

But don't leave your manhood behind at the therapist's door.
Find a counselor who will honor the strengths you bring to the marriage. The therapeutic process *can* be helpful for you to learn more
about your wife. You can learn about marriage as it specifically
applies to you. You can learn how to recognize fixable problems and
learn how to work through more complicated emotional issues. If
you take on this challenge without the preconceived notion that

there's something wrong with your male traits, you can feel elated about your ability to improve your marriage. And that's an emotion you can recognize and talk about!

I'm all for improving your marriage. In fact, I don't want it to be just okay; I want it to be great, and I want you to feel great about it. But the reality is that a lot of men—and women—don't, or can't, access good marital therapy. That's where I come in. This book isn't a substitute for therapy, but it's my firm belief that if you learn the secrets of happily married men and apply my step-by-step approach to your marriage, you won't need a therapist. So read on and begin the process of helping yourself be your best.

3

The First Way
Make Your Marriage Your Job

Want to find men who have the skills that are vital for building a good marriage, such as listening, relating, managing, and empathizing? Look no further than the line at the train station at 7:00 A.M., or glance through office building windows at the figures bent over their desks late at night. Take a good look at the guys constructing, painting, and landscaping homes and businesses in the extremes of both hot and cold weather until their bodies scream for relief. That kind of single-minded dedication to doing a job and doing it right is exactly what can be used to build a strong and healthy marriage that lasts. Men do have special skills that have been socialized, practiced, and perfected over years in the workplace. Many of us really do learn how to

Focus

Prioritize

Develop strategies

Problem-solve

Pay attention to details

Negotiate and compromise

Resolve conflict

Work through a step-by-step process

Achieve our goals

These are the skills we frequently use at work and to support our families and pursue our careers. So ditch the Tom Hanks romance movies that make you look like a schmo and look to roles models like Nelson Mandela, who show us how to use these skills in the spirit of commitment, perseverance, diplomacy, and compromise. Then we can effectively approach our marriages as the most important job of our lives.

In this first step, we'll look closely at a variety of ways in which your natural work habits can be used to win your wife's heart forever.

OUR REAL CAREER CHOICE

Take a look at your earliest notions of work. What did you want to be when you grew up? The first time I remember having to choose a job was in fourth grade for a school project about careers. I was going to be an artist. Other classmates laid claims to being professional athletes or astronauts. Of course, real life didn't work out that way. To my knowledge, no one from Muhlenberg Elementary School has ever been featured in *Sports Illustrated* or has ever landed on the moon, and anyone who has seen my attempts at drawing will acknowledge that I was wise to switch my plans to medicine.

If you think about it, though, these childhood dreams about jobs revealed something about the kind of kids we were, about how we envisioned a future for ourselves. That being said, despite the forward-looking nature of early career goals, what percentage of boys do you think describe their future job as "husband"? In fact, how many grown men do you know who currently see their main job as being a husband? Probably not very many, because we haven't been raised to see marriage as a lifelong career. That's about to change.

The Language of Work

Thinking about marriage as a job is not something we are raised to do. In fact, the suggestion that marriage is like a job often raises strong objections from women. Because our culture has romanticized the institution of marriage and given it a mystical, touchy-feely quality that separates it from all other types of relationships, many women believe that a good marriage is based on subjective and emotional elements such as romantic whispers of sweet nothings in the night. Well, that's all great, but I don't think that's the whole story. Yes, a man can enjoy romance, intimacy, affection, even frivolity and play. But in order to sustain a long-term marriage, other approaches are needed.

For example, a man's highly attuned visual-spatial skills and his drive for dominance can come in very handy for sustaining a long-term marriage. In a much earlier period of our development, such visual-spatial skills helped us aim our spears at a clearly defined target, such as a grazing animal to be brought home and served for dinner. In today's world, we still stalk dinner, but we try to make our killing in the world of business or professional life, not in the grasslands. We seek a target, we meet the target, we kill the target, and we move on.

That's why the language of the workplace is so suited for men: it talks about objectives and targets, deadlines and drop-dead dates. In the workplace, we enter the meeting expecting to "knock 'em dead" and "beat last year's figures." These expressions resonate with men because they are action oriented and goal directed.

(Psst!)

SecretsofMarriedMen.com

I'd have to say that marriage is like my job in one very specific way: For either to be worthwhile, dedication and hard work are required.

—Jim, age 39, married 12 years

The Language of Love

There are some really spectacular differences in the way men and women express their feelings about marriage. Basically, women are more prone to talk about it or to express their love with words and feelings (and some deeds too, of course). Men, on the other hand, are usually more comfortable with showing their love through actions that many women may find hard to interpret as tender and emotional, such as, well . . . mowing the lawn.

Nevertheless, mowing the lawn, taking out the garbage, and carrying large boxes of old, wet newspapers down to the recycling center are part of an authentic language of love for many men. The act of performing such tasks completes an emotional circuitry in a man's brain. Through those actions he believes he has clearly expressed his intent and feelings of love. It's hard for women to understand, but males *need* to exert physical effort to deal with inner emotions.

Most women simply don't know this, so they expect that their husbands should express love verbally as they do. So when a husband doesn't say "I love you," that omission gets translated by the female brain into "I don't love you."

There are many and complex reasons why some men have trouble expressing love with words. For example, I've treated many men who have been taught as children—often in very subtle ways—that they should shove their feelings out of their consciousness. Studies show that parents are much more likely to admonish a boy to stop crying than they are his sister, so he learns to hide his feelings.

This social conditioning is no surprise to Brenda, married for seventeen years, who writes to me, "Why don't they talk about their feelings? Because somewhere back in their childhood, some egotistical male influence told them it wasn't masculine enough. They got picked on when they cried, and laughed at when they tried to show their feminine side."

I know this to be true in many cases, but some very important and quite recent research in the difference between male and female brain development has shown us that there are also major biological reasons why "big boys don't cry." Men have a smaller hippocampus—the brain area linked to memory—than women. Men also have less connection between their hippocampus (memory bank) and the limbic brain (the emotional centers). So men are more comfortable when they can release feelings physically, rather than store them emotionally. The ultimate product of this biological need is work.

Of course, from a woman's perspective, it would be ideal if a man could sort through the emotions that course through his brain, quickly process what they all mean, and then verbally express how they make him feel. But the man's less developed corpus collosum—the connection between the two brain hemispheres—may impede the rapid translation of emotions into words. Compared to women, men are delayed in their ability to process what they're feeling. They've already started to act long before they can figure out what to say. And in many ways, that action speaks louder than words.

The bottom line is that it's likely you'll find it much easier and more personally rewarding to use your many transferable job skills to build a strong marriage; it beats relying solely on your skills at articulating emotion. If you haven't yet put marriage in the top spot on your career choice list, go ahead and do it right now, immediately—even if your wife thinks you're crazy. It's an effective and productive way for a man to give himself the best marriage possible.

Psst!

SecretsofMarriedMen.com

Very early in our marriage we posted a piece of anonymous wisdom on our refrigerator that has helped us through good times and bad. It read, 'Marriage is like running a farm, you have to start all over every day.' It takes serious managerial work to have a good marriage, and lots of it!

—Saul, age 66, married 41 years

WANTED: A LIFETIME CAREER
OF LOVING FOREVER

The whole setup of dating and marrying has such strong parallels to the work world that it's amazing that men haven't hooked into this idea much sooner—but then we've been so distracted by the TV shows, movies, and magazines that keep telling us to be more like women if we want our women to love us. Yet the parallels between work and love are remarkable.

Interviewing for Marriage

Think back to when you last went on an important job interview. You polished up your résumé and wrote the perfect cover letter. Then you went in for your interview, making sure to dress right and arrive on time. You came rested and mentally prepared. You presented yourself in the best possible light, showcasing your strengths and answering the difficult questions tactfully. The dating period with your wife was very much like a long interview. You probably won your wife's heart by employing some of the same skills you used in nailing down your job. You showed up at her place on time and tried to dress cool. You told her a little about yourself and showed her that you were bright and fun-loving without coming on too strong or overselling. You listened intently to what she had to say and picked up on common interests or dislikes. You showed your strengths and hid your weaknesses.

The months or years you dated your wife may have seemed like installments of Donald Trump's *The Apprentice*. But you knew the drill; as you moved closer to popping the question, you kept up your best behavior. There was too much at stake to mess it up.

After selling your strong points to your future wife, you closed the deal on your wedding day. The marriage certificate is more than a legal commitment. It literally puts you "under contract." You're now cochair of Matrimony Inc.

It's easy to see that dating and courtship are almost identical to the job search and the big interview, but I want to be specific about why it's important to make this comparison. A potential employer is looking for value and commitment. He or she wants to feel confident that you are ready to work at the appropriate level and that you will show up every day determined to get better and better, that you are eternally loyal and devoted.

Now here's the point: a potential wife expects no less. Saying "I do" is only the beginning. Now the real work begins.

Psst!

SecretsofMarriedMen.com

While I was dating, I did have some formal and informal "criteria" that I considered in a mate. Some women were more qualified than others. And much like a formal interview, the process was usually mutually evaluative—we would both look for things that would make the relationship a good match.

—Josh, age 26, married 2 years

ON THE JOB

What happens after you get hired? Well, much like your wedding day, the first day on the job is usually filled with excitement and expectation. It's not coincidental that you probably picked out your best clothes to wear on your first day on the job, much the same way that you selected the perfect tuxedo for your wedding day.

The first day of work is typically very promising. You may get a visit from someone with a gift basket of office supplies ranging from pens, pads, and paper clips to expensive cell phones, notebook computers, and wireless palm devices. Or maybe you got a new uniform and a badge. Everyone welcomes you. Your bosses or peers invite you to lunch. In the best circumstances, your first few weeks on the job mark a festive celebration of a new beginning that compares to the honeymoon period after your wedding.

When the excitement calms down and you're faced with the finer details of your new job, you have an interesting biological advantage over women: you are preprogrammed to achieve. That's right. Research and sociological studies consistently reveal an incontrovertible truth: most men are born with a drive to compete, to be better than the next guy, to seek to prevail. It's in our genes. It shapes our brain. It forms our character. It affects the way we think and what we do.

Some folks may not like to hear this, but it's true. This competitive advantage first shows itself as early as kindergarten. Whereas girls tend to develop close friendships with one or two friends and give equal status to all, boys create what psychologists call a dominance hierarchy. They play in large groups that generally have one leader, several of his close friends, and a few other members who are allowed to tag along. The boys at the top of the hierarchy can then safely challenge the ones below who have less social status and power. This dominance is established by threats and challenges: a boy will boldly take a toy from another boy to see how that child will defend or retaliate. One of them will come out with the toy. A male's concern with being better and stronger than the other boys is far greater than his need to be friends.

And if you're wondering whether that pattern persists into adulthood, just ask the guy in the Hummer with the bumper sticker saying WHOEVER DIES WITH THE MOST TOYS WINS.

This biological structure that has put men on top in their childhood adventures and in their careers also has the power to transform relationships into unions that not only last but also contribute to the quality of our lives. I can't say it better than Jim, married fifteen years, who feels that a bad marriage is like having a bad job: "Just because you stay there for the long run doesn't make it a successful venture. Is my dead-end job a success because I've been there for decades? Just like a job, marriage is successful only if both parties derive mutual benefit and gratification from it."

FACING A CHALLENGE ON THE JOB

Inevitably, even in the best of jobs, many men discover that the business they loved during that honeymoon period changes, develops in unexpected and unpredictable ways, and can become far from perfect:

- After a few weeks on the job as a magazine editor, Jerry was unhappy to realize that he had to copyedit and rewrite hundreds of pages of terrible, unpublishable gibberish. There was far more drudgery associated with his work than the fun he had anticipated and experienced at first.

- Keith, a financial investor, soon found that his supervisor had quirks and habits that drove him nuts. For example, every afternoon when the market closed, he insisted that Keith observe ten minutes of silence and reflection. Not only that, he didn't believe in email and wanted everything typed and delivered.

- Coworkers who greeted Anthony with enthusiasm when he began his teaching job soon seemed threatened by his presence. They started quizzing his students about any new and potentially controversial books he was assigning and didn't invite him for the regular Friday drink after work.

This is life—and when a man is faced with these kinds of disappointments and setbacks, his drive to achieve is not easily dampened. Men are generally quick to realize that they need a strategy to get past the problem and keep their career on a growth trajectory. In other words, they come to grips with the reality that all the hard work that went into getting the job was only the beginning. They have to work even harder to make the opportunity pay off.

To do this, good businessmen leverage their successes and their failures into new and better chances to show that they should be valued. They learn from their mistakes in order not to repeat them. At work, these adaptive skills make all the difference in their level of contentment. Historically, however, these talents have been deemed nontransferable when it comes to marriage. I don't buy it.

These days, when I talk to my clients about their marriages, they don't understand why they should stay married if they are unhappy. Many have adopted a consumer approach to their life. They want to feel good, now! They see marriage as a disposable commodity: "If you're not happy, move on."

But hold on. What happened to the work ethic that helps men realize that when things go wrong they have to work even harder to make the opportunity pay off? To look at setbacks and mistakes in a marriage as insurmountable obstacles and to say they are evidence that you have no choice but to dissolve the marriage, fire your wife, terminate the contract, and split, is what, in my neighborhood, we call a large receptacle of excrement.

Certainly, sometimes it's best to quit a job that makes you miserable and to find a new job. But few men would do that without first trying to resolve the problems and find agreeable solutions. Remember, the male's need to fight for dominance is a strong one, and this tendency makes it hard for him to admit defeat in the workplace.

When it comes to marriage, too many men are easily convinced it's their fault that their wife is not happy and the relationship is not the proverbial bed of roses. They figure it must be their fault when the marriage fails because most often they're not the ones who ask for a divorce. And their wives repeatedly tell them, "You just don't get it."

When this happens, some husbands forget all about their innate work skills that help them solve problems. They need to remember how they overcome obstacles at work. For example, they could

- Ask a colleague for advice.
- Brainstorm solutions.
- Stick to it until they make it right again.

Instead, when they face a marital problem, they clam up and push themselves into that "failure" category created by the media and the society we live in. They see their disappointment as an either-or situation: either I stay and resign myself to a life of misery, or I give up and look for something better.

I'm suggesting a third option: we can use our work mentality to come up with a strategy that will get us through the rough times and keep the relationship on that growth trajectory.

If you're open to this third option, keep reading.

Psst!

SecretsofMarriedMen.com

A successful marriage occurs when you have passion, intimacy, and commitment. Passion will ebb and flow. Honor your commitments. Strive for intimacy. A wise man once said, "Love is a decision." Reviewing this formula helps when you don't feel "in love." I don't always feel like getting out of bed or going to work, but I do it anyway.

—Paul, age 52, married 30 years

THE JOB DESCRIPTION

We can all see how getting and starting a new job is a lot like finding a wonderful woman and getting married. But here is where the obvious similarities end. Here is where you have to let yourself take the work skills that you so naturally apply at your job and make a committed effort to apply them in your marriage. This can be the hard part, because even when men are ready and able to put time and effort into their marriages, they really don't know where to begin.

When it comes to the work world, we have a pretty good idea going in what the job is going to be like. From the first moment we crack open the want ads, we find a list of very specific duties and requirements. If this information isn't in the job posting, chances are you'll be informed at some point in the application process.

Not so with marriage. Picture this scenario: back from your honeymoon, you arrive home at your new "office," put your feet up on the desk (or coffee table), punch the speed dialer on the speaker phone, and call your best buddy. You bubble over with enthusiasm about your new job of being a husband.

"That's great," he replies. "What exactly do you do?"

There's a long silence. You don't know how to answer. The fact is, you've put all your energy into getting the job. But what are you supposed to do now that your nameplate is on the door? You didn't answer an ad spelling out the job requirements. No one from HR will be dropping by with a company handbook. There is no prewritten job description to which you can refer.

So if you're serious about supporting your marriage on your own terms in ways that fit naturally with your gut feelings about what it means to be a man and a husband, you've got to do some research, interview all the relevant parties, think hard about it, and write out your own job description so that you have a concrete statement of what exactly you're supposed to do.

Psst! SecretsofMarriedMen.com

When I do something that puts a smile on my wife's face, that is one of the most fulfilling things in my life. I thrive on doing things that make my wife happy. They may not always be things for her directly but the little things truly do count. Maintaining the house, getting dinner ready. Greeting her with a glass of wine at the end of a hard day or taking the children with me when I run somewhere. Telling her that I love her out of the clear blue. Her alone time and seeing that she is relaxing is important. My wife and I have known each other for 17 years. The rewards have been great!

—Bryan, age 35, married 11 years

In the business world, creating a job description begins with a position analysis—a process in which all aspects of the routine are laid out. In industrial jobs, the analysis is as specific as estimating the maximum weight a person might be required to lift or the speed at which widgets are churned out. For our purposes, let's look at a part of a position analysis that can be of value in writing your job description as a husband.

Duties and Responsibilities

What are you expected to do for the company? This would appear to be self-evident in the job title, but if it were that easy, companies wouldn't need job descriptions. Individuals need clear ownership of certain outcomes. When an employee signs off on the responsibilities listed in his or her job description, it signifies an agreement that there will be no excuses.

Right now, take some time to jot down specific duties and responsibilities that apply to your personal job description as a husband. If this were a job description you were filling out for Human Resources, you'd want it to show your strengths as well as stake out a claim for those challenges you know you can meet. As a doctor, psychiatrist, and marriage counselor, I've given a lot of thought to the job of husband, and I offer the following general job description of a marriage to help you write your own position analysis.

To Love, Honor, and Respect Her

These words are in standard wedding vows for a good reason. Fulfill these three duties and you will be successful in this job. From these roots grow all the good things in a marriage.

To Be Sexually and Emotionally Faithful

No one issue better defines marriage than the promise of sexual fidelity, and I believe that all men know this. But emotional cheating can be as detrimental as a night at Motel 6 with your secretary. Your wife expects you to stay open to her, to turn to her to share your feelings and emotions.

Sometimes you may not know what's on your mind—you may have no particular feelings to show. Take it from me, that's okay. But here's what's not okay: if you are having problems at home, you *must not* share these problems with any woman outside your family. You may have an old high school friend or a coworker who seems to understand you better than your wife does. Do not turn to her as a support. The only friends that should be included in your confidence are those who are friends of the marriage. Even though your intentions may be pure, you can be sure that your wife will see your closeness with another woman as emotional infidelity. And part of your job is to help your wife feel secure in your faithfulness.

(Psst!) ————————————————————————

SecretsofMarriedMen.com

Infidelity should be a capital offense. I have given thought to the subject, and that is where it ends. I love my wife very much, and would never break our vow. I know how I would react if she were to cheat on me, and would expect the same from her.

—Jimmy, age 23, married 3 years

————————————————————————

To Listen Without Being Judgmental

When 95 percent of all Nobel prizes go to men, you've got to believe that men know how to solve problems. But your wife may not need you to solve her problems; sometimes she just needs to know you're there by her side. So when she tells you something important that's going on with her, don't jump in right away and tell her what's wrong, what she doesn't realize, or what she should do. Just listen. (You can find more on the details of listening in Chapter Seven.)

To Support and Nurture Her Ambitions in and Outside the Home

Roles are changing, and it's a good thing too, for everyone. More men than women work outside the home. But there are more stay-at-home dads than ever, and an increasing number of women—up to 30 percent—who earn more than their hubbies. As your children grow up and opportunities open up for your wife to pursue her own dreams of fulfillment, will you be there to support her? She needs to know that you stand by her side during all phases of her career evolution.

To Make an Effort to Understand How She Is Different Emotionally

I know, I know, the world would be so much more manageable if women would just see the world the same way men do. But they don't, and that's the way it is. We've looked at some of the differences between men and women, and you'll be hearing more as you go through this book. Your job is not to change her to be more like you, but to acknowledge and respect your differences.

To Be Honest at All Times and Always Do What You Say You Will Do

I was doing a presentation to a group of husbands a short time before drafting this chapter, and a man asked me about how honest he needs to be with his wife. Can a man lie and still call himself a good husband?

First, the stats. Studies show that lying is part of everyday communication outside of marriage. About a fourth of all conversations will involve lying. Within marriage, studies show that more than 46 percent of spouses will lie about how much they paid for an item. Almost everybody lies about something, and many men who consider themselves happily married do admit to an occasional white lie. For example, there is the classic question, "How do I look in this dress?" When you're facing this one, you need to be tactful. Be discreet. Exercise sound judgment and weigh the alternatives.

Let's be clear. When I talk about being honest here, I mean there is no room for lies about infidelity, addiction problems, or other important matters that reflect on who you are (such as belief systems or underlying medical problems). You need to hold yourself accountable for what's important—the core issues, the crucial stuff, your promises. Rightfully, your wife has set up expectations for you based on your promise to protect and serve her. You must respond with a sincere effort to do your best.

To Share in Child Care and Domestic Work

Statistics show that when total time worked (outside plus inside hours) is added up, an average man contributes nearly as much time to the household as his wife. But when you are outside the house, your wife may not see what you are doing as contributing to the household. You know that you're doing your share, but your wife simply doesn't see it the same way you do. And it's true that men spend much less time doing housework at home.

So if you are to be successful at husbanding, you must take her perspective into account. It's useless to argue that you *have* already

---

Psst!

SecretsofMarriedMen.com

My wife Jessie and I have found a way to make our marriage happy for both of us. We take things in turn. Just like our parents made us take turns with our siblings when doing chores. We have just had our first child, Phoenix, and Jessie is off work, so she stays with our daughter during the day. But at night I take over by changing nappies, bathing her, etc. This gives time for Phoenix and me and gives Jessie time to relax. Then, later, we have our time together. This was an idea that we both came up with and I swear it works. My wife is happy. I am spending time with both of my beautiful girls and my daughter gets both of us.

—Rolf, age 22, married 2 years

worked enough today—use that same energy to pick up a dishcloth and start drying. I know it's not fair, but rest assured she doesn't think she's getting a fair deal either.

To Be as Attentive, Fun-Loving, and Adoring as You Were During Courtship, or Close to It

Sometimes it feels like the weight of the world is on your shoulders—particularly when you come home from work at the end of a stressful, high-pressure day. It's not hard to understand why you lose some of the lightness of being that made your wife's eyes sparkle when you first dated. But you have a choice about how you deal with stress. If you take a positive approach to challenges at work and home, and remain upbeat and optimistic, you put others at ease and make your environment more pleasant.

Studies of upbeat people show they are less affected by bad events and bring about brighter responses in other people. As a psychiatrist, I sometimes see people who suffer from depression and have lost the ability to see any good in themselves or their futures. Professional help is available for depression or substance abuse. We'll talk about this further in Chapter Ten, but for now, know that you don't have to be hopeless.

To Be Affectionate

To your wife, affection means more than cuddling or holding hands, and it definitely means more than wham-bam-thank-you-ma'am. Your wife desires a sense of closeness from you because knowing you care is paramount for her being able to stay in the relationship with you.

Maybe I didn't say that clearly enough: *if your wife doesn't feel connected to you, she will leave.* Don't rely on her sticking by her vows if she doesn't feel loved. She might, but most women I treat who decide to call a divorce lawyer don't do so because of abuse or infidelity. Women leave men because they feel emotionally disconnected. Even in the worst of your arguments and disagreements, you must somehow let your wife know you care.

YOUR TURN TO WRITE
A JOB DESCRIPTION

We've looked at some of the duties that I've come up with. Now you give it a try. Choose some of the responsibilities described here that fit the needs of your marriage, or write up your own unique job description that seems fair and doable to you. Don't be afraid to stretch a little. Give yourself responsibilities that you haven't yet tried to fulfill or that you gave up on over the years. Look at the individual tasks that, when put together, define a lifelong commitment. What I'm saying is simple: put a little bottom-line thinking into your marriage.

After drawing up your job description, take time to evaluate your progress—something along the lines of making a chart with days of the month and recording the number of times you expressed appreciation, or keeping a weekly list of all the promises you made your wife, with a duty to return back to that list a week later.

As you get good at this job, you will rise to higher levels of proficiency that may change some of your duties and responsibilities. So, as you settle into your bed each night, review how things went. Which interactions with your wife would go into the profit column, and which would go on the loss side? How can you better manage your life and your relationship so as to maximize profits and minimize unnecessary costs? Think marital black ink, and your job performance rating will soar.

Table 3.1 shows a sample chart that you can use as a guide to building your own weekly calendar for evaluation. Schedule in specific actions you want to apply to your marriage and then assess the results. Each week you can create your own chart and To Do list. Every time you check off a box, you're a step closer to winning your wife's heart forever.

Table 3.1. Sample Job Description Evaluation Chart—Week of October 12.

ACTION	SUN	MON	TUES	WED	THUR	FRI	SAT
Told her I adore her	✓		✓	✓			✓
Suggested fun-loving activity		✓	✓ Brought home bubbles		✓ Took her to park	✓	✓ Rode bikes
Helped with child care	✓	✓	✓	✓		✓	✓
Helped with chores	✓	✓	✓	✓	✓	☺ Wife gave me day off!	✓
Said "I understand" her emotions	✓	✓	☹ Argued about kids	✓	✓	✓	
Supported her interests	✓	✓	✓		✓	✓	✓
Listened without judging		✓		☹ Said she was wrong	✓	✓	✓
Praised her	✓ Noticed her haircut	✓		✓		✓	✓

To Do List

Write thank-you note to her parents	☑	Bring down her sweaters from attic	☐
Make dinner at least one night	☑	Send her a card "just because"	☑
Buy extra cards to stash in my desk for later	☑	Pick up clothes at the dry cleaners	☐

What went well this week: _____

What went wrong this week: _____

New objectives for next week (include all promises to wife): _____

EXPECT CHALLENGES

Creating a job description of marital duties and responsibilities is an effective and manly way to get your marriage on track, but it is certainly not a guarantee of perpetual wedded bliss—which brings us back to how our experiences in the workplace can help us have a better relationship and marriage.

At work, we try to think through the possible consequences of every action, because we know that our relationship to our employer is a two-way street. We show our loyalty to the organization by demonstrating to our bosses and colleagues that we're committed, even driven, to seeing the company succeed. In exchange, we are rewarded for our actions, and that keeps us happy and coming back for more.

But sometimes, even on this two-way street, you're not rewarded. Sometimes, no matter how hard you try, you have an absolutely awful day. Your diligent efforts go unnoticed, or you make a costly mistake. Yet still you go back and try again. Why? Because even on the bad days there are benefits. You still get a check at the end of the pay period. Your health plan is still in effect. Your employer is paying for disability insurance. You may even have a pension. Even if you are self-employed without fringes, you are learning from your mistakes so that tomorrow can be better.

Marriage too has its bad days. But if we have not learned the skills of a good marriage and have never learned how to fix our problems, these crappy days make us feel incompetent and helpless—very unmanly emotions. And so we throw up our hands in frustration. But when we start to think of marriage as a job, to keep at it we can activate the male traits that seek mastery. We'll see that even on the worst of days there are positive gains. We've gained the benefit of being married for one day longer. We've stood by our wife's side, even if in anger, and let her know we are committed to her. We've added experience and been given an opportunity to learn. We have gathered data, improved our alliance, survived conflict, and added to our portfolio of long-term investment. And if we've been paying attention—especially if we focus on what we said and did rather than rationalize or defend our behavior—we've learned to eliminate one more costly mistake. This optimistic attitude will keep us going back to our marriage day after day hoping for the best.

Notice I said, "especially if we focus on what *we* said and did." It does no good to leave a disagreement and ruminate over what your wife said and did. After all, in the business world, it does little good to blame the customer if you lose a sale. Yes—if you look at marriage like work, then you will see flubbing up as an opportunity to analyze *your* actions. One of the greatest lessons we can all learn is not to blame our wives for our reactions to marital stress. We're men: we can fix it!

Whether you're a starting pitcher for the Dodgers or a toll taker on the George Washington Bridge, an air traffic controller at O'Hare or a shoe salesman in Houston, I am absolutely convinced that your work skills will help your marriage survive setbacks and disappointments. To make both your job and your marriage work, you'll haul your butt out of bed on the good days and the bad ones. You'll master certain management strategies, apply due concentration and diligence, and take each opportunity you find to improve your performance and stay at it for the long haul.

REMEMBER THIS
Don't Get Stupid

The concepts and theory of business skills are directly applicable to your marriage, but, of course, you'll have to adjust the vocabulary. I strongly discourage your gazing longingly into your wife's eyes over a cozy candlelight dinner and saying, "You know, sweetheart, I now think of you as a wholly owned subsidiary with about a $3 million market cap. I worked up a little PowerPoint presentation on my laptop that I want to show you later. All I have to do is run our marriage like Spacely Sprockets, and I will reach my goal and objective of, pardon me for saying it, getting some peace of mind. I read it in a book on my flight back from Grand Rapids, and we start at 8:30 sharp tomorrow morning." That's just plain stupid.

WHEN TO START

Anyone who shows up on the first day of work ready to coast is out of his mind. There is a name for these guys: former employees. And those who get off to a good start and then rest on their laurels go by another name: expendable. Whether you've been married two weeks or thirty years, you don't want to become expendable, and certainly not former.

So start today to protect your career as a husband by treating this day as though it were your first day on a new job called marriage. One of your To Do lists for this job is printed here. But this list is just a beginning. In the next chapter, we'll talk about how you can get to know your wife. You will learn to gather the intelligence you'll need in order to carry out your new list of marital duties and responsibilities. As you go through each of the remaining chapters, remember to keep your work ethic front and center. If you maintain your can-do attitude, you will achieve tremendous happiness in your marriage—and you'll love it like no other job you've ever had.

TO DO LIST

- Free yourself of Hollywood romantic stereotypes and apply those strengths that come most naturally to you—the skills you use and refine every day in the workplace.

- Focus on the benefits of marriage, not on the day-to-day frustrations.

- Show your wife the same traits that make you valuable as an employee: focus, discipline, reliability, devotion, loyalty, stability, intelligence, flexibility.

- Be determined to get better and better at this job of being a husband.

- Learn from your mistakes.

- Commit yourself to the duties and responsibilities of your marital job description and reassess your progress as you go along.

4

The Second Way
Know Your Wife

N ow that you've made a decision to put in some hard work on your marriage, how exactly do you go about it?

The first thing I recommend, based on my clinical practice, the many letters and emails to my Web site, and my own life experience, is this: get to know your wife. Don't assume that you already have her all figured out, even if you've been together for years. Take nothing for granted, roll up your sleeves, and get to work, just as you would on the job.

We all know that no matter what our occupation, success depends largely on the information available to us. To do a job well, we need to do our homework, do the research, and get the data, statistics, sales figures, trends, budgets, cost of goods sold, tax liabilities, terms of the contract, history, projections, or whatever else is appropriate to the job. After all, we are only as good as the data we command.

So . . . if you want to be a better husband, you have to find out as much as you can about how your wife operates. Who is this woman, and, in the famous words of Sigmund Freud, what does she want?

REMEMBER THIS
Check Your "Facts"

Aristotle, whose basis of philosophy was grounded in collecting information about the world, asserted that women have fewer teeth than men. Although he was twice married, it never occurred to him to verify this statement by examining his wives' mouths.[1] The truth is, of course, that women have exactly the same number of teeth as men, so watch out for these false myths and for assumptions in general, and beware of applying them to your wife in particular.

THE BIG MISUNDERSTANDING

A lot of us feel very strongly that we just don't understand our wives. So if you too have this sense of dread, ignorance, even fear—you are not alone. Recall the agony of Professor Henry Higgins in My Fair Lady after Eliza Doolittle tossed his slippers in his face and left him in a rage. He wonders why she did such a thing, compares her behavior to that of a man in the same circumstances, and famously asks, "Why can't a woman be more like a man?"

Higgins—the master linguist who expects everyone to conform to his academic standards—sees the world through his eyes only. For Higgins, obsessed with his desire to teach the coarse-cut flower girl from Drury Lane how to pass as a refined lady, knowing or understanding Eliza was the last thing on his mind. He simply refused to accept that women are not inclined to distinctly male thinking or behavior. This is the big misunderstanding that so unnecessarily causes anger, hurt, and untold numbers of arguments and divorces among married couples.

I don't have a magic formula for figuring out the woman in your life. However, I am certain of these points:

Women don't think or express themselves like men. Just as their bodies are different, women's minds work much differently from ours.

No man thinks the same way his wife does. There really is a big difference.

No man knows easily what his wife is thinking, even if he thinks he does. And therefore . . .

It may be a big mistake to take everything your wife says as truly reflecting what she's really thinking or feeling. So . . .

Don't ever take it for granted that you know what your wife is thinking or feeling just because that's what she says she's thinking or feeling.

For example, when I hear a man say that his wife "doesn't understand me," or "always accuses me of being negative," or "dismisses everything I say," I know that the primary reason communication has broken down is because this guy assumes that he knows what his wife is thinking or feeling. When one person misunderstands how another views the world, what he or she says or does takes on a different, sometimes contentious or annoying meaning.

So stop thinking like Henry Higgins. Forget everything you think you know about women and how they ought to behave. Enter your wife's universe.

Psst!

SecretsofMarriedMen.com

Sure, we're different, but that doesn't mean we can't be understanding and thoughtful when it comes to our wives' needs. If
we thought and acted alike, how boring a relationship that
would be!

—Jim, age 48, married 24 years

GIVE HER A CLEAN SLATE

There's a joke that runs in therapy circles that goes like this: There
are two times when a man doesn't understand a woman: (1) before
marriage, and (2) after marriage. Alas, getting to know your wife
may seem like a hopeless endeavor. But it can be done. So let's get
down to it.

Drop All Your Past Assumptions

For this exercise in getting to know your wife, it's best to take a
"clean slate" approach. Being open to the new and unpredictable is
what true learning is all about. And that's how you can best discover
the unexpected and unknown in your wife.

My wife and I, for example, were married for thirteen years when
I realized that an assumption I had made about her was absolutely
false. I had resisted buying jewelry for my wife for a long time.
From my practical, male-brain point of view, it didn't make sense to
spend my hard-earned cash on some substance found only on the peri-
odic table and in South African mines. Minerals? Crystals? Little rocks
from the earth polished up? What for? And they're so expensive, too.

Once in a while I gave in and bought her a little bauble, and she
had also acquired some pieces through inheritance and gifts, but I
was locked into my assumptions, and they seemed very reasonable

to me. I presumed that my wife wanted jewelry because she was materialistic, competitive with other women, even greedy. I held a rather self-righteous viewpoint that I was superior to her on a moral level because she cared about this possession stuff and I didn't.

Then one day, as I took my wife to the hospital for a one-day outpatient procedure, she became full of anxiety. As she was about to go into the prep room, she said to me, "If something happens to me, I want Alena [our daughter] to get my jewelry." As one would

Psst!

SecretsofMarriedMen.com

In my marriage, the secret of our success is contained in the word "you." When I focus on my wife's happiness and well-being, sometimes to the temporary exclusion of my own, wonderful things happen. In the past, most emotionally laden conversations with my wife ended with, "How do you suppose that makes ME feel?" Now I ask myself, "How do you suppose that makes HER feel? What does SHE need?" The answers to those questions determine my course of action. This philosophy recently came to a real test. She wanted a separation. She was unhappy (for reasons related to intimacy). She determined that her "need" was to be away from me, at least for a while. I tried to see the situation from her point of view. We agreed on a six-month trial separation. I took her to the airport. I kissed her goodbye. I told her I loved her and that her happiness was my only goal. And off she went. And guess what? She came back three weeks later.

Although every one of the problems is not totally resolved, we're both thrilled just to be in each other's company and she sees me in a very different way.

—Carter, age 47, married 15 years

expect, I gave her whatever reassurance I could as a couple of scrub-attired nurses ushered her off into the back room.

Then I got to thinking. My wife was faced with possible death (she recovered just fine, thank you), and her last thought was of what should happen to her jewelry. She had been telling me she likes jewelry for a long time, but just then, in that instant, I heard in a different way what she had been saying. I understood that she saw jewelry as more than just an ornament—she saw it as a precious extension of herself and an enduring symbol, a legacy to pass on to future generations. I never thought of it like that before, and it taught me a lot about her. It wasn't that she was materialistic or greedy. Not at all. Jewelry for her was more symbolic, a metaphor for love, permanence, loyalty, devotion. Like a lot of women (and men, too), she agreed with that famous and oh-so-effective advertising slogan—whatever you may think of it—that "diamonds are forever." I had held an incorrect assumption and never even thought to challenge it.

Take a Closer Look

Think about all the day-to-day details of living with your wife that you take for granted because you assume that you understand them. Then think about the following areas of your wife's life and ask yourself if any of them are worth a second look. Do you understand how she feels about . . .

Her Being a Mother

Some women are totally okay with being a full-time mom, but many women feel deeply conflicted by how motherhood confines them and defines them. Early child rearing can be extremely demanding, and your wife may feel inadequate because of how stressful taking care of children can be. Is it possible that some of your wife's unhappiness or anger may not have anything to do with how she feels about you, but rather about her conflicting feelings about being a mother?

Her Relation to Her Own Parents

Starting a marriage with you may have caused your wife to rerun all the old tapes about her relationship with her parents and their relationship to each other. Do you really know how your wife feels about her childhood? It's possible that the way she reacts to your anger or even love is a leftover response from unfinished business in her original family.

Her Relation to Your Parents

Your parents, and your relationship to them, can get in the way of a strong marriage. You'd be surprised how your mother's offhand comments about her daughter-in-law's competence and your reaction to those comments affect your wife. Do you know how she feels about your frequent phone calls to your mother or your decision to keep your distance from your parents? She may seem to be angry about having to cook more than her share or clean up after you, but the problem may really be rooted in her role as a daughter-in-law.

How She Wants to Raise Her Children

This subject could be whole book. I'll give you one example of how couples may not understand each other in the parenting arena. Invariably, when I talk to women about raising children through their teenage years, they say how very tough it is, how it's the biggest challenge of their lives. When I speak to men, they shrug, say it could be worse, and deny feeling much stress about it. Men are much more likely to see their children's acting out as part and parcel of being a kid. From this point of view, a husband will have no idea why his wife collapses into tears after a run-in with one of the children.

Her Career

Man, if you could walk in your wife's shoes for *one minute* on this one! Career issues may be quite straightforward for you, but they are anything but for her, especially if she is not only working outside the home but also juggling day care for your children, looking after you, and being the one most responsible for preparing meals and doing other domestic chores. Trying to prioritize a stuffy nose in relation to a board meeting is absolutely nerve wracking, yet those kinds of issues are often overlooked as a source of major stress on the marriage. Or perhaps your wife is one of the women who, at a rate much higher than men, take time out of the workforce to raise children. Sounds like the ideal situation, but try to imagine just for a moment what that does to a woman's sense of identity. It's certainly enough to feed family tensions when you least expect it.

Her Attitude Toward Material Things

I recognized that my connection to jewelry wasn't the same as Susan's. Have you figured out how your wife relates to material stuff, such as clothes or cars? It's worth paying attention to what she treasures and what she gives away to Salvation Army. We'll talk about this one more in Chapter Eight.

Her Notion of Important Ideas

What topics of discussion are interesting to your wife? Making assumptions about this, you may read detailed stories from the newspaper aloud to her in the morning. But have you ever noticed if these are the things that interest her? Pay attention to the ideas that get her charged up and the ones that leave her flat.

Look at your wife with new eyes. This is your chance to ask her questions, watch her actions, get to know who she has become since the day she married you. We all change—how has your wife changed? This is your challenge: give her a clean slate so that you can discover her all over again.

Psst!

SecretsofMarriedMen.com

My ex-husband assumed that I was just lazy after I gave birth to my daughter. I could barely get myself out of bed each day, never mind clean up the house before he came home. He didn't know I was actually suffering from post-partum depression. He never thought for one second that something was wrong with me, and after listening to the advice of other people, he pushed harder and harder to make me "snap out of it." Finally it ended our marriage. Always listen to your mate and to your heart to know how to treat your wife.

—Rebecca, age 31, second marriage of 7 years

FOCUS ON SPECIFIC BEHAVIORS

Biologically speaking, males are ideally suited to learning through observation. They are more adept than women at using their left brain to collect logical and linear information, undiluted by emotional input. With less peripheral vision than women, less color discrimination, and fewer multitasking abilities to distract them, they are keen, focused observers.[2] When men make it their mission to observe, they can easily block out distractions to take in the information they need. Don't believe me? Take a close look at a man watching a football game or playing Gamecube. When we need to, we can focus, and we can learn.

Well, now you can use that skill to make your marriage great. You can learn a lot by staying in the background and watching your wife with this same intensity. For example, you might start your observations the next time you visit a supermarket with your wife. During this mundane chore, you can learn something about the way her mind works if you step back and let her take the lead.

Let her decide which items to buy, which aisles to peruse, and how long to stay. You'll soon notice something about the way she thinks and makes decisions. Her methods of shopping are more than just consumer habits—they're clear signs of her personality. If she takes time to check prices, choose the bargain of the day, *and* use coupons, you'll learn that she's careful about how she spends money; this is a clue as to why she gets so angry when you pick up the tab when you go out to eat with friends. (Money is at the top of the list of things couples argue about.) What else can you notice? Does she plan out her trip so that she ends up in the frozen food aisle last so those foods are less likely to melt, or does she haphazardly choose her items? If she goes for the ice cream first, you'll have some insight into behavior that may drive you crazy at home when she doesn't plan ahead or think of the consequences of actions in the same way you do.

You can learn a lot if you just watch. Does she know exactly what she wants, or does she browse? Does she use a list or buy on impulse? Does she use her sense of sight or touch to buy produce? If you don't know the answers to these questions, there's a lot you don't know about your wife.

Of course, the answers to the questions aren't right or wrong. They just give you information to help you get to know this person you're sworn to love. Individually, these observations don't mean a whole lot. But put them all together and you get a better picture of the person you're trying to relate to and communicate with, and they also give you the tools you'll need in later chapters.

If you start thinking of yourself as engaging in industrial espionage, you'll be surprised at all the places you can find to know your wife better. Consider the list here and reflect now on how much you really know her. What turns her on? What excites or bothers her in these situations? What are her facial expressions, her body language? What does she love to do and with whom does she enjoy certain

REMEMBER THIS
There's a Reason Men Don't Like
to Go Clothes Shopping with Women

Do you have any idea why it takes your wife two hours to find one pair of pants she likes? Well, watch how often she takes something off the rack, tries it on, and then rejects it. This habit drives most men crazy because they just don't see how this process can be called "fun." Yet social researchers have found that 61 percent of women say they "love" or "like" the experience of shopping whether they buy anything or not. But a full 53 percent of men say they don't love or like shopping and go to stores only to buy what they need and then get out fast.[3] There's no point fighting this. It's just the way it is, and once you tune into this habit of females, you can turn it off as a source of anger and frustration.

specific activities? As you consider this field research, imagine you need to prepare a report to your CEO and need to observe more closely in person. Look carefully. What do you see?

- On the sidelines of your child's sports game

- With her best girlfriend

- At the beach

- While reading a magazine

- At a restaurant or coffee shop

- Before sex

- During sex

- After sex

Well, you get the idea. There are many places you can monitor and learn from your wife's actions and interactions. Don't watch with judgment; don't watch to compare or be critical. Just watch and keep an open mind. Even though her mode of navigating through this world may not make much sense to you, in no small part it is why you fell in love with her and why she is your wife today.

SecretsofMarriedMen.com

There will never be a substitute for devoted friendship if you really want to see your wife for who she really is. It is much more difficult to build a relationship by starting with sex and moving into friendship, than it is from the starting point of friendship and then moving toward romance, sex, and family.

—Dave, age 25, married 1 year

ASK DIRECTIONS

While making an effort to get to know your wife, it won't be unusual to find yourself in situations where you don't understand what's going on. When that happens, *ask for clarification*. Too often, innocent misunderstandings lead to arguments that bring unnecessary tension into the marriage simply because we don't know what our wives are thinking.

Gene, for example, got involved in an online romance. Obviously, this was not good for his marriage, and when his wife found out about it, Gene promised to stay away from chat rooms for good. A month later when he had to go out of town on a business trip, his wife said she'd like to come along. Here was the point when Gene should have said something like, "You've never wanted to come on my business trips before. Why do you want to come now?" Instead, he jumped to the conclusion that she didn't trust him and wanted to keep an eye on him. They both went on the trip, but tension and resentment went with them. If he had asked, his wife would have explained that her desire for companionship wasn't about her lack of trust, but about wanting an opportunity to get away with him and rekindle some romance.

Don't ever be afraid to get to know your wife's thoughts and feelings by simply asking, "What do you mean?"—even if you worry that your question will at first be misinterpreted or received as criticism. You and your wife are equals in this relationship. You're talking to a person who is committed to the marriage and who loves you. But she may be startled when you start to question her. Expect and accept this reaction if it happens. Assure her that you are genuinely interested and want to understand her better, and that you need her help to do that. Then make sure that when you ask questions, you ask with sincerity and true interest, and resist the temptation to be judgmental about the answer you get. When your wife explains why she wants to give her third cousin by marriage once removed a $500 wedding gift, don't respond with "That's the stupidest thing I ever heard." Remember, you asked the question "Why" so that you could better understand her point of view—not to judge her.

Psst!

SecretsofMarriedMen.com

Always remember that nobody is perfect. You will make stupid mistakes. You will say stupid things. You will do these things because you are human. The question is how will you handle them. Don't hesitate to be compassionate, understanding and loving. Be man enough to admit when you are wrong.

—Frank, age 57, married 32 years

DEEP DEBRIEFING

So, you might wonder, what are you to do with all this information that you gather by observing your wife? Well, here's the answer. You can use it to make your marriage far better than it is today (even if you already have a great marriage).

To keep track of both the activities you observe and your insights about what you see, and to record your ideas about what you can do with those observations, I suggest writing it all down. (I'm just one of those people who need to keep lists and charts to stay organized and to keep track of what I'm doing and where I'm going. If you can keep this info in your head—great. But stay on top of it.)

Table 4.1 gives you an idea of how you can track your progress in getting to know your wife and doing something about what you learn. It is followed by a short list called "Psychological Profile." This is the kind of debriefing material you need in order to turn your observations into action.

Table 4.1.   Daily Observation Chart.

Activity	Observation	What Can I Do About It?
Argued on phone with mother about vacation plans	After she hung up, she was upset and went straight to the refrigerator to eat.	Next time I see her picking at the fridge, ask, "What's up?"
Had a conversation with me about a problem I'm having at work	She starts clipping her nails and buffing them up with an emory board.	When I see that she's looking at her nails when I talk to her, I should realize she's bored and change the subject or ask her about herself.
Went shopping in mall for clothes for the kids	She always goes to the item that is on the mannequin as she walks in the store.	If I want to have her notice something, I have to dress it up and make it distinct so it gets her attention.

Table 4.1.   (Continued).

Activity	Observation	What Can I Do About It?
	She has no patience when two people are talking at her at once.	When I see both of the kids wanting her attention at once, I should take one of them aside and either keep him entertained or try to get what he needs.
	She was really attracted to the red scarves.	Something to put on the Mother's Day shopping list!
Watching TV in bed at night	She complained that her feet are cold—a common complaint.	Pick up a pair of those heated socks I saw in the boutique or bring her a hot water bottle.
	She wants me to join her for *Law and Order*.	Arrange to be in bed by 10:00 for *Law and Order* on Wednesdays.

Psychological Profile

- Things she likes

  Red scarves

  Law and Order (the original one)

  Whatever is big, bold, neatly detailed, and in front of her

- Things she doesn't like

  More than one person talking to her at once

  Conflict with her mother

  Hates it when her feet get cold at night

- Nonverbal cues

  Looking at nails = bored

  Hunting in fridge = upset

- Things to add to my list for next week

    Pick up a red scarf at the mall.

    Pick up a pair of heated socks for those cold feet of hers.

    Wednesday night: bed by 10:00 P.M. for *Law and Order*—set PDA alarm to remind me.

These observations and reactions may be the best things to happen to your marriage *if* you follow through and use them to show your wife just how serious you are about having the best marriage ever.

REMEMBER THIS
Love Is an Action Word

First and foremost, getting to know your wife is an act of love. Because many men grew up never hearing "I love you" from their fathers, they often express emotions through their actions, rather than with words. That's okay. Getting to know your wife is a good example of how you demonstrate love through your action.

KNOW YOUR WIFE TO LOVE HER, NOT TO CHANGE HER

We don't get to know our wives so we can hammer the gavel down and pronounce guilt or innocence, right or wrong. When she says she likes reruns of *Eight Is Enough*, your opinion about the quality of the show isn't at issue. What's important is taking time to think about what she likes and why.

We're also not trying to understand our wives so we can get around them or manipulate or trick them in any way. Rather, we want to know our wives better so we can have the tools necessary to improve our relationship and love them for who they truly are. When I urge you to know your wife, I am suggesting that you should open your mind to ways of acting and thinking that may be different than your male instincts. You do this not just because you love your wife but because this is a good way to be a better friend to her and to acknowledge your desire to build that friendship. By scrutinizing your wife's behavior, you'll learn a lot about what makes her tick, and that is the goal.

Keep this goal in mind as you move on to the next chapter. You're going to be asked to stick around the house more often so that you have more opportunities to observe your wife and get to know her better. If that's still what you're after, then keep reading.

Psst!

SecretsofMarriedMen.com

Accepting my wife for who she is has been the greatest discovery ever. I have a whole new platform for my relationship.
—Allen, age 66, married 40 years

TO DO LIST

- Drop all past assumptions about your wife. Look at her as if you just met her today and try to discover who she really is.

- Use your keen powers of observation to watch your wife and learn more about her. Pay attention to how she acts in various life situations. What do these actions tell you about her as a person?

- When you can't understand her point of view, ask for clarification.

- As you observe your wife, open your mind to ways of acting and thinking that may be different than your ways.

- Keep track of your observations on a chart and create a Psychological Profile to guide you into action.

- Love your wife for who she is—not who you think she should be.

5

The Third Way

Be Home Now

Harken back to your shop class and you may recall the tools needed to build a house: hammer, lumber, 10-penny nails, gypsum board. If your shop instructor was anything like mine, he taught you about the physical elements of construction, but he didn't say boo about the metaphysical part of actually living in that house. Of course, when you are married and have a family, you do need a physical place to live (even if it's in the basement of your parent's ranch house), but once the final trim is painted you still have a lot more work to do before it becomes a real home.

In this chapter we're going to talk about the very simple yet oh-so-hard-to-do third marital rule: Be Home Now. To win your wife's heart and build a lasting marriage, you have to be there, in person, day by day, Mr. Regular, at home, in the building—and that's that.

WHY COME HOME 101

It's a straightforward but overlooked truth that successful husbands spend time in their house in order to build a home. I know this sounds simplistic, but don't slough it off as trivial.

One of the most common complaints I hear from wives, especially those who haven't been married too long, is that their husbands divide their nonworking lives between two pursuits, neither of which includes them: hanging out with their pals and sitting alone in front of the television or computer monitor oblivious to the rest of the world. It's sad but true. An astonishing number of young, newly married men seem to think that after all the fuss surrounding the wedding ceremony and honeymoon, they can get back to their bachelor routine: golf every Saturday, beers a couple of nights a week after work with the guys, slow-pitch softball league, football season tickets with their college buddies, and the occasional road trip. In other words, life as an independent person. This is being a guy, right? Well, kind of . . . if you want to stay nineteen all your life.

Breeding for Wanderlust

There are a few interesting reasons why men more than women are likely to stray from home. It's no excuse, but we men can claim that we were brought up to be this way. Men in our culture are conditioned at a very early age to cut the apron strings and move away from home base. Child development experts have watched generations of parents comfort their sad or fearful sons with a quick hug and then an encouraging push to "get back out there," while they placate their daughters by holding them close and soothing them longer.

This affects how males and females learn their gender roles. Researchers have found that when mothers placed their thirteen-month-old babies in an unfamiliar room filled with toys to play with, the girls spent most of their time near their mother, came back to her frequently if they strayed away, and maintained continuous contact through touching, glancing, and talking. The little boys were quite different: they were more likely to go all the way to the far side of the room, to spend less time close to the women who cared for them, and to check in with her less frequently.[1] Sounds an awful lot like the husbands I talk to in my practice each day.

Evolution may also have had a hand in this natural need to wander. After all, hunting on the savanna required the caveman to roam for days on end, usually with other guys. Sure, they did their share of climbing through the dense brush in search of weak and unsuspecting wildebeests, but come on, they couldn't have been so serious the *whole time* they were away from home. I have no doubt that primitive man would pause along the hunt, find a nice smooth stone, and shout, "Thog—go deep!"

So if it's hard-wired in us men to be hunters, adventurers, and explorers, why should our wives expect us to spend time with them at the cave? Because they need us there, and because it's also possible that our reasons for staying away have nothing to do with our breeding.

Psst!

SecretsofMarriedMen.com

I find it fascinating that a man would ask if the time spent together sleeping counts as time spent together. But I am sobered by the fact that my husband might indeed think so. Men and women do think of time spent together in entirely different terms. No, gentleman, we do not consider serving you pretzels during the football game as a moment of deep connection.

—Rochelle, age 30, married 13 years

The Art of Avoidance

Natural inclination and evolutionary imperative aside, those of us who spend less time at home than we should or could need to take an honest look at our motives. The causes of the real problem are usually within our control. As you read through the following discussion, be brutally honest with yourself. Do any of these reasons for staying away from home hit home with you?

To Avoid Conflict

Research has consistently shown that men avoid conflict with their wives because when their brain gets flooded with emotions, they are less competent problem-solvers than women.

I know this sounds surprising. Certainly, with their higher levels of testosterone fueling aggression and competitive urges, most men are very competent at handling conflict. Yet they'll avoid going home just to hide from confrontation with their wives. Sounds like a paradox, but it's really quite understandable.

At work, most of us know what to do when we get there. And we have a road map to guide us through trouble spots. We know our destination, and we know where the exits and alternate routes are if we hit a roadblock or traffic jam. But at home, we don't always know what to expect when we arrive, and we don't feel confident that we know how to achieve our goal—or even what that goal is.

I had a couple in my office recently who illustrated this kind of conflict avoidance. I asked the husband, who is a competent child psychologist, "Do you really need to spend so much at-home time in your study with your computer?" He quickly answered, "I could try to be with the family more, but when I try to get involved, we usually end up arguing before I even sit down for dinner about something I did or didn't do with our kids. It feels to me that I can't meet her expectations because I can't figure out exactly what she expects from me. So I just stay away."

This is so typical. Outside the home, this man is trusted to know what's best for children, but when he comes home, he knows his wife will jump all over him for some misstep with his own kids. So he avoids the conflict by spending his time isolated from his family. Ironically, he spends more time each day with other people's kids than he does with his own.

None of us want to go home when we know we'll be walking on land mines.

To Avoid Loss of Control

Have you ever walked through the front door of your home and suddenly felt like an outsider or an interloper? Or worse: like a hired hand? If you have, it's probably because your wife has taken charge and left you with no important or well-defined household role to play. This is especially likely to happen in marriages where the wife spends more time in the home and therefore establishes the rhythm and routine of that environment. She decides when everyone eats, where everyone goes in the evening or on weekends, when she and her husband go to bed, even how they'll spend their money. This wife may have a long list of things for her honey to do that he doesn't want to do, and still he often feels that he's interrupting and in the way. That can be unnerving to a guy who's used to feeling powerful and in charge. In this situation, it's not long before the man will be spending more time at work or with his friends than at home with his wife.

A man I have been counseling for his severe depression has long felt that he has no say in the way things are run in his marriage. He recently told me a story that illustrated exactly why he has this feeling. His wife went in for a surgical procedure that brought her to the brink of death after unexpected and severe complications. But she survived.

As she came out of the anesthesia, her first words to him were, "So, I guess you think *you'll* be taking over now." She was more worried about who would have the power in their home than about her possible demise.

"No, no," he assured her, "don't worry, you'll still be in charge of everything as soon as we get home."

This fellow gave his wife complete control of their relationship, but then wondered why he battled such severe depression.

To Avoid the Stress of Parenting or Household Work

Being at home can be very stressful. The job of parenting or of maintaining a home is time consuming; it's stressful, strenuous, and demanding; it's often just not fun. In households where there is extended family or close friends nearby to step in and ease the burden while mom and dad take short (or sometimes long) breaks, there is less need to hide from the demands of home life. But far too many couples live apart from their parents or siblings. There is no hope of relief, so the inevitable stress of family life becomes a reason to avoid going home.

Men have an opportunity to stay away to avoid family responsibilities more often than women because society lets them. A wife who works overtime and weekends while her family struggles at home without her is not admired by her family for her work ethic. Despite all the progress made through the feminist movement, if there's no one else to watch the kids, it's the woman who's expected to be at home when she's not required to be at work. But a man gets a break and can easily use work as an excuse to stay away from home—and many do.

To Avoid Intimacy

Some men stay away from home to hide from their fear of intimate situations. This is different from being afraid of having sex. It's about being afraid of marital situations that would push them to show the vulnerable side that does exist in every man.

By sharing another person's emotional world, we risk exposing our own emotional world—something that's very difficult for many men to do, especially for those raised by fathers who taught them to bury their feelings.

It's far easier for many men to keep up their defenses by being the warrior, rather than to admit to being a "dandy in distress." I've seen married men who feel this vulnerability much more than their single friends because more people's lives are depending on the married man, so it's just too emotionally risky to show any cracks in the armor.

Complicating this fear is the fact that some men who have shown those cracks have learned that their wives are not as sympathetic or supportive as they had hoped they'd be. Although women claim they want to see the more "feminine" side of their men, true vulnerability more often than not scares women. I've seen men who break down during my counseling sessions feel horribly ridiculed by wives who say, "Grow up. Be a man!"

What does that mean? It means "endure pain silently," "don't show your feelings," "keep your vulnerable side to yourself . . . I really don't want to hear about it." To do this, some men will spend more time at work or with friends, where they do not have to deal with their intimacy issues.

To Avoid Having to Grow Up

When married men are at home, they can't act like they did back in their bachelor days. Keg parties every night are out. Being an irresponsible slob is frowned on. Hanging out with the guys while there are kids to be watched and a lawn to be mowed is bound to cause marital upset. Some men who just aren't ready to be responsible husbands find it much easier to hang out at their friends' homes than to face the responsibilities in their own homes.

This lack of maturity is at the top of the list of things that put the first years of marriage on shaky ground. There was a study of ten thousand households in which 645 marriages were observed over a period of five years. Many of those couples expressed deep unhappiness in their marriages. When the researchers looked at how those couples fared five years later, they found that 23 percent of them had divorced. But the most remarkable thing about the study was that of the couples that stayed together, the vast majority felt much better about their marriages and described themselves as "happy" or "very happy" in their unions. Very few of these marriages improved through the wise intervention of therapists or ministers. In fact, most couples reported that they just kept going, putting one foot in front of the other. But when the researchers talked to fifty-five of these couples to find out what had tripped them up five years earlier, according to the report, one of the most common complaints was, "men behaving badly." The researchers commented that many wives described great levels of unhappiness because their men were staying out at night, acting reckless, hanging with their buddies, or using drugs or alcohol.[2]

Psst!

SecretsofMarriedMen.com

How do I get the attention of a Peter Pan? He is fifty-one years old and prefers the company of his little brother. We have been married for twenty months and he can't find anything to do with me. I suggest we go here or go there and he agrees, then his brother stops in and asks him to go out and he forgets about me.

—Pat, age 55, married 20 months

This immature, adolescent lifestyle is hard for some young men—and some not so young men—to get over because of what the mass media and pop culture tell us about "real men." Open the pages of *Maxim* or *Men's Journal* and you will see a glamorized depiction of manliness. These publications reinforce the notion that a real man spends his leisure time scaling the Himalayas or tasting the forbidden nightlife of Amsterdam or Bangkok. The real man masters all the electronic gadgets, drives the hottest cars—a Range Rover for adventure, a Porsche for dating—and dresses like Brad Pitt or James Bond. Inevitably, in these magazines, women are seen as the ultimate accessory. They average about 105 pounds, dress with their perfect breasts seductively exposed, and gaze, pouty lipped and hungry eyed, awaiting the opportunity to satisfy their man sexually.

In men's popular culture, the underlying message can be summed up in two words: freedom and adventure. So it's no wonder that many men resist the Be Home Now rule and choose to stay away from the place that reminds them of their real responsibilities.

To Avoid Getting Caught

I hate to say this, but some of the more dastardly married members of our gender actually think they still have the right to chase after women. For them, staying out of the house is one way to keep from being questioned or to minimize any guilt that might ensue. You know who you are. This is the best way to destroy a marriage, but it does happen. No excuse. No rationale. No support from me for this, so cut it out and grow up. The affair is over.

To Avoid Feeling Like a Bad Provider

Some men think they must sacrifice their own need for love and intimacy precisely *for* their wives and family. These men risk their mental and physical health to work overtime or maybe even two jobs to give their families everything the men think they need. Although at first glance it seems admirable that these men have such a strong sense of duty, in many cases the time spent earning more money is another socially condoned way of avoiding being at home.

If you are one of these hard-working men, you need to evaluate how this work is contributing to or detracting from your state of happiness. It's possible that your wife would actually prefer living in a smaller house, taking fewer vacations, or remodeling less often, if it meant you could be at home more to work on having a good marriage.

Harkening back to our evolutionary roots, it's true that we've been given superior muscular strength, single-minded focus, an independent spirit, and a well-honed fight-or-flight system to provide for our clan, but let's not forget that our skills have been honed over the ages to *protect* the family as well. After the hunt, we must come home. When we finally arrive, carcass slung across our shoulders, our wives and kids are waiting for us around the fire, now feeling safe and secure once more. It is at home that we receive our reward for being such good providers.

There are many reasons why a man might choose to stay away from his home, but there is no way to avoid the truth: the only way to build a lasting relationship based on loyalty, devotion, and commitment is to be at home, spending real time with your wife.

REMEMBER THIS
You Can Be "Home" Even Away from Home

You can enjoy the benefits of being home even when you and your wife go out together. I mean really together. Not to dinner with another family. Not to a charity ball with four other couples from the office seated at your table. I mean going out together to dinner or a movie, or taking a walk on the beach or a drive in the country and stopping for an extravagant picnic lunch. No kids, either. Being home, in the context of this chapter, means being wherever you and your wife temporarily set up shop and you are really together. It's the time spent face-to-face that counts. A motel room for a night, a cruise cabin, or a tent in the wilderness can all be your home. Every happily married man knows that when he's really with his wife, he's at home in the world.

EARLY ADJUSTMENTS

New husbands shouldn't expect "I do" to be the last words they hear before being fitted for a ball and chain. But getting married does require a change in habits. Before marriage, men are more likely than women to engage in reckless behavior. Data from police reports, epidemiological surveys, and insurance companies tell us that men drive faster, eat more fast food, and are more likely to have one-night stands. Additional data show that entering into the fraternity of husbands slows a man's driving speed, cuts down his drug abuse, and reduces his number of sex partners.[3] But these men don't change all at once (except, we hope, for the sex partner thing). Adjusting to the weight of that gold band around the fourth finger often happens in fits and starts.

SecretsofMarriedMen.com

Happiness in marriage is spending time and standing by the man/woman you say you love. Yes, you make your happiness, but also it takes two. For a marriage to work both parties have to take the time to sit down, talk, and compromise.

—Marilyn, age 22, married 4 years

First Mistake on My First Day of Marriage

I recall a vivid example of this adjustment in my own marriage. In fact, it happened on the very first day of my honeymoon. My wife and I stayed in a beachfront hut on the Pacific Island paradise of Tahiti. We chose a Club Med honeymoon, one that is known for ease and convenience and lots of socializing. Soon after we arrived, I collapsed on the too-small bed for a nap, and to give me peace and quiet, Susan went off for a short stroll. I quickly regained my energy and decided not to look for Susan—but instead to join the 2:00 P.M. volleyball game. I left a note on our bed that said, AT VOLLEYBALL, and I took off.

At this point my female readers are no doubt gasping in horror at my gaff, while my male readers might be more inclined to follow the logic of my impulsive decision. But by the time you've finished reading this chapter, you'll be better able to understand why this seemingly innocent action was so devastating to my wife. When she finally tracked me down, my wife expressed her feelings clearly: I had screwed up. She felt deserted, unloved, and low on my list of things to do. To her, home is where the hut is, and I wasn't there for her. (Not only that but my team lost the game.)

Scenes like this play out for almost every married man in some fashion or another, especially in the formative years of marriage—the years when roles are first defined and tasks are assigned. I wasn't trying to assert my independence. I didn't set out to show my new wife that I could not be tied down. I just wanted to play volleyball. Now that I know my wife better, I can clearly understand how she felt when she returned to an empty room. But I honestly didn't know I was supposed to wait for her.

The bottom line: marriage requires a whole new set of rules.

Psst! SecretsofMarriedMen.com

I'm in my mid-fifties, so my tomcat days are long past. I would rather be at home than any place else I can think of with the possible exception of being out fishing somewhere, which I don't do very often. My relationship with my wife is much more important to me at this stage of my life than any other.

—Damien, third marriage of 6 years

INDEPENDENCE VERSUS TOGETHERNESS

So what are the rules of marriage? As a bachelor, I had a pretty good grasp of acceptable and unacceptable protocol for life in general. But when I got married, I wasn't sure anymore. Was I still allowed to buddy up to my pals? Could I talk with friends about the great sex I had with my wife last night? Suddenly, after a brief matrimonial ceremony, the rules changed. Now what?

Now you must master a balancing act. Imagine a tightrope suspended high in the air. If you stay upright on the rope, dead center, you're promised the joys of living together: building the life you have always dreamed of; enjoying sexual intimacy and nights, weekends, and vacations together; creating a lifelong partnership; getting to know someone so well that you rise to levels of intimacy and understanding you never imagined; raising or not raising a family; and growing old together.

Lean too far to the right, however, and you tilt toward total independence. If you slip in this direction, you may achieve your work and career goals, maintain exclusive friendships, spend solo time enjoying hobbies and activities, and veg out alone. But your wife will be deeply unhappy. And so, ultimately, will you.

If you lean too far to your left, you enter a world where you risk losing your individuality. When that happens, you return home from work each day, braced to succumb to the whims of your wife at the expense of your own interests. Your hopes and desires are stifled as your spouse appears to be realizing all her needs. And after all that, she still wants more!

Successful husbands must somehow find a way to stand balanced in the middle of the tightrope where they honor their own dreams while attending to their wife's needs. How do you strike this balance? How do you divide up the hours of the day in a way that is acceptable to both you and her? How do you answer the demands of your day job and the call of your wanderlust while also preserving the great priority of building a home with a devoted and contented wife?

I'll tell you the way to start: be clear about your priorities. If you care about your work and ambition but know that none of that kind of achievement can happen, nor would mean a darn thing, if you didn't have your wife and family as the number one reason to be alive, helping you establish who you are in the world and providing the home base for everything you do, then keep that attitude at the very front of your mind and at the top of your list as you continue reading this book. You'll soon learn how to put it into action.

If, however, putting your wife and family front and forward feels to you like trying to speak a foreign language, don't put down the book assuming that I'm not talking about your marriage. Instead, rethink your priorities and ask yourself whether you can make it your goal to rearrange them. On your wedding day, you probably had no trouble with the idea of putting your wife first, so if you realize now that you've drifted from that commitment, it's time to drift back. Besides, you already put your hard-earned money into this book, so you might as well read it through to the end as you figure out how to balance the all too few hours of the day between career and home or, as Dr. Freud used to say, the two essential goals for a human being—meaningful work and intimate love.

Looking for Love in All the Wrong Places

Stephanie is a forty-nine-year-old woman in her twentieth year of marriage. Her concerns reflect those of many wives whose husbands have not learned to make a house a home: "His work and career are his first love and utmost priority," she laments. "He gets up, goes to work (where he finds his comfort and happiness through accomplishments and adoration from fellow workers), comes home, expects the maid (me!) to have his shirts ironed and meal on the table so he can escape our home for another 16 hours the next morning."

Although I admire Stephanie's husband, Jeff, for his drive and business acumen, he's missing a key ingredient in his life, an ingredient that Stephanie thought was supposed to come with marriage. She continues:

> I sometimes think of myself as a single mom with a paycheck. When the kids were growing up, he often went days without seeing them, leaving early in the morning before they were up and returning after they were in bed. Yes, he provides well for us monetarily, but at the cost of offering no father figure for the children and no life partner for me.

When he speaks about work or people at work, one can tell that's his whole life and the place he loves to be. He never gave us a chance to be his comfort zone here at home, because he's never been here at home.

Being home gives the message to your wife that she is central to your life. It's crucially important to *her*. Your being home starts to make your wife feel more comfortable, more trusting of you, and more aware of your commitment. Being home becomes a way of acting out your commitment tangibly, in a way your wife can understand. Stephanie, for good reason, doesn't experience that trust:

> Do I think he's having an affair at work? Well, he has one cute little employee he's brought along on his coattails every time he's changed companies, because "she's such a good worker!" Yeah, I'd like to know exactly what it is she's so good at working on! Once, at a family gathering, my brother asked me where my husband was. I said, to my mother's shock, "He's with his mistress." I explained that I meant his work and computers were his mistress. After about an hour, he appeared, smiling and euphoric about a project that he had just completed successfully. His words upon entering my brother's house were: "Wow. What a great feeling. It's better than an orgasm!" There you have it. Some men love, love, love their work, and their families and wife are merely incidentals, trophies and caretakers, kept just to support his needs and get him ready for another day at the office.

Although Jeff may have truly felt that he was working so hard because it was important to his family, I would argue that he wasn't home enough to really know his wife (as you have come to know your wife because you paid attention during the last chapter). Had he done so, he would have recognized the pain that he caused her.

Stephanie concludes, "I wish I had the guts and financial ability to walk out on him. Let him iron his own damn shirts!"

Finding Your Balance

If you were Stephanie's husband, you might have many excuses for your work habits. You could point to the outrageous credit card payments, the private school tuition, or the many people you help in the community. From your perspective, it is understandable why you would not be spending as much time together as when you dated. Understandable for you as a guy, yes. But it may not be understandable for your wife, and she's the one more likely to get fed up and hand you back the ring.

Of course, spending more time at home isn't an instant cure for what ails your marriage. But you should definitely give it a try, without getting discouraged by the challenges of walking this tightrope between your need for independence away from home and your need to build your marriage by staying at home. If you concentrate, practice every day, and expect to fall down once in a while, you'll learn from your mistakes, and someday you'll be capable of performing without a net—maybe even executing a back flip now and then.

QUALITY TIME

There is a small catch to the Be Home Now rule. Simply being in the house more often is a good start, but it's not the ultimate goal. If by your presence you become just one more thing for your wife to trip over while she's mopping up the mud you tracked in and cleaning up your empty beer cans, you will find that this idea of being home more will probably backfire. You have to make your at-home hours count by using the time to give your wife your attention, help, and love.

Stacy, a mother of two, met her husband, Russell, when they were still in high school. Stacy tells me that ever since their children were toddlers, Russell had climbed the ladder of success as a merchant seaman—a job that required him to be away from home nine months out of the year. When he was gone, she pined for him. Yet when he returned, he disappointed her. After a quick hello upon his return, Russell would spend the night drinking and occasionally drugging with his old friends from the neighborhood. He'd return and demand sex, whether she wanted it or not. He slept late in the mornings and waited impatiently for her to prepare a large breakfast when he awoke.

In his fashion, Russell thought he was spending time with his wife when his ship was in port. In her view, he wasn't. In reality, Russell couldn't adapt to the expectations of being a husband. For him, being home meant being a part of Stacy's life—on his schedule and on his terms. Stacy is now divorced, and Russell is still calling her to "hook up."

Most husbands are not as dense as Russell, but many of us have trouble seeing the imbalance that often exists in the quality-time-at-home department. We all need to rethink our priorities and recognize that we may be using work, ego, ambition, and other "rational" reasons for not being at home as much as we should be to strengthen our marriages—emotionally as well as physically.

Psst! ——————————————————————————————

SecretsofMarriedMen.com

Stop expecting so much from her. And take the cliché about being toughest on those we love most and give it the porcelain swirl. The people we love deserve our lightest touch, and that means expecting her to be, allowing her to be, and loving her for, nothing more than herself. It is the only thing any of us can reasonably, and justly, expect of anyone.

—Ed, age 45, married 18 years

THE PAYOFF

About now you may be asking yourself, "If I stay at home more, my wife may be happier, but what's the payoff for me?" Trust me on this. The payoff for you is direct and bountiful. When you spend more time there, home is the place where you will receive love, friendship, support, emotional nourishment, peace of mind, fun, intimacy, and sexual satisfaction—in other words, happiness. This is not just about pleasing the wife but also about taking care of yourself and your needs as a man.

Feeling Safe at Home

Home can be a safe place where you can put aside your insecurities and not worry about finding your next date, not worry about finding someone who loves you and will be your companion. It can be a place where you go when you're tired of the rat race. Sure, your old posters may not be tacked on the wall the way they used to be, but that doesn't mean you can't get comfortable—if you make the effort to spend more time at home.

As you begin to settle in, your wife will get to know you better. She'll start to notice your tastes, your favorite TV shows, your habits (like reading the paper in the mornings), and your favorite places in the house to hang out. Being there is a way of subtly establishing territory for yourself within your own home.

Being home also gives you a chance to pursue your hobbies. Remember the days of picking up a book, collecting stamps, or playing fantasy football? Get back to these hobbies again or look around for new ones. Your kids might lead the way on this. My son played a game called "Magic: The Gathering"; it was a card game similar to "Pokémon" that he picked up in fourth grade. At first I was reluctant to play because it was his thing. But after a while he taught me, and I really loved the game—in fact, even though my son stopped playing by the time he started middle school, I continue to collect cards and play with other Magic enthusiasts.

Whatever the hobby may be, when you spend more time at home, you'll have time for exploring pastimes and hobbies new and old that help center you, relax you, and give you a sense of control over yourself and your world.

When you put your hobbies aside, parking yourself right in the middle of family action is also a good way to find out how things work—and that alone can increase your sense of competence and security around the house. An awful lot of men have no idea how their household is run. Where are the spare keys kept? What brand of peanut butter do the kids like? Which plumber always comes when the drain backs up? How do the microeconomics of the household work? How is the address book organized? (Is your next door neighbor's number filed under "B" for Betty? "R" for Ricci? "N" for neighbor?) If you don't know the answers to questions like these, you haven't been staying at home enough.

Being at home is not just a gift you give to your wife and kids—there's something in it for you too. Being home allows you to slow down and take a breath. It gives you a chance to look inward at yourself and the role you play as the man of the house.

Watering the Roots of Your Marriage

Your marriage is rooted in your at-home relationship with your wife, so being at home is the best way to nurture it—even if you do nothing more than talk about your day-to-day stuff. When you rush home at 7:30 just in time to eat and check the mail, all you really have time to do is put out fires, review the kids' math homework, discuss the critical issues of the day, then crash—because even if you're up for more conversation, the odds are that you and your wife are exhausted, particularly if you have kids.

When you're home at a decent hour, you can chat about the more ordinary stuff that's going on, so your wife can be aware of the little things that feel big to you in your daily life. That way, when there is down time, she can tune in to you and communicate about things that you feel are important. When you make time for this on a regular basis, there's a better chance that your wife will get to know your values, needs, and priorities.

Another advantage of being home is that you can anticipate your wife's needs better. If you see that she has run out of her morning eggs, you can go pick them up before the next morning. This isn't to your direct benefit, but ultimately you'll realize that it's an act of enlightened self-interest. When your goal is to build a strong and loving marriage, these little things count a lot.

As positive as all this sounds, be forewarned: if you suddenly start hanging around the house more, your wife may be suspicious at first. To calm her anxiety, stay in the background for a while. Observe, watch, and plan. The purpose of being home more often is not to challenge your wife's role of authority in the household. It's to get to know her routine well enough to complement and support her efforts.

Growing Kids

Kids benefit when Dad is at home more often, and because we all want the best for our kids, what's good for them is good for us. For starters, spending more time at home makes you less likely to be one of the dads who don't get to celebrate the baby's "firsts": first smile, first word, first step. Being there at milestone moments connects you to your family and brings you into the insider's circle. It's a bonding experience.

When you are at home, you also have a better chance of giving your kids a sense of connection and harmony. As you and your wife learn to coexist peacefully, you become your children's role model for how to live with a life partner. And you know the ol' trick that kids learn at an early age: mom versus dad? When you stay home, you reduce their ability to raise the household tension level by playing one parent against the other. That means more tranquility at home and less tension all the way around.

Spending more time in the home also gives you a chance to know your kids' needs and to respond better in an emergency. Just last week I heard of a young husband who was at home alone with his ten-month-old son when the child had an asthma attack. The baby had suffered these attacks since birth, but this was the first time the dad had ever seen one, and he had no idea what to do. In a panic he called his wife's cell phone begging her to come home immediately. He felt incompetent only because he hadn't been around enough to learn how to handle this situation. Dads should know just as much about their children as moms.

Being home with your kids is just plain good—and can have far-reaching benefits as they get older. Kids who eat sit-down meals with their families do better in school and score higher on standardized tests. Getting into the habit of eating together can have a lasting impact on your children in other ways. Research shows that regardless of a teen's sex, family structure, or socioeconomic level, those who eat frequent family dinners are less likely than other teens to have sex at a young age, use drugs or alcohol, get into fights, or be suspended from school, and are at lower risk for thoughts of suicide.[4]

This is impressive stuff, but I'll bet the farm that it's not the sit-down meals that give kids these advantages, but rather the fact that these children have parents who spend time at home and therefore have the opportunity to sit down with their kids, listen to them, talk about important stuff, and let them know that they are valued and loved. That's the key to life success for kids, and just one more reason why you should spend more time at home.

PUT YOURSELF TO THE TEST

Okay. Enough of *thinking about* being at home. It's time to answer the question, Are you home enough? To find out, honestly answer yes or no to the following questions:

	Yes	No
1. I spend more time per week doing my own thing than my wife spends doing her own thing.	_____	_____
2. Commonly, when I tell my wife that I got home late because I was working, I was actually hanging around the office shooting the breeze with coworkers.	_____	_____
3. I've lied to my wife about working late, when the truth is I stopped at a bar for a quick drink with pals on the way home. Or worse.	_____	_____
4. I erase email or phone messages because I don't want my wife knowing about my interests outside the home.	_____	_____
5. In the past three months, I've complained when my wife announced plans of her own that I felt conflicted with my personal plans.	_____	_____
6. In the past three months, my wife and I have exchanged harsh words over how I am spending my leisure time.	_____	_____
7. My wife agrees with the following sentence: My husband gets to do more cool things with his friends than I get to do with mine.	_____	_____
8. When I am at home, more than 50 percent of my time is spent on a solo activity (such as watching TV or sitting at the computer).	_____	_____
9. Even when I'm home from work, the housework and child-care load still falls primarily on my wife.	_____	_____

Rate Yourself

Level One At-Home Guy: If you passed with flying colors by answering no to all these questions, good for you. It might mean that you are very considerate about maintaining fairness in this area. Or it may mean that from the very beginning of your marriage you and your wife agreed that your mutual happiness is a matter of quality time together.

Level Two At-Home Guy: If you answered yes to two, three, or four of these questions, you may need to evaluate whether you are leaning too far toward independence on your tightrope. This may be easily remedied by your making a few changes in your routine.

- Call your wife daily and ask her how she is doing. If she lists the problems of the day, don't jump in with solutions. Do listen. Do promise her you'll help out as much as you can when you come home.

- Take a look at how you are organizing your day—can you lump your tasks together more efficiently? Try arranging your trip to Best Buy to coincide with your trip home from work, or use the Internet from work to order your new DVD player and get home an hour earlier. (Don't tell your boss I told you this.)

- If your sweetheart usually prepares dinner, plan to give her an occasional night off. Arrange to pick up a meal from your favorite Chinese restaurant or Boston Market. Call ahead of time to shave minutes off your time away from home.

Level Three At-Home Guy: If you answered yes to five, six, or seven of these questions, it is more than likely that your wife would like to see some change.

- You may need to reexamine your job priorities and assess the number of hours you work. Are you constantly being asked by your employer to stay late or come in early? Sometimes you've got to do it. But all the time?

- If you do have after-hours obligations, either work or social, let your wife know as soon as they are planned. Either write it down or call your answering machine to remind your wife to remind you. If you have kids, offer to find child care for that time, so that your wife is not always left on duty. If there is any chance that your wife can come along, invite her. Most times she'll say no, but she'll feel pleased that you considered her.

- You may need to reevaluate your recreational priorities. You may want to be a champion tennis player at the club, but if that takes you away from your time at home, then it's up to you to put those dreams on hold, particularly if you have kids in the house who need you.

- Being a husband means being a little less available to your friends. You can't be perfect in every area of social obligation, and your wife comes first. Most men don't have many close, close friends—if you do, it's important to keep those connections alive. But if you have a few guys you like to hang with just to do some brainless activities, try to limit these get-togethers to once a month or less.

- Any time you're staring into the mouth of a beer bottle rather than the eyes of your wife, she's feeling cheated. Cut the after-hours drinks out of your repertoire. Go home after work, not to the bar.

Never-at-Home Guy: If you answered yes to eight or nine of these questions, it is likely that your wife feels angry and resentful—whether you've noticed or not. You may have spent your whole life getting things right and perfecting a lifestyle that works for you. But getting married isn't about balancing your life alone. It's about balancing your marriage.

It's time to sit down with your wife and ask for an honest accounting of what she needs and what you're not providing. Maybe you'll be lucky, and despite all your yes answers, she'll tell you she thinks things are going well. If not, read on.

- Pull out your schedule for the next three months and find a way to separate the unessential chaff from the necessary grain. You need to set limits on yourself. Can you cut back work commitments or scale back on major obligations—even if it means postponing advancement in work? If you do, your wife may have less money in her pocket, but at least you'll still have a wife.

- If you work a full-time job but feel compelled to exercise, practice an instrument, or read, keep the activity down to an hour a day if possible, or reserve these activities for after your wife has gone to sleep (unless you play the drums). Big time-bandits like golf or sailing may no longer be possible every week. Perhaps you'll have to cut those back to every other week for a while, or at least you'll have to include your wife.

- Any plans to complicate your life, extend work hours, or add on another social obligation must first be enthusiastically endorsed by your wife. Otherwise, ditch the idea.

If you fell short of the ideal on this test, you haven't necessarily committed a fatal marital error. More than likely, the value of at-home time is something you just hadn't thought about in this way before. After all, there is no master switch that gets flipped into the "married" position after exchanging your wedding vows. But now that you do see the importance of being at home, you should think about making some adjustments.

REMEMBER THIS
Being Home Increases Fidelity

You don't need a scientific study to tell you that when you're home more often, you're less likely to have affairs—and so is she! If you're hanging around your house, you know no one else is!

YOUR TURN

Here's one example of a man who found a way to keep the right balance on that tightrope and reaped the benefits. George is a forty-nine-year-old married man, in his second marriage of fourteen years, who sent this note to my Web site:

> My wife and I have learned to support each other by spending more time together and more time with our kids. I've been surprised to find that my own feeling of freedom has increased since I've started to do this. My advice to other husbands would be to get home in time to be with the kids, and sometimes why not make dinner and wash the dishes? After the kids are in bed, then do whatever work is waiting for you. If you realize that you don't spend much time with your wife, give up watching TV and surfing the web. These are just excuses for avoiding her. If you give her your attention, you'll get paid back nicely with your wife's gratefulness.

Whether you've been married one week or forty years, you should think seriously about making improvements in this aspect of your marriage. Maybe that means *asking* if it's okay, rather than simply *telling* your wife, that you're going to the range to hit a bucket of golf balls after dinner. Perhaps you'll call from the office once in a while and say, "I think I can get out of here right at five. Why don't I pick up take-out, and we have a relaxing evening together?" Moreover, it may mean telling your boss that you plan to leave work today on time—the McMillan report can wait until tomorrow morning.

Like most of the recommendations in this book, this one works best together with the strategies discussed in other chapters: increasing at-home time gives you more opportunities to apply your work skills at home, to learn more about your wife, and, as you'll learn in the following chapter, to better handle inevitable conflicts.

TO DO LIST

- Ask yourself why you're not spending more time at home.

- Unlearn behaviors to which you've been accustomed during your dating and bachelor years. Doing this isn't automatic or easy, but it's a must.

- Don't foster close friendships away from home that exclude your wife, particularly if they are with other women. Your wife should feel that you're her best friend.

- Evaluate the quality of your at-home time and make changes if you find yourself falling short.

- Let go of resentment if you need to put some of your interests on hold. In time the permanent rewards will far exceed what you temporarily give up.

- Make a list of the benefits you personally receive by staying home more often: emotional stability, intimacy, sense of loyal support and devotion, commitment, fun, partnership, sexual satisfaction—and if you're not all the way there yet, consider these to be the best possible goals in your marriage and your life.

6

The Fourth Way

Expect Conflict and Deal with It

In considering conflict in relationships, I'm reminded of what I learned in medical school about a broken clavicle (collarbone). Because clavicles heal so readily, there is usually no surgery required to treat their fracture. In fact, they patch themselves up so easily that we doctors joke, "Just put two ends of a clavicle in the same room, and they'll eventually grow together."

As a scientist who examines marriage, I have discovered that intact relationships are nothing at all like clavicles. My conclusion is, "Put two partners in the same marriage, and they'll eventually argue." Kidding aside, there's no such thing as a conflict-free marriage. All couples argue, fight, and fume. It's the nature of the beast.

Quite by coincidence, as I write this chapter, the *Wall Street Journal* has a headline article that opens with the line, "A growing body of research suggests there is no such thing as a compatible couple."[1] Although this sounds like a startling assertion intended to grab reader attention, I'm convinced that no couple is compatible all the time. As you'll find in this chapter, research studies make it quite clear that both happy and unhappy couples have just about the same number of arguments and, in fact, tend to argue over the same issues. It's not the arguments themselves that are the problem; it's how a couple handles the inevitable disagreements that really matters.

Your job as a husband who wants a good marriage is to learn how to accept the inevitability of conflict in your marriage and then learn how to deal with it in ways that respect your relationship and keep your love for your wife always at the forefront.

I'M RIGHT, YOU'RE WRONG

It was supposed to be the perfect ski vacation. Tim and Laura had rented a small condo in New Hampshire during school vacation week—one of those with a hot tub, swimming pool, balcony, and game room for the kids. It was a snowy winter in New England, and the conditions on the slopes were just right.

One morning Laura left Tim and her two preteen children at the slopes so she could treat herself to a manicure and some shopping. Two hours later, when she returned to the ski area, she was pleased to show off her "new" nails to Tim, who, sitting outside, hot chocolate in hand, nodded absently at them. (What is the proper response to a wife's manicure, anyway?) That's when the question rushed into Laura's mind: "Where are the children?!" "They're skiing," Tim calmly replied.

"Alone?"

"Well, they're not with *me*, are they? I went down a few times with them, and they know what they're doing. Besides, Bobby wanted to do some of those moguls, and my knees can't take that. Here, have some hot chocolate."

Laura's anxiety escalated as she pictured all the horrible possibilities, everything from child abduction to fatal collision. As the minutes crept by, she scanned the mountaintop for some sign that her children were all right. When her daughter flew down the hill and snowplowed to a halt next to her, Laura was only partially relieved. After all, it wasn't the older, more conservative girl she worried about. Having her daughter by her side only highlighted Bobby's absence. Where could he be? She looked back at her husband angrily: "How could you have allowed him to ski by himself?

It's the end of the day; he's tired, less focused. It's dangerous for him."

Moments later, Bobby popped out of a bank of trees, rode up on the crest of the hill, rested for a moment, and then made his final descent, fists raised high in the air. Slightly out of breath, he beamed with pride at the rest of his family as he pulled to a stop. Yes!

That was the last run for the day and the last day of family harmony on this vacation. Laura was fuming at Tim. In her eyes, he was irresponsible and thoughtless. Moreover, he jeopardized the welfare of her children.

Tim defended his actions, pointing to the triumphant and safe return of both children. But still Laura countered with accusations of stupidity and carelessness. What was Tim to say? He wasn't sorry; he had used his best judgment and had been proven right. It was infuriating to be put down in front of his kids for being a bad father. Laura fumed through the rest of the vacation over her husband's lack of responsibility; Tim fumed over being falsely accused.

The *Wall Street Journal* sure got it right this time: this was one incompatible couple.

A PROFESSIONAL OPINION

Laura still wasn't feeling very good about Tim when she came to my office, alone, the week after the vacation. She explained what had happened and looked to me to help solve the problem. I was the judge, the arbiter of human love and childhood safety. Had he, or had he not, screwed up?

Note to aspiring therapists: this is not a situation you want to be in. I did, of course, fall back on my classical analytic technique of asking her, "Tell me more" and the ever-inquiring, "What do *you* think?" But as I explored and cajoled, she still looked for some third party to validate her views.

I took the plunge. "You're right," I began, "skiing is a potentially dangerous sport, and children need guidance. But it looks like your husband tried to take that into consideration when he made the decision he did. There are lots of reasons that made you feel that Bobby shouldn't have skied alone. I have absolutely no doubt that if you were in charge, considering the circumstances, you would never have let him go by himself. That's how *you* do things." She nodded her head.

I continued. "But Tim probably had an equal number of reasons why Bobby should ski alone, so that's what *he* decided. It's how Tim does things." I could see her disbelief in her eyes. She was no doubt considering her sheer incompatibility with Tim, so I added the following warning: "Imagine what would happen if you were divorced. He'd take them for whole weekends, and you wouldn't have any control over what your children did on the ski slopes." I thought I saw a sense of understanding and relief spread across her face. Our session ended, and both of us survived.

I saw Laura in my office one month later and asked how things were going. "Much better," she said. She had told Tim what I had said during our previous session, and that seemed to put an end to their dispute.

"Really," I said, excited that my strategy paid off.

"Yes," she announced. "I got home and told him that you said I was right!"

Oh, well. I'd tried my best! Actually, I'm not surprised by Laura's interpretation of what I said. I believe that unconsciously she heard my defense of Tim and processed it before being able to calm things down at home. Ultimately, this time, the problem was shelved, not entirely resolved, and the couple is now able to go on, to the benefit of themselves and their children. Nonetheless, Laura's approach to the ski-trip problem illustrates what so many of us are used to in the world of Coke *or* Pepsi, Republican *or* Democrat: seeing things one way means you can't see it any other way.

What we all need to understand as we try to improve our marriages is that conflict is part of a loving relationship and that in many instances neither partner is entirely right or wrong—and that's okay.

REMEMBER THIS
Conflict Is Inevitable

The reality of marriage is this: conflict happens. Worse, if you've been making an effort to follow my advice to spend more time at home, you may find, at least temporarily, that conflict actually increases. And worse still: most of your disagreements (researchers say a whopping 69 percent of them) are *never* going to be resolved.[2] In fact, that's why there has been a recent shift in couple's counseling toward learning how to fight constructively, rather than learning how not to fight at all.

THE END OF THE FAIRY TALE

Let's start with some statistics. Virtually every couple has tension, serious tension, in their lives. We know that about half of all marriages in the United States fail. But the other half aren't all that ecstatic either. Up to 80 percent of marriages have had one member consider divorce at some time. In 2003, a German study showed that after the vows, newlyweds experience a 10 percent jump in their happiness quotient. Fast-forward two years, and these people are no more or less happy than they were before they walked down the aisle.[3] These were not pairs who separated; they were not divorced. These were just "average" couples whose wedding-day euphoria lasted about as long as Americans' zeal for Furbies—and that's fine.

I recall a client who attended her regular session with me for her quarterly "med check." She felt well enough, had no side effects to her medication, and was sleeping and eating well. As the session drew to a close, she added, parenthetically, that she was divorcing her husband. "Why?" I asked.

"Because we argue with each other." In this young woman's mind, the very fact that arguments happened was evidence that her relationship was flawed. From its blissful origins, her marriage took an unexpected turn, and now it was time to get out. This couple's experience reflects what I see all the time in my clinical practice, and I think it's important for all of us to understand its significance.

Yes, fairy tales end with the promise of happily-ever-after marriages. Yes, Hollywood perpetuates this belief with feel-good chick-flicks which prove that love conquers all. And yes, raised on these messages, we expect Cupid's arrows to set our hearts aflame forever. But real life doesn't happen that way.

The Letdown

My work with married couples demonstrates a predictable finding: during the first postnuptial decade, the longer an individual has been married, the greater the chance I hear about relationship strife. The honeymoon glow dims. Couples are less happy than they were on their wedding day, and husbands and wives express belief that something must be wrong with their marriage. They have yet to learn that contentment is not a given in marriage.

Of course, staying married, continuing to grow with another, and nurturing your best friend and confidant all lead to a higher level of happiness, but these things don't happen overnight. When researchers survey couples two years after their wedding day, they generally find them to be "less happy" than they were the day they said "I do." That's because learning how to love beyond the hormonal "high" of infatuation requires the development of a deep and maturing love. Unlike going out and buying a Furbie (can you still buy Furbies?), deep marital satisfaction takes time to develop.

Psst!

SecretsofMarriedMen.com

There will always be conflicts as long as people are different. But the ability to work through differences relies on two individuals in a relationship deciding that they will be committed to being the best friends no matter what. This means being honest, talking about what bugs them, talking about what makes them happy and doing it on a regular basis. Is it worth staying together even if it entails periods of discontent? You bet.

—Dave, age 25, married 1 year

WARRIOR MEN

Although conflict is inevitable, if you want to be happier in your marriage you're going to have to take time to understand how you react to conflict, how your wife reacts and why her reaction is very likely different from yours, and how the two of you can come to terms on issues that cause conflict over and over again.

He-Man Hormones

Human biology has actually wired men to be good at conflict. On average we weigh 8 percent more than women, and we are 6 percent taller. We have greater muscle mass and less body fat. It is no accident of history that most great warriors and soldiers have been men. Men have a highly attuned internal alert system. When we are pressured to act, our arousal system kicks in with fight-or-flight body changes—changes well suited to solve conflict. From gladiators to matadors to hockey fans, men are designed for confrontation.

Not all men, of course, have the physique or physiology of a fighter. But because of the male hormones that flood their brains, men are more likely than women to have a physically intense response to stress. As tension builds, they experience an increase in muscle tension (including tightening of the jaw), an elevation in blood pressure, flushing, an increase in heart rate, and more rapid breathing. Because men were designed for gross motor activity, their sensitivity to pain decreases, as does their receptivity to sound in response to stress.[4]

Women, in contrast, often soften as conflict escalates. Shelly Taylor, a researcher from California, discovered that quite unlike men, who lapse into the fight-or-flight response when they are stressed, women frequently lapse into a tend-or-befriend mode in which they deal with stress by caring for others and sharing an emotional connection. It is theorized that this happens because of women's dependence on oxytocin (the brain chemical that controls maternal nurturance and empathic bonding) as a stress fighter.[5] Of course women do experience autonomic activation of fight-or-flight too, but it's not their natural inclination, whereas for men, the high level of arousal is performance enhancing.

This intense physical response was absolutely necessary to help males in the wild manage conflict. When faced with confrontation, their bodies give them an immediate rush of adrenaline and dopamine. These neurotransmitters cause a mild state of euphoria and an extra burst of energy during battle—it's the same chemical reaction that enables a father to suddenly lift the corner of a car to save his child pinned beneath. Moreover, the threat of conflict gives the male a surge in testosterone as he comes face-to-face with his nemeses.

A man's testosterone acts to help him maintain focus on one item, at least while it is a threat to him. From an evolutionary perspective, that's good, because if there's a rhinoceros bearing down on you in the grassland, you want to be able to keep your eye on it.

Moreover, testosterone has perfected the "cause-and-effect brain." When a man feels threatened, his brain's ability to assess visual-spatial data is critical. Once he locks in to the challenge, his one-track mind allows him to send information quickly to the motor cortex of the brain, so his body is called into action. There's no time for multitasking here. All that's really required as the perissodactyl bears down on you is to . . . RUN!

You would think, then, given all the biological reasons why guys are made for a good fight, that we would welcome the opportunity to engage in a little conflict with our wives. You would think wrong!

The Challenge of Taming Instincts

Historically, man may have been perfectly suited for fighting off his enemies or protecting his cave, but in modern society there aren't any marauding hoards to defend against. In fact, there aren't even any hearth-and-home caves left to protect. So even though he is designed to fight, a man at war doesn't fit comfortably in the domesticated world.

Let's look at our modern man when he becomes enraged. As his blood pressure elevates, veins pop out above his collar, his eyes bulge, his face reddens. Because he hears less, he shouts. Because he feels less, he pounds his fist against the table. He becomes locked in on the object of his fury—whatever it is that he and his opponent disagree about—and refuses to let go until all surrender. He gets puffed with adrenaline and seeks frantically, above all, to win. This is not at all attractive to his wife. Go figger!

In our culture, posturing, puffing, and clenching of jaws are viewed as danger signs in relationships, and smart men avoid such displays of rage and usually the marital conflicts that cause it. That's why it's not surprising that wives initiate over 80 percent of all household complaints.[6] When men are confronted with irritating marital issues, they are much more likely than women to withdraw from any discussion of the subject. Their biology tells them to fight back, but society, conscience, and common sense tell them they must not. So a man feels cornered when his wife gets angry, yet he must attempt to keep sheathed his most natural fighting tools.

In today's world, a man must use his higher cortical functions, not the instincts based in his brain stem, to solve problems. This is the he-man approach of the future, as we all know from countless *Star Trek* episodes which prove that brute force never wins. The clever and creative Captain Kirk teams up with the logical Mr. Spock; together they design an ingenious, nonviolent plan to get out of the terrible, often life-threatening, predicament. That's our goal.

This chapter is about using your higher cortical functions to solve problems in your marriage. I think you'll like this chapter, because all the observations and recommendations are based on fact. They are scientifically tested, rigorously studied, and statistically proven. This isn't touchy-feely stuff—it's straightforward, and it gets results.

TOP FIVE REASONS WE FIGHT

In the opening line of *Anna Karenina*, Tolstoy writes, "Happy families are all alike; every unhappy family is unhappy in its own way." This idea makes for great literature, but actually it's not true. In fact, studies show that the major areas of conflict are similar from home to home.

In the first year of marriage, money problems stand out. In the years that follow, the introduction of a new child will shake the foundation of the marriage. Sometime after that, unhappy couples will point to sex as a common bone of contention. If you've got problems in these departments, you're not alone.

Without meeting you face-to-face, I cannot make your relationship fit some easily understood pattern. Certainly each marriage has different strengths and weaknesses. Through my clinical practice, though, I have found five issues that are the hot buttons in many marriages. In no particular order, these are

1. Money

2. Sex

3. In-laws

4. Housework

5. A new baby

It could be, of course, that you never argue over these issues because you have all the money in the world, you have no kids, and your wife begs you for sex to the point of exhaustion. Even so, consider each of these areas and think about how you and your wife might differ. Right now you might not believe it, but as you continue to read and explore these typical stumbling blocks, you may find that recognizing these flashpoints may actually help stimulate long-lasting improvements in your relationship.

REMEMBER THIS
Some Conflicts Are Deal Breakers

The top five issues that cause conflict in all marriages most frequently spring from differences of opinion and personality: How important is it really to keep the house immaculately clean? Why is it necessary to spend that much money on another pair of shoes? But there are also marital issues that tear at the values and nonnegotiable needs of married couples. These include such problems as addiction, alcoholism, infidelity, and untreated mental or physical illness. In these cases, although this chapter may be of some help, you or your spouse may require individualized professional guidance.

Money

"Show me the money," shouts the football star to his agent in the movie *Jerry McGuire*. I don't know much about professional sports, but I know that at the end of each pay period, that could well be the content of every husband and wife's conversation. Each marriage is defined, in part, by the way the couple shares their financial resources. Truth be told, the paycheck conversation is not about the money. It's more about differences in values.

I suppose there are some marriages in which both partners spend and conserve equally. But it's rare to find 100 percent equality in pecuniary values—usually one partner spends more than the other thinks is acceptable. So it makes sense that money is the root of many marital conflicts. Because women handle 75 percent of the family finances and control roughly 80 percent of family purchasing decisions,[7] statistically speaking it's more likely that the husband will feel as though the coffers run dry because of his wife's actions.

Perhaps that accounts for the joke, "Before marriage, a man yearns for his wife; after marriage, the Y is silent." Clearly, that's a man's perspective, particularly if he's the main breadwinner. Now, however, it's time to try to understand money issues from your wife's perspective as well. This will shift the focus away from scrutinizing what your honey purchased and toward helping you better understand what need that purchase fulfills for her.

To begin, *ask*. Talk to her about money. What does it mean to her?

Take a step backward and try to define your wife's core values, the deep feelings that determine where she feels money is well spent. By "core values," I don't mean whether her next car should be a Jetta or a Jaguar. I mean really digging deep, looking at her spiritual beliefs and lifetime goals. This isn't the kind of thing you can expect her to start whipping out in a few seconds—it takes time to reflect on these values. Give her time to think about what's really important to her; doing so can reshape your view of her spending habits and help both of you find ways to reconcile your differences on this subject.

Here are some examples of core values that your wife might consider:

Financial security	Generosity
Possessions	Productivity
Health	Justice
Family	Friends
Learning	Lifestyle
Personal growth	Contribution to society
Personal appearance	Spiritual fulfillment
Peace of mind	Work
Home comfort	Entertainment
Education	Children

Of course, your wife may have other values that she deems important that aren't listed here, such as fame, travel, or diversity. But let's imagine that your wife says her main values are learning, truth, and family. If all goes well, most of the nonessential spending will go toward reinforcing those values. Keeping this in mind, if at the end of the month you've overspent your budget, together you can then review where the money went, with an eye on what's really important *as your wife defines it.*

Let's say you see on the credit card bill that your wife purchased a book last month. You can say to yourself, "Okay, that's money well spent. It matches her values regarding learning and truth." And you can give her some positive reinforcement for such a reasonable purchase. (When was the last time she heard you praise her for spending money?) But then let's say you also see that she bought a new pair of shoes. Now you have a reason to question how her spending matches what's really important to her. You can ask, "Is that really helping you achieve your core values?"

In the same way, if the stated core value is travel, you can help her see that she is siphoning money away to renovate the bathroom. If a core value is home comfort, is she blowing money on dinners out? If her core value is entertainment, is she putting money into her wardrobe instead of a plasma HDTV? This method allows you to help her examine her spending habits without coming off as a drillmaster or control freak. Purchases that support her values are praised, those that do not can be limited or eliminated without excessive nagging or criticizing.

Get the idea? Now put it into action. At some quiet moment (when you're *not* fighting over money issues!) talk to your wife about core values that lead to the fulfillment of lifetime goals. If she wants you to do the same, go ahead. This is a good sign that means she's looking to understand you better too. Remember, there are no right or wrong values. You are not allowed to disagree or argue that your wife's values are incorrect. But you should ask lots of questions so you can really get to know her. Dig, explore, strive to understand. The information you will gain will far exceed what you can buy on your MasterCard: it's priceless.

Of course, as you work to improve your relationship with each other, it will be important to explore *your* values as well. You'll get your chance to do that in Chapter Ten. But for now, your task is to sit down with your wife and tell her you want to understand her better.

Sex

Jane Austen once wrote, "One half of the world cannot understand the pleasures of the other."[8] So let's start with the premise that, like most hot topics, sex is one on which men and women will differ in their interpretations. You'd have to be pretty dense to ignore that during sex you and your wife experience seemingly identical moments in entirely different ways. And that fact, my friend, is exactly why sex is so often a common source of conflict in marriages.

What do women think about sex? For one woman's perspective, listen to Jenn, a twenty-five-year-old, married for two years, who wrote to SecretsofMarriedMen.com:

> When my husband and I first met we had the most earth-shattering sex. He would want me over and over again. Since then some things have changed. Once I found out we couldn't have children my sex drive decreased to almost nil. He is still as horny as ever and looking for it every day (no exaggeration). He doesn't seem to understand that for a woman it is about love and, for me especially, it's about the prospect of having a family. The fact that our lovemaking will never lead to a child makes me feel as if sex is empty and worthless. But how do I explain that without hurting his ego?

Hmmmm. From this woman's perspective, sex is far more than a pleasurable, physical act. It is the by-product of an intense emotional connection and part of a much greater innate need to reproduce. Her husband probably has no idea she feels this way. He's sitting home somewhere out there assuming his wife no longer loves him or finds him attractive. Or worse, maybe he thinks she blames him for not being able to give her children. There's bound to be a lot of tension and conflict in that marriage.

And then there's the perspective of Lou. Married thirty-four years to a wife he adores, he certainly sees the differences in sex drive between husband and wife far differently than Jenn. According to Lou, "Nothing says a woman has to have the same drive for sex as a man. But that doesn't mean she should turn him away. In this case, sex should be like walking the dog on a cold morning or doing the dishes. Some things we do not because we have to, but to make things nicer for our mate. There's nothing wrong with giving sexual pleasures—even when you don't feel like it."

Both Jenn and Lou are absolutely right—from their perspective. But if two people who share their beliefs were to decide to marry, sex would doubtlessly be a major source of conflict—*if* they were unable to talk about their differences and *if* they didn't even make an effort to understand the other's point of view.

Because the letters s-e-x spell something entirely different for husband and wife, you can lessen the impact of sexual conflict on your marriage if you make an effort to understand why your wife's attitude is different from yours. Through observation, touch, talk, and faith in your love for each other, show your wife that you want to learn about her sexual feelings and attitudes. You can't solve the conflict if you don't know what's causing it.

I wish I could promise that as you come to understand her perspective on this very personal issue, your wife will become hornier.

REMEMBER THIS
Women Have the Power

Not long ago I heard Sandra Scantling, who penned *Ordinary Couples, Extraordinary Sex,* speak at a Harvard conference. She offered this startling perspective: "It's the low-sexualized person who has all the power." Think about that. If your wife is always eager to tickle your funny bone, then it's up to you whether or not you fulfill your fantasies. But if she isn't in the mood and you want sex tonight, guess what? It's up to her whether or not you're going to get together. Because of these differences in sex drive, in many marriages it's women who have the larger share of the power.

Maybe she will, and maybe she won't. But she will love the attention you're giving her in your effort to better understand her. And that's the first step toward helping you solve your sexual problems together. Then, see Chapter Nine for a more detailed discussion of sex and marriage and specific things you can do to reignite the fire. This very complex marital issue requires its very own chapter.

In-Laws

Stand up at the altar for an hour or so, and by the time you turn around and walk back down the aisle your family size doubles—and so do the opportunities for family squabbles. Contrary to the in-law shticks of male stand-up comics, most problems arise between *women* and their mothers-in-law. Surprised?

Think about it, men. If you didn't talk to your mother-in-law for several days, and she called you and said, "What's the matter? You don't know how to use the phone anymore?" how upset would you get? The men I know would probably quickly turn their head from the phone and yell, "Honey, it's for you!" But women are not likely to shrug off the same comment from their own mothers-in-law. In most households, the wife assumes the domain of household management, so when her husband's mother passes a critical comment, even with the best of intentions, it is not usually well received.

Given that your wife is probably more sensitive to in-law comments, how do you react when she complains about them? Do you spend more time defending the supposedly impolite behavior than listening to what your wife is saying? Do you make a distinction between what someone said or did and the way it made your wife feel?

It's okay to wish you didn't have to cope with in-laws, but it's wrong to tell your wife that you're tired of her whining. Remember: the male brain is adept at focusing on the immediate facts and reacting on a case-to-case basis to render a verdict of guilt or innocence. Women, in contrast, tend to think more globally and see the big picture that includes all other family members' feelings and a fear that irreparable damage has taken place within the family.

In order to move ahead on the in-law issue, you must commit yourself to getting on the same page with your wife so you both can see the problem as a mutual challenge. This is simple to do: make sure you support your wife. That doesn't mean you have to sacrifice all you believe in. It means you have to work hard to respect your wife's needs and make sure that she knows you're on her side. Here are a few ideas to get you headed in this direction. From there you can apply your support as needed:

- Always consult with your wife before planning family get-togethers.

- Never spend money on your siblings or parents without talking it over with your wife.

- Don't compare your wife's cooking with your mother's cooking (or your wife's parenting style, or her methods of housekeeping, or her clothing, or her beliefs, or . . . her anything!). The only exception is when the comparison is a positive one: "My mother wasn't half as good a parent as you are" is okay.

- Set limits with your parents so that they know where the boundaries are between helping and criticizing.

- Don't tolerate any show of disrespect toward your wife. Let your parents know it's not okay to criticize her.

- Establish a sense that you're a unified team by consulting your wife on all decisions regarding the in-laws.

- Never complain to your parents about your wife. This is a common big mistake, especially early in marriage, and it can come back to bite you when you've moved past that earlier lack of impulse control and good boundaries.

Psst!

SecretsofMarriedMen.com

I lived in total depression for so many years that it nearly took my life as well as the life of my wife. I was very sick. She stood by me through the worst until my eyes were finally opened to the destruction caused by my family of origin and my inability to say no to them. I come from a very enmeshed family with no boundaries. My silence during their abuse of my wife told them that I was agreeing. Finally, I realized where my unhappiness was coming from—my inability to say no to my parents and to protect my wife and my marriage. My brother did allow our family of origin to destroy his family. He chose to divorce his wife and send his children to a kind of emotional death. I was offered the same—my family promised: "Divorce that bitch and you will have a farm here where you belong."

I have come to realize that the more dysfunctional the family is, the harder it is to break the ties. That was certainly the case for me. It was clearly my inability to break the emotional ties of my parents and cleave to my wife that caused us years of problems.

It is said that if you want to know the true character of a man, look into the face of his wife; what he has invested in her or withheld from her will be seen in her countenance. I looked into the face of my wife and wept at what I was allowing to be stolen from us. I am appalled at myself for allowing my parents to nearly destroy my marriage before my eyes were opened. After twenty-eight years, we finally pulled away from my family of origin and started on the journey of a healthy marriage. My wife's stamina saved us all from that curse. She never gave up on me. My wife is still with me and I have spent the last three years doing nothing but serving her.

—Don, age 56, married 31 years

Housework

Christine, a thirty-four-year-old stay-at-home mom with two daughters, came to see me in my office. Now in her tenth year of marriage, she and her husband were at a critical crossroad:

"He had been making great strides in his work as a real estate account executive, and had put more and more effort into advancement," she explained. "I just never saw him anymore. I was exhausted from the work I had to do at home. I wasn't getting any emotional support from him. None. He didn't appreciate what I was going through in the slightest. I had just had it."

One night he came home from work, and she tried to tell him how she felt. She said, "Why do you even bother coming home?"

A short time later, he announced he was moving out.

Chris was distraught by the time we met. "I don't know why he can't stay to work it out," she told me. "I didn't mean that I didn't want him here. I was angry; I wanted to let him know. But I didn't see myself as rejecting him. I just wanted to open up lines of communication."

Chris wanted her husband to notice that she needed him and that she needed his help around the house. In her mind, she vocalized that sentiment. What he heard her say, though, was, "I don't want you here."

Obviously there is more going on here than simply misunderstanding the meaning of a single sentence. Chris's husband no doubt had his own view of the division of labor in his marriage. He focused on work and assumed she had the same focus on caring for all things domestic. He failed to understand how differently she felt about her "job," and how great a distance they had grown apart.

Chris and her husband are now back together, but they learned a bitter lesson. Problems associated with housework are often really about a simple misunderstanding of roles, yet they can grow into a make-or-break issue. Here's how it happens. You frequently hear that women do more housework than men. Statistically, it seems to be true.

Studies show that women do more housework than men—about eleven hours more per week. Many women may resent their unfair burden, but they're not getting the whole story. When researchers factor in housework *and* work outside the home, men and women make nearly equal contributions to the household; the difference narrows to twenty minutes a day.[9]

Psst!
SecretsofMarriedMen.com

My wife and I share housework. At least I think so. We both do laundry, although she probably does more. And I do empty out the dishwasher. But I am working 14 hours more each week than she is, so I don't understand why she gets on these tirades about how she's the only one doing anything around the house and cleaning up all my mess. Hey, I also take care of the yard! Oh for the fifties when women did everything!

—Stu, age 48, married 20 years

So the I-work-more-than-you-do argument does not automatically, nor abundantly, favor women. Nevertheless, it can have validity in those homes where guys like Chris's husband don't chip in their fair share. If there's tension in your house over who does what, here's another opportunity for you to use your distinctly male skills of observation. Take a hard look at who's doing most of the grocery shopping, cooking, dusting, mopping, vacuuming, laundering (collecting, sorting, washing, drying, sorting, folding, putting away), picking up toys, emptying trash cans, and a dozen or more things that keep the household running. If you see that it's your wife who's the worker bee in your home, it's time to pick up some slack, or at the very least shower her with appreciation.

While writing this section of the book, I went into the kitchen for a break with my wife, and experienced firsthand just how easy it is to fall short in this area. Both of us had had a busy day, and the kitchen still had signs of use scattered about: the plastic screw cap from some now discarded bottle, the crumpled-up foil wrapper from a Pop Tart eaten hours earlier, things like that. I opened the microwave door to discover a small spillover of whatever last vacated the spot.

So I said, "Even this is a mess!"

That's right. You paid for a book by a guy who is stupid enough to blurt out a marriage-booster like that. I quickly did some verbal repairing and cleaned up the mess myself, but you can be sure that my wife didn't take my comment as the innocent observation I claimed it was. I know her well enough to know that she felt I was criticizing her domestic abilities; I was putting her down for not keeping everything perfectly clean all the time. Knowing this about her, I was asking for an argument. Fortunately, I caught myself and apologized before what I thought was a simple observation escalated into a war.

How does your wife react when you make a comment like that? Let's say, for example, that after searching all over for your golf shoes you mumble, "How can anyone expect to find anything in this pigpen?"

Your wife, who overhears the comments, says, "If you think the place is so messy, why don't you skip your dumb golf game and clean it up!"

Before you say, "It's not my responsibility to clean the house. I work hard enough at my own job," stop and remember how she probably feels.

Just for fun, why not try saying something like, "You're right. If I'm not pitching in to make this place cleaner, then I don't have a right to criticize. Tell you what: as soon as I get back from my golf game, I'll spend some time sorting through the back hallway and put my ski gear away. Does six o'clock sound okay?"

Of course, you could have told her you'd skip the golf game altogether, and frankly, if you were just out playing eighteen holes earlier that morning and were going back to the links for another round, you better believe I'd recommend staying home. But otherwise, skipping the game you've been looking forward to all week isn't necessary. What is necessary is to acknowledge your wife's efforts to manage the household, to define specifically how you would like to help her and when you plan on doing it, and then follow through.

But why wait for a snide remark to get you thinking about helping out? To avoid the typical "I'm tired of being the one who has to keep the house clean" argument (and, remember, to win your wife's heart), find a specific task that you can help out with today. Ask to learn how to fold the wash, or offer to put the laundry away. Of course this will cut into your time to check up on your stock portfolio, but small contributions can mean a lot. This plan is far better than just wishing your wife could shrug off your negative comments about housework. It's not going to happen, and there's no doubt that criticism will not advance your desire to have a strong marriage. The quality of many marriages depends on how much the husband helps with household chores and how often he expresses his appreciation

REMEMBER THIS
It Might Not Really Be
About Housework

If you feel you're doing enough around the house but your wife still sees an inequity, she may be upset about more than the workload. Engage her in a dialogue about the kind of work she would rather be doing or what she would prefer doing with her elusive spare time. Listen with an open mind and respond supportively, not defensively. Try not to redirect the conversation to how hard your own job is. It won't fly. Let her talk about why she feels burdened and what she'd like to do to change it.

for the work his wife does inside the home. The good news is that when men share housework, the husband and wife both report more satisfying sex lives.

A New Baby

A new baby in the house changes everything. It changes money. It changes in-laws. It changes sex. It changes housework.

A new baby creates new routines, increases exhaustion, shortens fuses, and signals an end to the pre-baby relationship you had with your wife. Because of all these things, a new baby definitely puts a marriage at risk—two-thirds of the newlyweds who become parents cite marital dissatisfaction within three years of their baby's birth.[10] Other than that, having a baby is the greatest experience in the world!

Whether the little intruder is their first or seventh child, husbands and wives react and adapt differently to the changes in their lives that are bound to occur. That's why you can't assume you know how your wife is feeling or judge her actions by your own standards or feelings. To avoid the conflict that your bundle of joy can cause, you should make a sincere effort to understand how your wife feels about this life-changing event.

Occasionally I meet women who radiate with joy when discussing the daily routines of motherhood. Their rousing testimonials about caring for newborns and toddlers day in and day out are summarized in this one short, oft-repeated phrase: "I love it!"

But be forewarned: You can't assume your wife feels this way.

Most new mothers, and not-so-new mothers for that matter, don't find child care as rewarding as they expected it would be—especially while they're in the midst of it. Find out how motherhood is affecting your wife, and you can prevent many common marital battles that tend to rock an already shaky boat. Strike up conversations that allow you to hear how she feels: Does she feel like she isn't doing it right? Does she feel guilty because she is too exhausted to be elated? Does she seem exceptionally unhappy? Don't jump in right away with suggestions or corrections. Just listen.

Be especially alert for signs of depression. It's quite common for new mothers to experience some form of postpartum blues in the first weeks after leaving the hospital. Symptoms can include frequent crying, loss of energy, and sleep problems. But in about 10 percent of cases, women go on to develop a full-blown, major depressive illness after childbirth. Symptoms may include severe insomnia, appetite changes, intense preoccupation with death or harm to loved ones, loss of interest or pleasure, or suicidality. She may even lose touch with reality, including hearing voices or having paranoid beliefs that others are out to get her.

Depression (or psychosis) is not an attitude. It's an illness that requires immediate medical attention. Husbands can be the first ones to detect the symptoms of depression in their wives, which is just one more reason why knowing your wife is so important—it can save her life.

Even after the first two months of the postpartum phase, and even in the absence of a depressive episode, motherhood is hard. Yes, I know that the role of a new dad is no picnic either. But the goal here is to better understand your wife's feelings about this change in your life and relationship so that you can better avoid comments, attitudes, and actions that will increase the tension and stress that can strain the glue of your marriage during this time. If your goal truly is to have a great marriage that stands strong through difficult times, then take to heart this simple advice: let your wife talk about her feelings, and tell her frequently that you appreciate how difficult it is to be a new mom.

Men these days are getting the idea. Almost all the men who come into my office who have children still in the home see themselves as much more involved with their children than their own fathers had been. William, a thirty-four-year-old director of public relations, says, "Our father would never change our diapers or take us to Little League; that was always Mom's job. I'm determined to act differently." Many husbands follow William's example by changing diapers, getting up at night to do feedings, attending school functions, transporting children to activities, and so much more. Taking a more active role in child care will improve your connection to your heirs and make a lasting impression on your wife.

KEEPING LITTLE THINGS FROM ESCALATING INTO BIG THINGS

Most of the disagreements on those five hot-button topics aren't about big things. The fights aren't really about a mother-in-law's comment or a new pair of shoes. They're not totally about a messy closet or a baby's incessant crying. They're about feeling listened to, cared for, and respected.

When one spouse or the other (or both!) feels that his or her feelings are being slighted, ridiculed, or demeaned, a simple difference of opinion can quickly escalate into an all-out fight.

Come on. You know it happens. Your wife says your car needs a cleaning, and you feel she's calling you dirty and lazy. You say your wife should pick up a take-out meal for the two of you on her way home from work, and she feels you're saying you don't like her cooking. When it comes to conflict, *feelings and assumptions* often get in the way of solving problems.

Here are four common ways major fights get going and some suggestions to help you keep the small stuff from getting out of hand.

Feeding the Fire

Do you remember the Atari game "Breakout"? It was like "Pong," but you didn't need to play against an opponent. Your challenge was to break though some video bricks by hitting a video ball with a video paddle. When the electronic ball first got pitched into play, it came at you straight and steady. But soon it started to come faster and faster. Each time you hit it at an odd angle, it careened off the bricks in an

even more unpredictable way. Before you knew it, you were frantically trying to keep up with the ball as it frequently flew right past your
paddle. It took a lot of quarters to perfect that game.

"Breakout" is a good metaphor for the way we sometimes feed
the fire of anger in our marriages. For example, suppose your wife
throws out a negative comment. Naturally, you respond with indig-
nation. Her turn. She volleys back with a comment of exasperation,
you counter with defensiveness, she hits you with sarcasm, and,
well, things get easily out of control from there. But they don't have
to. In fact, you can control the rate and speed of the disagreement
and even stop the mounting tensions dead in their tracks.

Again, it's kind of like playing "Breakout." You can slow down
the action of this game by having your paddle swallow an electronic
pill that lets it catch the ball. Then you can make the paddle release
the ball at your leisure and regain control of the game. Don't you
wish you had a pill like that at home?

You do. You have a few pills that are easier to use than you
think. Next time you begin to feel things spin out of control, try the
following techniques:

- *Soften your tone.* Your wife will respond to the side of
  you that shows compassion, warmth, or hurt. Her natural inclinations are to nurture, not attack. A show of
  anger, on the other hand, stimulates fear in her, and
  she will respond with an attempt to annihilate the
  source of her fear—you!

- *Look for areas of agreement.* Make an honest effort to
  hear something in the dialogue that you can agree
  with—and focus on that. Men have an attuned sense of
  exactness for words or meaning and can get hung up on
  detail without seeing the right-brained "big picture."
  Today, for example, as I was driving with my wife
  through Pennsylvania, I pointed to the Queen Anne's
  lace that grew on the roadside. Laughingly, I wondered

aloud "how they dare sell these commonplace weeds at florists." Susan suggested that the ones sold at the florist might last longer than the natural weed. My first instinct was to scoff—it sounded like an absurd proposition. What could be hardier than a weed? Then a voice inside me said, "It's possible she's right. After all, florists do keep them refrigerated, so they won't wilt from the heat as you cut them." To my wife I said, "Point well taken." Escalation averted.

- *Stay positive*. Keeping a positive outlook, even in the face of negative news, stymies escalation. For example, let's say that you and your wife have an appointment with Barry, the guy who helps do your taxes, but she gets held up at work. And because it's been that kind of day, of course your cell phone battery has run out so you can't call him to explain that you're running behind. Fighting traffic all the way, you finally arrive fifteen minutes late to the meeting—only to find that Barry left the office two minutes before you got there. This is a moment of decision for you. If you choose to get PO'd at your lady because she made you arrive late, you have nothing to gain except an angry, awful ride back home. So try instead to turn it around. "Hey, babe. How often do we have one hour together with nothing scheduled to do? Let's leave Barry a note to reschedule and then run down to Ben and Jerry's and have a few scoops of Cherry Garcia!"

- *Hold that emotion*. You don't have to accept the gauntlet just because it gets thrown down. I recall a client, Brenda, who worked as a secretary for a corporate vice president. Whenever her boss received an upsetting memo, he invariably dictated a scathing multipage response and then gave it to Brenda for transcription.

After a few of these tirades, Brenda realized that her boss would jeopardize his credibility, and possibly his job, if he continued to send out these biting communiqués. So she developed a strategy. When one of his dictations came across her desk, she would transcribe it and then suggest, "Why don't I hold this for a few days before we send it?" He agreed, and almost always threw out the memo a few days later. As her boss learned not to jump on the emotional tidal wave that overcame him—at least not to share that emotion with others— he improved his standing among his colleagues as a rational and reasonable guy. The same strategy can work for you in your marriage—despite what you have heard from counselors and therapists.

REMEMBER THIS
It's Okay to Hold Back

One of the great failings of modern psychotherapy is the insistence that the improvement of interpersonal relationships depends on free and open expression of internal emotional experiences at all times. That's a load of bull. If what you express escalates the dialogue of hurtful comments and accusations, it will destroy successful communication. It's okay to hold in negative emotions. (Look back at Chapter Two for a more detailed discussion of why talking about your feelings is not always a good thing.)

Withdrawal and Avoidance

I may not need to tell you this, but studies show that women tend to criticize more than men. Men, in turn, sometimes give it right back, but more often than not, they don't. When a complaint is made, men are much more likely than women, by a 5:1 ratio,[11] to turn a cold shoulder to the problem rather than deal with it. And that's a reaction that drives women crazy. Withdraw from her or avoid the issue and you might as well throw gasoline on the spark of an argument.

Here's an example of withdrawal that is oh-so-typical: I heard my friend Mark talking on a cell phone to his wife, Beth. Mark had his daughter Nicole with him and was bringing her to her grandparents' house for the weekend. Beth asked if Nicole had everything she needed, and Nicole chirped up, "No. I forgot a bathing suit." Beth then asked Mark, "Does she expect me to drop everything and bring her a bathing suit?" Mark was silent for a moment and then replied, "Well, if it's too much trouble for you to bring it for her, then why did you ask if she needed anything?" With that, he did the most amazing thing: he folded the phone and hung up . . . while Beth was still talking.

Lots of men reading this are probably raising their fists in solidarity with Mark. I have to admit, inwardly, that I was impressed. The pure logic of his verbal response was irrefutable. But do you really think his relationship will be stronger for it? Get real! Any man who's been married knows that Mark didn't really win this one.

There are lots of ways to withdraw besides the obvious hanging up the phone or walking out the door. Sometimes you probably use the ever-popular:

- Absentmindedly saying, "Uh-huh"

- Throwing your hands in the air and muttering, "Whatever"

- Turning your attention to the TV or computer screen while your wife is still talking

You might also use withdrawal's twin brother: avoidance. Whereas withdrawal involves walking away from conflict, avoidance happens before conflict is even born. At the first sign of potential clash, the avoider changes the subject, veers off in another direction, or suddenly remembers something urgent he has to do. Most men are very good at dancing around issues. They interrupt and redirect in their effort to keep conflict at bay. But it rarely works. Women, as you may have noticed, are not so easily distracted. They persist and persist in trying to engage you in discussion of the offending issue because, believe it or not, the act of engagement makes them feel better.

I firmly believe that men withdraw and avoid for two basic reasons:

1. It's a way to suppress that strong (but socially unacceptable) urge to fight to the death. Men, more so than women, have a harder time calming their bodies down once their fight-or-flight system kicks into gear. So they try to prevent those emotions from stirring up in the first place.

2. They don't realize that they have any other tools for dealing with conflict. Well, you do, and once you finish with this chapter, you'll be able to look conflict straight in the eye and without fear say, "Bring it on!"

Negative Interpretation

Quite out of keeping with American jurisprudence, in our own marriages we often assume our spouse is guilty of trying to harm us until proven innocent. Sometimes we all tend to read unintended negative meaning into what our spouse does or doesn't say, without any real evidence to prove that she meant us any harm.

Sometimes "I don't feel like going to the farmer's market" means just that. What makes things confusing is that when I tell my wife she looks beautiful, she's as likely to ask, "Okay, what do you want?" as she is to say, "Thank you." But as Freud said, "Sometimes a cigar is just a cigar."

Sure, sometimes partners do mask communication, and sometimes a cigar is more than a cigar. But the point here is that to keep a small comment from escalating into a major battle, *you cannot assume*. We discussed this in Chapter Four, and it applies here too. Don't read in negatives that are not there. Don't accuse your spouse of something she didn't say or didn't intend to say. The problem with falling into this trap is that you end up responding to something that was neither stated nor intended, and, gosh, that can be confusing to your wife.

Moving a conversation in the direction of negativity will pull you directly away from your goal. If you want to instill a sense of comfort, warmth, and trust in a relationship, you must transmit all those qualities in your interactions.

Finger Pointing

Criticism is high on the list of things that can turn a casual observation into a major marital battle. Think about your reaction when your wife says, "You're such a slob." If you can't ignore her completely, you probably get self-conscious and feel compelled to respond. It's a gut feeling, an instinct born of a wish to defend oneself against hurtful accusations. Also, it reminds you of being a child scolded by an adult. Do you see an opportunity for escalation here? Of course! Having not yet read this book, you respond by saying, "Why can't you lay off me for once?" You meet harshness with harshness, and the result is quarrel number 17b—the "clothes on the floor" argument, perhaps to be followed later that day with quarrel number 31—the "you never put the toilet seat down" argument, or any of a number of other squabbles in your repertoire.

There's an alternative, and you'd be surprised to see the way altering your approach to a disagreement can radically change the direction the discussion goes. We use this technique all the time as psychotherapists. We learn in our training that when you say to your patient, "You're angry," his or her first response is to say, "No, I'm not." So instead, we use "I" statements such as "I'm sensing that you're angry," and it changes the course of therapy. I'm expressing the same idea, but instead of pointing the finger at my patient, I'm pointing it at myself. This way, there's nothing for the patient to defend himself against, and he's likely to ask, "What do you mean?" In response, instead of saying, "You're foaming at the mouth, and your fists are clenched like the Incredible Hulk," I would say, "Well, it looks to me like your body is tense." Again there's no finger pointing, because, after all, I'm just talking about my own perceptions.

"I" statements can be a very powerful tool to steer any discussion away from a looming argument. The truth is, being upset about something really is about you and not the other person. So if the Mrs. were to apply the same principle to your sloppiness, she would say, "I feel distressed when you leave your clothes behind you wherever you go." And, because you want her to feel no pain, you are more motivated to help her with her problem.

In the likely event that she does not use an "I" statement when you throw your clothes on the floor, *you* can defuse the potential argument by applying the strategy yourself. Rather than reacting with denial or anger, try saying something such as: "I get the feeling that you really hate it when I don't pick up after myself."

PATCHING THINGS UP WHEN THE FIGHT IS OVER

Scientists have learned a lot about how and why couples fight and how their fights affect the quality of their relationship. The leader in this field is John Gottman, a relationship researcher at the University of Washington, who has researched marriage the way Jonas Salk researched polio. And like Dr. Salk, he has actually found ways of curing sick marriages.

Dr. Gottman has a laboratory in Seattle, referred to as the "Love Lab." Within the walls of this lab are a number of rooms, wired with microphones and cameras. Gottman invites married couples into his lab and hooks them up to medical monitoring devices that assess their blood pressure, pulse, galvanic skin response—almost like being wired for a lie detector test. He even puts sensors under their chairs to see how they squirm. Then, with his blessing, the couples are told to argue. By watching couples this way, Gottman has learned about what works and doesn't work in marital debates. He can predict, with up to 90 percent accuracy, which marriages will fail and which will succeed.

His conclusion, in a nutshell: after tempers flare and hurtful things are said, the future of the relationship depends on how the couple makes up—or at the very least engages in some sort of damage control.

This reconciliation (or patching up) does not necessarily involve groveling and jewelry. It can come in the shape of a simple loving comment: "You really do care about this, don't you?" Or it can be a giving act, such as getting your spouse a cup of tea. Or it can happen with humor, such as a playful raspberry sound. Or you can take a respite by suggesting that you each take a few minutes to get your bearings. Actually, it's not that hard to patch up. You simply need three elements:

1. You must want to help your partner not feel pain. When you are disagreeing, you may not be conscious of the deep love that brought you together and the wonderful future you can have together. But at least ask yourself, "Is my objective to hurt my wife?"

2. You must be calm. You cannot be flooded with emotion. For repair work to take place, you need to engage your "I have a job to do and I intend to do it well" mentality.

3. You must have your patch-up attempt accepted. Sometimes your mate isn't always receptive; perhaps she's distrusting of your intentions or too emotionally swamped herself to allow the repair to take place.

REMEMBER THIS
Good Reasons to Make Up
After a Fight

Patching up is the single best tool for happy marriages. In a study of newlyweds, the couples that could not patch things up after a fight had a rate of divorce in excess of 90 percent. But when couples were successful at making up, the odds of staying happily married soared to 84 percent.[12]

When spouses get into a cycle of one-upmanship, they hold on to the idea that they must make their point known before they can move away from that point of conflict. This approach doesn't allow for patching to happen because these spouses are too busy trying to win the other over to their side. It reminds me of the old joke: "I finally married Mr. Right; I just didn't know his first name was Always!"

In my household, my wife and I share responsibility for patching-up efforts. Sometimes when we're getting stuck on something and nerves are beginning to fray, Susan will make a face at me or start to chase me around the room. We shift from fuming to having fun and are able to lose the intensity for the fight. I know that Susan feels better when I open myself up emotionally, so if we've parted ways annoyed at each other, I'll take time out but then come back with an effort to acknowledge her perspective and a wish to heal things. Sometimes I'll bring a peace offering (although I don't call it that to her) like a cup of tea or our pet rabbit.

There are many creative ways to patch things up—going out for a walk, making the other person laugh, or just acknowledging that, despite the fight, you still love and admire your spouse. I know it's not easy to do it sometimes, but think about the alternative: living in an emotionally cold, distant, or angry household with chronic tension between the two of you. Compared to enduring that, *anything's* easy!

Your greatest challenge is to foster, within your wife's heart, a real and lasting faith that she can trust you. That's why you've demonstrated to her that you want to learn about her, and that's why you've decided to be by her side at home. As you help her manage the potential torment of conflict, you will continue to demonstrate, over time, that you are trustworthy and strong. When she knows she can rely on you, she'll be more open to your efforts to patch things up after a major squabble.

PRACTICE WHAT I PREACH

It's a lot to keep in mind: how conflict works, how to prevent it, how to diffuse it, and how to patch things up when you give into it. That's why you may need to read this chapter several times. It's not enough just to know that conflict happens; you've got to know all the stuff in this chapter inside and out. You've got to make it second nature.

You may not get it right the first time, or the second, or maybe even the twentieth. But as you do get better at it, you will see the patterns of conflict in your relationship, and you'll find ways to handle the sparks before they become forest fires. Best of all, as you master these skills, your wife will notice the change. She'll be reassured that you care more about her than you care about being right—and that's going to be good for your marriage.

TO DO LIST

- Accept that conflict is a natural part of marriage.

- Continue to get to know your wife so you can better understand the moods and motives that cause conflict in your marriage.

- Learn to recognize that conflict isn't necessarily bad; your wife may need it as a way to clear the air.

- Hold back hurtful and hateful comments—you don't always have to destroy your opponent of the moment.

- When tempers flare, you may need to take some time to let things cool down, but don't disappear, hang up the phone, or switch on the TV. Stay open to communication.

- Don't assume that your wife's comment has an underlying malevolent meaning. Try to assume the best motives, take her words at face value, and move on.

- Cut back on critical comments and don't point fingers. Use soft-tone "I" statements to address your wife's annoying habits.

- Never let arguments fester. Be the bigger guy and step in to patch things up. Use positive comments. Fight if you must, but then you might as well put the fight behind you and continue to reach toward your goal of having a happy marriage.

The Fifth Way

Learn to Listen

Y ou never listen!"

Sound familiar? Wives all over the world hurl this accusation at their hubbies, who distractedly nod and throw in a couple "Uh-huhs" whenever the conversation drags on longer than their get-to-the-point-in-two-minutes-or-less limit. This chasm between the communication styles of men and women is the cause of much marital discord. Of course the truth is that we all need to be heard—especially by those to whom we're emotionally and intimately connected—so women do have a point. But often it's just so hard to hang in there with rapt attention.

This chapter will help you turn your distracted "Uh-huh" responses into a type of active listening that will help you hear what your wife is saying and also help you understand the feeling and meaning behind the words—without getting that glazed-over look in your eyes or nodding off to sleep.

THE POWER OF LISTENING

I recall once, when I was still in college, returning home from a trip to Boston, where I had just split up with a girlfriend. My best friend was giving me a ride back down to Providence. As I climbed into the car, I began to talk about the breakup, about my feelings of loss and my sense of emptiness. I was in a lot of pain. A few minutes after I began to talk, my friend broke in asking if I had bought my books yet for our histology class.

I don't have the words to explain how crushed I felt at that moment, but I do understand why I felt that way. I had just been through a distressing life event, and I needed to share it. I needed support. I needed understanding. When my friend, the guy whom I felt closer to than any other person, changed the subject, two things happened: (1) I got a clear message that what I was saying was not important to him, and (2) I lost an opportunity to process the event out loud. As a result, I kept the feelings inside, giving the emotional pain more time and room to grow.

Later that week I had lunch with another college friend, Gretchen. We met outside in a small park, and I told her about my painful breakup. My friend quietly took in everything I said; she barely spoke a word. I talked about how special the relationship with my ex-girlfriend had been. I talked about how hard it was to lose her. I talked and talked and talked. And Gretchen listened. In the end she affirmed that I had lost something wonderful and that my pain was valid. And that was all she said.

I remember Gretchen fondly for that moment above all others, for she had given me what my best buddy had not. After I spoke to her I began to feel whole again; my loss was real, the relationship had been real, my pain was real. All those things that had swirled inside my head took on form, and I felt I could handle them. All because she listened.

SEEKING VERBAL ACKNOWLEDGMENT

How many times do you begin a conversation about something important to you, only to hear your listener say, "That's just like me. I . . ." and begin to tell his or her own story? Sometimes, of course, that's a normal and healthy part of conversation as two people compare notes and express empathy for something they've both experienced. Most of the time, though, if you have an important story to tell or information to pass on, what you are looking for is some acknowledgment that what you say is significant and has an impact on the person because that person cares about you. You're looking for a "Really?" or a "Thanks for telling me." To seek such a reaction may sound selfish or egoistic, but really it's neither. It's human nature. If you don't believe me, just think about how you feel when, at the conclusion of your statement, the teenager next door—or worse, your own daughter—responds, "Whatever."

Verbal acknowledgment from the listener is what allows communication to happen. When a thought is put into words, it's like a scout being sent out by an army regimen. The entire army awaits news from the scout: Are there dangers ahead? How many troops does the opponent have? Is there a place we can seek refuge? Until the scout gets back, the army is temporarily paralyzed—it really doesn't know in what direction to move. At last the scout returns, and the army can then advance or retreat as necessary. Or it may do neither and simply send out another scout to assess other options.

Like the scout that rides off into the battlefield, our verbal communication gets sent, and the speaker waits for a response. Once he gets that news, he knows how to proceed.

You've probably experienced this principle when talking on a cell phone. Have you ever found yourself speaking at length and suddenly realizing the call got dropped? You know the feeling of embarrassment and annoyance. (Why can't they make cell phones that don't cut out, anyway?) Moments before you realize you're disconnected, after you've stopped talking, you wait for confirmation that your message was received. Once you realize that your intended recipient failed to receive your message, you're forced to call once more and transmit the information all over again.

These principles of communication also relate very closely to your interactions with your wife. When she talks to you, she needs to know that someone's home on your end. From the male point of view, there's often good reason to shut down when listening to a female weave her way roundabout to the point of a story. Unlike women, many men believe that the sole purpose of communication is to convey information and solve problems. That's why in the workplace you seem to be able to communicate just fine. When a newspaper reporter rushes into J. Jonah Jameson's office and shouts, "Spiderman was just spotted at the wharf," the editor of the *Daily Bugle* responds immediately: "Get Peter Parker there immediately to snap some shots." Listen to message; respond with action.

But when we apply these same skills at home, they are rarely of use because the female of the species very often talks without having any clear message, and when she's done, there's nothing to jump into action about. For example, she might say, "You know that little girl in Katie's class who lives over on Parker Ave? [You nod.] Well, she's having a birthday party Saturday, and she didn't invite Katie. [You nod and add "Oh?"] So I called Katie's teacher to see if there was a reason that that little girl doesn't like Katie, and she said that she hadn't noticed any problems in the classroom, so I can't figure out why Katie wouldn't be invited to the party. Katie doesn't seem to care, but I think it must bother her. But I guess little cliques exist even at this age, and there's nothing we can do about it." [You nod again.]

That's it. That's the whole story. What can you possibly say to that except, "Uh- huh"? Yet that response is likely to anger your wife, and you'll hear the ever-popular "You're not listening!"

WOMANSPEAK

In Chapter Three, when we talked about getting to know your wife, you learned that you must rely on your powers of observation to master marriage. One area that we will turn to in this chapter is the specific lessons gained from watching your wife use language.

Learning to understand what your wife is saying begins by listening to her talk to other people. Notice how she expresses herself in conversation with the children, her friends, the delivery-man. Each time you hear her speak, ask yourself, "How does she communicate, and what can I learn from that?"

I listen in on my wife when she's on the phone. Don't worry, it's not from a hidden phone in another part of the house, like some scurrilous no-good on *Days of Our Lives*. I'm sitting right by her side, or at least I'm in the room where she is.

By taking the time to observe her telephone behavior, I learned that my wife and her girlfriends value verbal expression. They take time just to sit and talk. At times, at least from my vantage point, the content is almost irrelevant. My observation confirms scientific research that shows that women hear more than words in conversations. They have a greater ability to convey and receive emotional messages than do men, and women feel connected to others through conversation.

As a man, I don't envy my wife's hours of heart-to-hearts with her friends. I'm different. I don't want to stay on the phone longer than necessary. I consider a phone conversation strictly for the exchange of vital information, usually with an important goal. After two or three minutes, I've run out of things to talk about. And I notice a lot of men feel the same way about telephone calls. It's not an activity they consider open ended or without a specific goal.

But listening to my wife talk on the phone reminds me how important conversation is *to her,* and that I should make more of an effort to give her my undivided attention and do a lot more listening when she talks.

To the female mind, verbal interactions are precious and have real meaning even in the absence of tangible substance. That's one reason women are more likely than men to engage in talk therapy or to join book discussion clubs. In the women's universe, words create connections, and they are an important way of establishing and keeping a loving relationship.

It's so hard for me to understand the way my wife communicates even the most simple information. Let me give a real life example. My wife and I are having dinner guests this Saturday evening. A lot of preparation is going into this event. I have taken some time off work to help with all the plans. Earlier this week, I was mowing the lawn and cleaning out the flower beds. I was dirty and sweaty, following a very tight agenda. Instead of my wife stopping me for a moment to ask me to add something to the list of things to be done, I was stopped for 30 minutes while she relayed not only the task, but a long justification of why it had to be done. This long justification, an obvious attempt to influence the priority, was a waste of precious time. I like efficiency. It would have been easier for me if she just asked and said it needs to be done by such and such time. This just drives me crazy.

—Tim, age 26, married 2 years

Listening Between the Lines

When you're listening to your wife's words and learning about the way she uses conversation to connect with others, remember that the words you're hearing may not always convey exactly what she means. Unlike men, who generally express themselves in a straightforward way (what I say is what I mean), women's verbal communications can be pretty complicated, subtle, and oblique. For example, what does it mean if you get a new car and your wife says, "I think your new car is swell"? Does she mean:

1. I like your new car.

2. I'm upset you bought a new car.

3. I want a new car for myself.

4. I really don't care about your car one way or another.

Tough one, isn't it? Because even though the words convey one thing, you've got to sort through the tone, timing, and inflection, as well as how she *feels* about the subject, to get down to the underlying meaning.

This communication challenge comes between husbands and wives all the time. These are typical examples:

> Bobby, a thirty-eight-year-old husband, writes to my Web site that he feels confused when his wife complains that he doesn't open up more: "I have shared things about my past family problems, but the response from my wife was unsympathetic. Sometimes she even throws this information back at me. So I clam up. Heck, even when we use the same words, we seem to have different definitions."

> William, an Ivy League professor, answered honestly "No thanks" to his wife's query if he wanted to go out for dinner. Later he found out that she was disappointed and angry that he didn't want to spend time with her.

> Aaron, forty-six-year-old, writes, "It's what I call 'womanspeak.' She will say: 'Someone should take out the trash.' To me that means the trash needs to go out and one of us should volunteer. To her it means the trash needs to go out and I'm supposed to do it. If I don't take this roundabout cue, not only am I an asshole for not taking out the trash, I'm an asshole because she thinks I don't listen to her."

The only way you'll ever be able to crack the code of "womanspeak" is to learn how and why the two of you don't express your thoughts in the same way.

SecretsofMarriedMen.com

I have always felt that I married my wife because I love her and want to spend as much time together as I can. Thinking along those lines, I figure I should help her with jobs around the house so we can have more time to spend together. But I've learned that men think differently than women, and that makes it hard to work together for this common goal. When my wife says, "The faucet is leaking," I think she means "You need to fix it." So I go out and buy a new faucet, not knowing she's on the phone calling the plumber. Next thing I know we're arguing. So now, I always get my wife to write down all the things she wants me to do. She complains and says I shouldn't need written notes, but it's the only way I can be sure of what she wants!

—Dustin, age 53, married 23 years

IT'S A GENDER THING

Communication skills are just one more area where men and women are different. No debate. No controversy. They just are. The more you know about these differences, the more likely you'll be to understand what your wife is trying to tell you, and you'll be better able to make yourself understood as well.

Using Left-Brain and Right-Brain Listening Skills

As we discussed in Chapter One, the logical, sequential, and mathematical left brain and the big-picture, creative, and spiritual right brain are compartmentalized in men, so logical thought and emotional feeling don't often overlap. But remember that women are better able to use their sizable corpus collosum—the fibers that connect the two sides of the brain—to intermingle thought with feeling. Unlike a man, when a woman speaks she can easily process information from the visual centers in the occipital lobe *and* the emotional interpretive site in the right hemispheric temporal lobe *and* the emotional expressive site in the right frontal lobe. This brings far more feelings and emotion into a woman's conversation than would typically be present in a man's. We men rely on the speech centers in the left side of the brain only, stretching from the temporal lobe (behind the ear) to the frontal lobe (behind the eye). This gives us a very direct, straightforward way of communicating.[1] Dustin gets the job done best when his wife simply puts things down in writing; this wise strategy helps him clarify the message by separating the emotion from the intent.

Women express far greater content by adding on those layers of interpretive feelings, gestures, and inflections that don't come quite as easily to men. This is why women are much more capable of putting words to feelings, and they are better able to recognize emotion in the speech of others. In other words, the ability to "listen between the lines" comes more effortlessly to womenfolk.

When this difference goes unnoticed by men, we find ourselves hitting our heads against the wall of frustration over and over again. Consider, for example, the common mistake of taking at face value extreme language such as *always, never, the best, the worst, everybody, nobody,* and so on. When your wife says, "You never put down the toilet seat," your more fact-based mind will be drawn to the literal meaning of "always"—of course that can't be true, and you're annoyed at the distortion of the truth. But in her mind, she's not lying, she's expressing how it *feels* to her. And to her, if that's how she feels about it, then that's how it is. When you take time to listen between the lines of what your wife says, consider that these words represent the *feeling* your wife has about a situation, not a factual absolute.

If you don't recognize this difference, you could find yourself *arguing with* her rather than *learning from* her. Once you see the distinction between your left-brained-literal world and her whole-brained-expressionist world, her words can give you a window into her emotions and help you see ways to communicate better with her. The next time she says, "You always want to watch basketball," don't reply by pulling out the Laker's schedule for the year and noting all the games you missed—because of family responsibilities. React instead to the intent of her comment: "I feel like I don't get enough of you."

If you don't respond to the emotional content in her speech, she leaves the conversation believing you don't understand her—which you probably don't. To pick up more clues, pay attention to what she says through body language.

REMEMBER THIS
If Practice Makes Perfect, Women Are the Better Communicators

Biologically, women are more attached to expression through words. Right from birth, girls are more attuned to verbal sounds and learn to speak earlier and have larger vocabularies than little boys. As they grow, the imbalance continues: the average woman uses seven thousand words in a day, using many gestures and up to five tones. Compare this to a man's paltry two thousand daily words with only three tones, and you can see the attachment women have to speech.[2]

Listening to Her Body Language

Women are known to have a keen sense of intuition. It's real, and scientists hypothesize that it comes from their superior skills at reading quick flashes of emotion. This is probably because traditionally women have evolved to nurse and raise children and need to be attentive to their many nonverbal messages.

Most men, in contrast, don't have that keen ability to read nonverbal cues—thus, one more obstacle in communicating with women. You might assume that because your lack of sensitivity to body language isn't really your fault, you're off the hook. But think again. Nonverbal communication is very important to your wife, so it's now important to you also. You *can* learn to pay closer attention to your wife's nonverbal speech—the inflection, tone, gestures, and feelings—that are part of her message.

When your wife says she's "fine," for example, pay attention to her facial expressions and body motions when she speaks. If her eyebrows are furled, her nostrils flaring, and her eyes squinting, it could mean that everything isn't really so hunky-dory. Using your higher-level listening skill can help you figure out what your wife is really saying so you have one more way to know her better.

REMEMBER THIS
It's Not All About Action

I'm still looking for the marital retreat that asks mates to mud wrestle or play one-on-one hoops in order to resolve a problem. Or, better, a course that insists that couples go to bed together at the first sign of distress and not come out until they've each had at least one orgasm. Action oriented as I am, I personally think talk is overrated, but it may be the best method of regularly communicating our inner world to our women. And taking quick action is usually not what our wives really want, nor does it usually do the trick. Wait. Listen. Wait some more. Listen some more. When you feel that inner pressure to snap into action, try to remember: don't just do something, stand there!

Learning a New Culture

Like it or not, we men have to learn how to listen—it's part of a man's responsibility to meet his wife's needs.

Does that sound patriarchal? Does it sound sexist? Women worry that if men aren't naturally able to listen, having an expert instruct them in those skills is a form of manipulation or mind control. To these critics I say, Get a life! The expectation that men should naturally or instinctively adapt themselves to women's style and hierarchy of needs is the stuff of fairy tales. Before diplomats go to a new country, they are taught the cultural norms of that land. When we attend a friend's church, we adapt to that church's service protocol out of respect to our friend's beliefs. Learning a new culture and modifying our behaviors to match pays compliment to that way of life. You can adapt to your wife's culture without sacrificing a thing.

SecretsofMarriedMen.com

My grandmother told me many times growing up that "God gave us two ears, and only one mouth!" That means He gave you twice the tools to listen with as He did to talk with. If men and women heed these words of wisdom, it would cut their number of battles in half. I have been able to reveal myself like an open book to my wife through the years because she has learned to listen to me, and vice versa.

—Herrick, age 37, married 18 years

COMMUNICATION SKILLS 101

Because men develop communications skills more slowly than women, and because women assume that men's skills should equal theirs, I have come up with very specific instructions on how to improve your listening skills. Some think it's insulting to list dos and don'ts of marriage because every marriage is different. But I'm suggesting it anyway, because the words of advice in this section have helped men master marriage and because the fact is, *if your wife doesn't* feel *as though you are listening to her, it's the same as you're not listening to her.*

Stand Still When She Talks

If you're racing around the house while your wife is talking to you, she will probably interpret that as not listening. You may know in your heart of hearts that you listen better when you're in motion, but she doesn't know that and won't believe you if you explained it.

Turn Off the TV

I've had a client come into my office and say, "Doc, I have a little bit of attention deficit disorder. It helps me to have the TV on when my wife is talking to me." Oh, I see. In that case, here's my advice: I don't care! Forget about that and turn off the TV! You wouldn't have the TV on if your boss came in to talk to you at work, would you? Turn off the TV.

Look Directly at Her

Many men actually attend better to conversation when they are engaged in action-oriented enterprises, such as straightening out a room or cleaning the barrel of a shotgun. It helps to relieve anxiety they feel about having to talk, particularly if they are asked to talk about their emotions. But it's important to women that you not only stop what you're doing and hold still but also look at them. As much as you say you care, if you direct your attention elsewhere, it sends a very clear nonverbal message that your feelings don't match your words. One exception: when you are driving or otherwise operating heavy machinery, you should keep doing what you're doing and not necessarily look in your wife's eyes until you can pull over.

Strive to Agree

You don't have to agree with everything your wife is saying, but if you are getting lost in too much verbiage, grabbing on to landmarks can help keep you focused. Suppose she is telling a story: "Remember the other day we went to the market?" Yes! I went there. But she continues on, and your attention wanders; then you hear her say, "Blah, blah, blah, and your brother Jim, he has that dog . . ." Yeah! The dog, Rover! Find things that you can relate to, even if what she is saying doesn't seem important to you, and then give her verbal encouragement by saying, "Absolutely," or say, "You're right," or just grunt or nod your head in agreement. Anything.

This verbal feedback is important because it's proof that you're listening. There have been times when my wife and I have been conversing, and she stops abruptly and says, "You aren't listening." I respond, "Yes I am, and I agreed with everything you said." She then persists, "But you didn't say you agreed." I tell her I'm sure I did, because *in my mind* I am agreeing with her, saying, "Yup, okay, I agree with that." I'm answering her back, but only to myself. My wife, and yours, need to hear it verbally—so say it.

Acknowledge

If you don't agree with the whole, find the part that you concur with and give your wife your support. It's taken me a long time to learn that acknowledgment is not necessarily agreement. I learned this, by the way, from *knowing my wife*. When I hear my wife talking to a girlfriend on the phone, her friend will talk about something she did that was outrageous. Her friend would say how pissed off her husband got. Then my wife says into the phone, "I can't believe he got pissed off at you. The nerve!" Susan stands by her friends 100 percent.

After she hangs up the phone, I begin my inquest: "Susan, it was clear from what I heard that Janie wasn't being fair to her husband. Why did you agree with her?"

"Because she needed it," she says.

My wife agrees with her friends. It's a way of showing friendship. She doesn't have to have this internal struggle, *Wait, am I being true to myself? If I say yes, does that define me as having a value that I can never escape from?* She doesn't worry about it.

Susan has taught me a lesson, the same lesson all husbands need to learn: acknowledging your wife does not necessarily mean that you are in agreement with her. It just means that you recognize where she is coming from. And that means the world to her. It's what friends do for each other.

REMEMBER THIS
Think Twice Before Being So Agreeable

Although it's almost always good to find ways to agree with your wife, there are some situations in which you should think twice before you readily nod your head. Two situations that jump to mind are when she tells you, "I've been such a bitch lately," and when she exclaims, "I'm getting so fat!" Do not—I repeat, do not—agree with these statements.

Express Your Love Verbally

We men may say to ourselves, "I went out and did all the things you told me to today. I made your coffee. I put away the groceries. Doesn't that say that I love you?"

Well, no. It doesn't. Because, fellow men, when it comes to communicating love to your wife, you have to actually state it aloud. As a man, I recognize that by engaging in work I am expressing my love for my wife. Unfortunately, she doesn't interpret it that way. She may a little, but it would probably mean more to her if I were to say I love her.

Admit Your Failings

If your wife says, "You're not listening to me," and you're really not listening, don't say, "I *am* listening." Try this for a change: "You're right, I'm sorry. My attention wandered. What were you saying?" You don't have to be perfect; you just have to make an effort to listen. To her, this says you care.

Give Her Time to Talk

Charles, married eight years, is a thirty-two-year-old man and a contributor to SecretsofMarriedMen.com. He says it better than I can:

> Roses, poetry, jewelry, cards. These are all great gifts, but one of the greatest gifts you can give your wife is time. Quality time! Just letting her talk about her day, her problems, her accomplishments for the week, the kids, whatever. I know it's sometimes difficult, but when she finishes talking don't give advice. Make very general statements. Just nod a lot, answer "Oh, really?" "Cool," "I didn't know that." Listening to her and just simply being with her can be the best gift you could ever give. When she's sitting on the couch one night just sit down next to her, put your arm around her and ask, "How was your day?"

If you haven't done this lately, don't be surprised if your wife doesn't believe at first that you really want to listen. But persist—and then resist the temptation to butt in, give advice, or turn the conversation back to your own day. Let her talk while you listen.

Psst!

SecretsofMarriedMen.com

Most men and women do think, relate, feel, cope, process, and communicate differently. You learn her language whenever she is expressing any emotion in any way, like even getting mad at you for what you said. Shut up. Don't argue or explain, even if her facts are all wrong. Just listen, respect and acknowledge the emotion, like: "I can see you are hurting and upset and I can see why." It doesn't mean you agree. Let go of that hang-up. It just means you are listening and care. This isn't phony BS. It's just listening effectively and giving what's really needed rather than the usual guy approach of trying to jump in and fix everything.

—Rich, age 51, married 30 years

RULES FROM PROFESSIONALS

After the basics of good communication discussed in the previous section become a habit, you and your wife will be able to communicate with greater understanding and insight. But . . . there will still be times when the sound of her voice saying, "Honey, we need to talk" will send you into a panic. Relax. There is a way to handle this kind of situation so it won't hurt a bit. There are actually some rules that professional psychologists and researchers have developed. These rules of communication allow for a more controlled, structured kind of communication. Calmly, cooperatively, you can agree on a time and place to talk, somewhere with no distractions. Freewheeling digressions and wide-ranging streams of consciousness are not permitted. This is how men like it, and it works.

Speak, Repeat, Respond: Reflective Listening

To use the highly effective communication tactic called reflective listening, you have to use words—but . . . you don't have to talk about emotions. Following the communication model created by Howard Markman, Scott Stanley, and Susan Blumberg, authors of *Fighting* for *Your Marriage*, let's say Dick and Jane want to have a talk:

Dick begins by saying what's on his mind. Not too much—just enough to get one major point across.

Jane has to keep her mouth shut until Dick declares that he is done. Then she does an ingenious and incredibly helpful thing. She repeats back what she heard, or thought she heard, from Dick. This is called "mirroring" or reflecting back exactly what she has heard, so Dick can be sure she's been listening and really understands what he's trying to say.

When Dick agrees that she has understood him (note: I didn't say "agreed with him"), Dick gives the floor over to Jane, who can then talk about her perspective.

When Jane is done, Dick must repeat back what he thought he heard.

Once Jane feels understood, Dick gets the floor again.

He speaks. She repeats. He confirms her repeat statement. She then responds. They repeat this process as long as necessary. It's really very simple.

Your distinctly male brain benefits from a technique like this. Here's why. The testosterone that saturates your brain has preprogrammed you to be competitive. Your natural instinct is to try to trump your partner. That's good for winning the high school debate championship, but not good for healthy discussions. When you identify the specific task of repeating back what you heard, however, you have a new target at which your mental arrows can fly. You no longer need to think about what you are going to say to prove how illogical your wife is. Instead, you are going to do the best job of listening you possibly can, so you can prove to her that you heard what she said. This is particularly wise because when you must repeat back what she says, you may in fact end up hearing or understanding much better.

This is an amazingly powerful technique because humans seek to be understood. Reflecting what your partner said to you is proof that you heard her.

This communication strategy might seem a bit one sided—you're doing all the work! Actually, it is a technique frequently taught in couples therapy sessions to both members of a relationship team so they can both use reflective listening. I have found, however, that one person alone can adapt these strategies. Your wife may not know it's her turn to speak when you let her. She may not know you're reflecting back, but whether she knows or not, it's still effective. Conversely, when she's done talking and you're expecting your chance to have the floor, you may be disappointed if she doesn't know how the rules are supposed to go. I'm not insisting that husbands teach their wives this strategy, but if she *does* read this book, she'll no longer be able to plead ignorance. In any case, men who adapt this technique to their communication eventually find that their wives respond in a similar way, even if they don't know they're practicing a technique called reflective listening.

Overcoming Obstacles

A heartfelt attempt to reflect back on your wife's concerns requires that you understand what she says. Sometimes we can misinterpret even the clearest communication because all of us distill information through our own experiences. These "filters" impair our ability to listen to and echo back what our partner is saying. Consider the following filters. Which do you use?

1. *Inattention*. When you begin a conversation and then suddenly your PC barks, "You've got mail!" or your cell phone starts to vibrate in your hip pocket, are you still paying attention to your wife? You don't convey the message that your wife's needs are important if you don't pay attention.

2. *Bad moods*. Do you shut your partner out when you've had a cruddy day? When people are down or depressed, they see the

world through gray-colored glasses. They are more likely to interpret actions negatively and are less creative about finding ways to fix things.

3. *Unrealistic beliefs or expectations.* Do you find yourself disappointed because your mate fell short of your expectations? You may have made assumptions based on your own needs or perception of who you think she is, not on what she really feels or believes. Imagine an incredibly frustrating conversation about a beach vacation you just paid a deposit on—she loves Bermuda, right? No. In fact, she is hypersensitive to the sun. Because you don't know this, you can't understand why she's so upset about your "selfishness."

4. *Difference in styles.* Is your wife accusing you of being too angry, rude, or passive? It may be because of differences in your communication styles, which are based on how you were raised. In my family, for instance, it's the norm to talk on top of another person. If your point isn't being made, you simply talk louder. In my wife's family, raising your voice or talking out of turn is considered rude. So Susan may be interpreting my assertiveness as aggressiveness, and I see her silence as withdrawal.

Before we can really listen to our wives, reflect back to them and learn from what they're saying, we need to remove the obstacles that get in the way. Remove the filters from your conversations and listen to the message as it is sent and intended.

It Really Is the Thought That Counts: Empathic Listening

It's important to practice reflective listening skills and apply your strong work ethic until you're good at it. Once you've made inroads into this listening technique and understand the obstacles that get in the way of this kind of true listening, I'd like to help you progress to the next level.

This section of the chapter teaches a skill known as *empathic listening*. When you use this advanced technique to listen to your partner, you make a conscious effort not only to understand the words but also to understand the experience from her point of view, as if you were in her shoes, so to speak. Empathic listening requires you to dedicate all your attention to what she is feeling—her thoughts, desires, intentions, and motives.

This may sound complicated, but it's really important to figure out your wife's intended message. Her words come wrapped in layers of emotion, so you must make an effort to look beyond the outer covering to get to the true meaning of the words that lie beneath. And while you do this, pay no attention to your own feelings. That's not what your job is here.

As you engage in empathic listening, you will find that you are more easily able to connect with the words that are spoken. You begin to develop the skills to see your spouse's problems from her point of view. And when you do that, you gain a deeper understanding of what your spouse's concerns are and how to address them. Think about it: if you truly understand what your partner is saying from her point of view, there is nothing to argue about.

Not sure what I mean? Think about this reflective listening conversation. Suppose she says, "I'm upset [notice the "I" statement] because whenever I go out with my friends for dinner, you seem to sulk at home." [Notice how she says "seem to" rather than assigning an emotion to her hubby.] When she finishes, her husband might reflect, "I hear you saying that whenever you go out with your friends, I look pouty and put out."

So now where does the husband take this? To the next level: empathic listening. Now, instead of simply mirroring back what he heard, here's how he'd respond:

> I'm hearing you say that when you go off to have fun,
> and I'm at home alone, you see me as getting gloomy.
> That must make it harder for you just to let go and have

a good time because you're thinking of what I'm going through. It's probably even hard to come home at the end of the evening because of what you're sure will be waiting for you at the door when you do.

This response might at first sound a bit contrived, but it works. When you react to a complaint this way, there's nothing to argue about. There's no point in saying, "I'm *not* sulking" because it doesn't address what she's experiencing. It's not of any use, at least initially, to say "I'm sulking because . . ." when you realize she's not looking for a reason. You don't even necessarily have to change your behavior; she just wants the feeling she has inside her to change. And that takes the pressure off of you.

Empathic listening focuses on what *she's* experiencing, not on what *you're* doing wrong. In this way, her comments are completely valid, so there's no disputing them. You can immediately leapfrog over the answering back, because you don't have to defend yourself. She experiences the event as painful. You don't want her to feel pain, so you can focus on helping, not on fighting.

This last step in advanced-level listening makes your spouse feel heard and understood. You let her know that you sense not only the words she says but also the thoughts and feelings behind them.

Fine-Tuning Your Listening

When you respond with empathic listening, you do put yourself on the line. After all, you are not a mind reader, so you may have missed the point entirely. But because you have expressed a real wish to understand your wife, she shouldn't be too offended if you're off base.

Let's return to the example of our party girl and sulking boy. Ideally, the husband's first empathic response is dead-on, and she says, "Yes, that's exactly right. When I go off, I *do* think you get gloomy, and that *does* make it hard for me to just let loose. Thank you for understanding." But suppose, in answer to his first stab at empathic response, the wife says, "No, you don't understand. I'm *not* worried about you sulking. I know you're a big boy. It's just that I feel guilty because I'm not used to doing my own thing."

By giving an empathic response, this man has helped his wife get in touch with her feelings more, and he now has even more information to help him understand her. But it's still not time for him to jump in with a solution, such as, "Why don't you just forget about your guilt and go have a good time?"

This method asks you to take a stab at an empathic response, await feedback, and then, with that new data, try another empathic response, and so on. In this case the husband might then say, "So you're really trying to branch out and establish your own identity, but you're not sure how I feel about it." He keeps trying to get at her feelings, not the right or wrong of things.

It is hard to overestimate the tremendous gift of yourself you give when you engage in this active process of listening. Not only will you drop your defensiveness, but your wife will begin to put down her shields as well. In time, perhaps you will both learn to share feelings and thoughts openly and feel truly understood by the other—and that's all you both wanted in the first place.

TO DO LIST

- Learn to listen for the meaning behind the words—not just the literal meaning of the words themselves. Also listen to your wife's nonverbal speech—the inflection, tone, gestures, and feelings—that are part of her message.

- Make sure your wife feels that you're listening to her by giving her your full attention, looking directly at her, and finding common points on which you can agree. Give verbal acknowledgment that goes beyond "Uh-huh."

- Consider asking your wife to write down important needs or tasks to make sure you are clear about what she wants.

- Don't let the filters of inattention, bad moods, unrealistic expectations, or different communication styles get in the way of understanding what your wife is trying to tell you.

- When the topic is an important one, reflect back what your wife says to you to make sure you understand her correctly. Then respond by asking questions that will help you understand the experience from her point of view.

- Don't listen to win her over to your point of view. Listen to understand.

8

The Sixth Way

Aim to Please

If Mama ain't happy, ain't nobody happy," read a T-shirt I once saw while strolling the boardwalk in Atlantic City. This glib observation caught my eye because it is backed up by an enormous amount of scientific research and many surveys that show that in most American households caring for the domicile, the domestic fortress, the hearth and home, is the woman's domain.

By caring for the home, I don't mean mowing the lawn and repairing small appliances. I'm talking about the day-to-day responsibilities of managing the household—everything from most shopping, planning, and preparing of meals, to keeping milk in the refrigerator and the pantry and freezer well stocked. Think about it. Isn't your wife pretty much the one who is responsible for keeping the house clean and relatively tidy, making sure everyone's laundry and dry cleaning are done, and sprucing things up when your parents visit? Usually, she is director of edible resources, culinary standards, household inventory control, and domestic sanitation, not to mention guidance counselor, transportation coordinator, short-order cook, family doctor, wardrobe manager, security chief, and many, many other things you and I can't even imagine.

More than that, the woman of the house is usually the emotional center, the force that holds everything together on a daily basis, creating, modifying, sustaining, and supporting the moment-to-moment warmth, nurturance, and positive collective feelings of the family. She's the mother, right?

And if Mama's not happy about how her home life is working out, there is very little chance that you are living a happy marriage. Although many responsibilities fall to her, it is *your* responsibility to find ways to make her life easier. And the best way to do this is to aim to please.

YOU ALREADY KNOW HOW TO DO THIS

In the workplace, most men don't have a problem pleasing people. Over the phone and out in the field, men are masters of relationship building. Think of the politician on the stump shaking hands and holding babies. Think of the car salesman, keenly honing in on the buyer's desires in order to make sure he or she leaves with a new set of wheels. Blockbuster service industries, from Wendy's to Wal-Mart, which were often built from the ground up by men, rely on the dictum that the customer is always right. Even the customers who are having a bad day. And the ones who are naturally ornery present nothing more than just another challenge. To succeed in this environment, you study the customers, you listen to them, you find out what they really want, you think through a strategy, and then you aim to please.

Given this skill and this willingness to please others, it's hard to understand why there are days when many husbands treat strangers better than they treat their own wives (which we all do on occasion—come on, be honest).

One reason we are less inclined to give special attention to our spouses is that, unlike a customer, who can walk away at the slightest provocation, we tend to take our partner's commitment to us for granted. Yeah, it's human nature. Because she's there all the time, we work under the assumption that she always will be.

If you're preoccupied when you walk in the house after a tough day, you may not remember to greet your honey with a warm hello.

Although you would hardly expect her to pack her bags and move back in with her mother because of this, it's one of those small things that multiply in impact over time. You certainly know that if you continually fail to treat your customers or clients with respect and warmth, eventually they may decide never to come back. Ever. You can't expect your wife's reaction to be any different. After months and years of feeling neglected, she will grow increasingly unhappy, and yes, she just might leave and never come back. Or she might stay put, but change the locks and have a constable show up at your work with a no-contact order.

One might argue that it works the same way for husbands—that they are just as likely to grow discontented as expressions of appreciation taper off. But studies show that the wife is much more likely than the husband to describe feeling unhappy in marriage.[1] Moreover, research shows that it's a husband's ability to accommodate his wife's needs—not the other way around—that is highly predictive of a lasting marriage.[2]

In a letter written to my Web site, forty-year-old Gilda attributes her infidelity to being ignored by her second husband:

> I became seriously involved with a man (also married with children) during my current marriage. He was the ultimate knight on a white horse. Very good looking, bodybuilder, romantic, poetic, the whole nine yards. He was quite a contrast to my husband who isn't one for major affection or romance. Women need to feel desired!
>
> Especially when we've gotten a little older and have some extra pounds to be reckoned with. Men you must learn that. If you want us to be sexy, act sexy, and be happy (not nagging all the time), you've got to make us feel like you desire our company—and our bodies. Make us feel special like you did before the marriage and children and the often-exhausting daily routine.

No, I'm not blaming my behavior on the way my husband treated me, but the door wouldn't have been open for someone else to swoop in if I had truly felt that I was the most important person in my husband's life. Married men, just remember that you get back what you give. If you want a great relationship with a great woman, you've got to believe that's what you already have and act accordingly—she'll follow form!

Gilda speaks for many women. Frequently when men come into my office after their wives have left them or filed for divorce, they say, "I never saw it coming." That's because they weren't looking! Listen to what this divorced woman says:

I was married for twenty-one years to a man who never bought gifts, flowers or small token gifts of love or appreciation for me unless he accidentally remembered my birthday. I never felt loved or nourished, although I spent my days loving and nourishing him. He felt that because he worked hard for the family he had fulfilled his obligations to his wife. When we divorced he was in total shock. In his mind he had spent twenty-one years giving generously to me. After all, he gave me his paycheck every two weeks. He was actually happy in our marriage. He felt loved and cared for; he was truly contented. I just felt alone and empty.

Some marriages have conflicts that simply cannot be resolved. In most cases, though, if you ask a wife why she is leaving, it is related, directly or indirectly, to the belief that her husband no longer makes her feel special. That's a problem you can do something about.

Psst!

SecretsofMarriedMen.com

You both must give 100 percent of yourself in your marriage if you want it to work. Love her the same as you did when you dated and make her feel like the most important thing on earth. You had better find the time or you will find yourself divorced. If you can't find the time to do this, why did you ever get married?

—Frank, age 48, married 25 years

BE ACTIVE: DO SOMETHING

The Aim to Please mantra reminds you that there are specific things you should be doing. I've listed a few here to get your started, from the obvious "Give gifts" to the more unusual "Play often." But don't stop with these suggestions. Wake up every day ready to please in new and fun ways.

I call this attitude *meeting payroll*. Each of us, male and female, is working round the clock for our spouse. Sometimes this work is obvious, as when she cooks dinner for your poker buddies or when you change the oil in her car. Most of the time the work is less obvious, as when your wife gets her hair done to look attractive for you or when you go out to the curb to pick up the morning paper each day.

In the real work world, you know that when someone does a job, you've got to pay the bill. But in the job called marriage, we too rarely pay back our spouses in ways that are both regular and appropriate. You can't just say to someone who works for you, "Well, you know that every six months or so I'll give you a paycheck." The employee wouldn't last that long. My secretary, Jennifer, does a great job for me, and we get along really well, but if I stopped paying her, she would disappear. And if I pay her less than others who do the same work, payday is not as meaningful as it should be. Everyone who does a job expects some sort of compensation—we need to be paying back our wives for all they do for us. You may choose to give gifts, you may choose to give some kind of emotional currency, you may choose to arrange a vacation or a day shopping at the mall. But no matter what you choose, you must be sure your wife knows that you recognize her contributions to your life and are striving to meet payroll.

Give Positive Feedback

The first payroll deposit your wife needs from you is in the form of positive feedback. Start with saying something nice. Research has shown that the ratio of positive interactions to negative interactions must be at least 5:1 for a spouse to opt in on the marriage.[3] This means that you must work hard to say or do five positive things for each time you complain, criticize, mock, put down, sneer, whine, roll your eyes, or turn a cold shoulder. Any fewer than that, and there's a good chance the marriage will not survive.

Saying, "Thanks for picking up my shirts from the cleaners" or "That was a nice meal" is a good way to start giving positive feedback. But remember that positives don't have to come in the form of attaboys. Here are some other ways to help tip the balance in the plus column:

- Say "I love you." Touch her arm. Hold her hand.

- Say, "That looks interesting. What are you doing?"

- Say, "Thank you."

- Say, "I understand."

- Ask, "Can I get you something?"

- Laugh with her more often. Share humorous stories. Tell a joke.

- Give her your full attention when she's talking.

All these actions are forms of personal attention that are too easily overlooked in our hectic lives. At the end of each day, look back and ask yourself if you gave any positive feedback during that day. Remember, your goal is to give five positives for every negative. How close to that goal did you come today?

Psst!

SecretsofMarriedMen.com

The secret to our success involves the use of language. Compliments—real ones—are required along with other expressions of love, admiration and respect. Tell her she looks pretty. Tell her something you admire about her. Tell her you think she's a wonderful mother. Tell her anything positive, so long as it's true . . . and specific. If she's not used to it, she might be suspicious at first, but persevere. She wants to hear it. She needs to hear it. Tell her today, tomorrow, the next day. And again. Then in case she hasn't heard you yet, tell her one more time. If it's true, she'll know it, and eventually she'll believe you. You'll find that the act of telling her in and of itself, coupled with her responses to you, will be tremendously gratifying for both of you.

—Jim, age 47, second marriage of 14 years

Match What You Do for Her to What You Know About Her

In Chapter Four we talked about the value of really knowing your wife. You can now use that information to aim to please. Taking her to a nice restaurant, for example, may seem like an effort to please, but if you choose to take her out to a lobster boil, forgetting that she's allergic to shellfish, she won't be very impressed with your thoughtfulness. Likewise, tickets to a Philadelphia Flyers game may not impress her if she's not a fan of fistfights on ice skates. (I know, it's hard to believe—there are some folks who just don't like hockey.)

In payroll terms, this principle reflects the need to pay in the right currency. Even though some South American tribes trade in seashells, I don't think my secretary would appreciate getting a large envelope of shells every Friday. Jennifer values dollars. In your marriage, you need to determine what currency your wife values; then you'll know what she's looking for in her paycheck. That's why knowing your wife is so important.

In my efforts to know my wife, I discovered something she really values. One staple in her makeup drawer is Lancôme eyelash stuff. It's the only brand she uses for lashes ever. So whenever Lancôme has one of those special buy-$25-of-makeup-and-get-a-free-gift-bag sales, I'll pick up the eyelash stuff so I can get the free bag with lots of other Lancôme makeup in it. (Of course the eyelash stuff she likes is just under $25, so I have to buy two—but boy, is my wife happy when she gets it.) Because the free bag comes with so many fun things inside (lipstick, different colored powders, cremes that are supposed to make wrinkles disappear, and so on), when she opens it up it's like a stocking on Christmas morning. And I get credit for each and every item that's in the bag.

What does your wife like? Think about this and try to come up with something that matches her needs and shows you're a thoughtful guy. Go back and review the list you have been making in your practice of the Second Way. What have you learned about what makes her tick?

If she's an outdoor person, you might adopt a wolf in her name or name a whale or a star after her.

If you see that she's looking tired or bored lately, arrange a day at the spa or buy her a gift certificate for a massage, manicure, or pedicure.

If she loves old stuff or bargain hunting, schedule an afternoon of antiquing or wake her up early one Saturday morning, cup of coffee in hand, and take her garage sale cruising without even being asked.

Thomas, age twenty-eight and married three years, says,

> Give a gift if there is an occasion to do so or if you feel like it. Contrary to popular belief, women do not sit around and dream about what gift they will receive next from their husband. I do not give gifts for adoration, seduction (well, occasionally), and certainly not appeasement! I do believe though that wives feel special when their husbands get them gifts. However, I think it is thoughtless to give flowers or one of the generically "women" gifts to your wife just out of tradition. Grow up and stop being boring! Hopefully, you know your spouse and the small things she might find funny or pleasing. For instance, my wife recently had a horrible day at work, and on my way home, I picked up her favorite high-cal, high-cholesterol McDonald's meal. The drive-thru took me about five minutes and cost about $7 for both meals. She was so happy and we had a wonderful night!

Thomas is right, but an awful lot of guys have trouble with this gift-giving thing. Jake, married eight years, wrote to my Web site saying that he takes a logical view of gift giving: "Tokens of love aren't necessary once the deal is sealed," he said. Is that so, Jake? I strongly disagree and suspect that the reason so many men are against gift giving is that the whole concept confuses and frustrates them.

I admit that I too used to struggle with the whole issue of gift giving. The running joke in my household was that I dreaded all the landmark days: Valentine's Day, my wife's birthday, our anniversary, Mother's Day, and the winter holidays. Just the thought of having to choose the perfect gift for my wife on each of these days made me very anxious. I couldn't figure out what the big deal was to my wife—why was it so important to her that I dare not "forget" to buy her something?

As a scientist, I'm fascinated by this kind of question. Although it's often hard to tease out those aspects of human behavior that are inborn and those that are part of our assigned roles in society, I do have a theory about why women put so much emphasis on the gifts we buy (or don't buy) them.

When it comes to the role of men throughout history, the theme that emerges time and again is that of the protector and provider. Men feel like they are at the top of their game when their loved ones express appreciation for their contributions.

So what role does that put women in? Are they the protectee and providee? Most modern-day women would reject that idea because they value their independence. In fact, almost all the advances in opportunities for women are contingent on their ability to fend for themselves. Yet when I talk to women, I still sense that in some fundamental way, they look to their men to prove that they can club a mastodon to death and drag it home to the doorstep. Well, not a mastodon perhaps, but something as simple but thoughtful as a card can give the modern-day wife the message that her husband is of strong and capable stock and that he is committed to the defense of the household. On an intellectual level, it's nice to be thought of. But in a very primitive way, it touches a chord deep inside a woman, a feeling that most men cannot relate to.

Whether you can relate to it or not, understanding who your wife is, what she likes, and what you can give her to make her happy is a great way to continually meet payroll. We men have to realize that we must never stop courting our wives. No kidding. We need to show them our love with attention, chivalry, presents, kisses, declarations of love, poetry, and on and on. We should never stop showing how we feel. So go ahead: start today and don't be afraid to think outside the Happy Meal box.

Psst!

SecretsofMarriedMen.com

Gifts for a special occasion are nice and appreciated, but are also expected on some level. You almost always know that it is coming. It is the gift sent for no reason and out of the clear blue sky that means the most to a woman. A gift sent even when you don't feel like sending one can usually be an enticement to get a problem resolved because she knows that you care about her in spite of whatever problem you have going on. It may just be the thing that gets your foot in the door to let her know how you feel about something and getting her to listen and understand your point of view. Letting her know that your differences have not changed your love for her is a good way to get her attention.

—Rhonda, age 31, married 7 years

Send a Card

Many of the greatest salesmen and professionals regularly send out communications to their customers to remind them that they are thinking of them. I know of a dentist, for example, who records his patients' birthdays when they first register with him and then faithfully sends each one a birthday card every year. This is a smart business model.

Send cards?! I can hear you groaning from here. Forty-four-year-old David told me his feelings loud and clear:

> I hate giving cards with a passion. My wife insists I do it despite the fact that she knows that simply going into a card store gives me the sweats. I've never found an appropriate card yet, and I'm always concerned about which type to buy: mushy, humorous? I'll be judged either way . . . and the card won't be a reflection of my feelings; only a reflection of what I settled for. I can't be the only guy who believes that card giving is a ridiculous custom, dreamed up by companies like Hallmark and only beneficial to them and the post office.

I know exactly how David feels. But we men need to focus on how our wives feel. Even though cards may not be meaningful for us, they are valuable currency for many women. Listen to what thirty-year-old Shannon says: "I really don't care about gifts, but every once in a while a card just to say 'I'm thinking of you' is nice and lets me know I'm on his mind when I'm not around. I would rather have an unexpected card than a gift that he has to get for a major holiday. With a card, he can say things and explain how he feels better than he can in person."

Considering how many women feel like Shannon, why not give it a try? Here's what I suggest (just don't tell my wife). Go out shopping one day for cards. Not just one card—lots of cards. Get some that are serious, some that are funny, and some that are artsy. Then take about a half hour and write a note inside each one of these cards. The note can be brief, but should express some specific thing you like about your wife and should include at least one positive emotion you feel about her. For example: "You've got such a great warmth and deep caring about others. I'm proud to be around you!"

Then address and stamp all the notes and put them away in your office drawer. Mark your calendar, Palm Pilot, or Outlook Scheduler to remind you to send out one of these cards at regular intervals, for various events, or as the impulse moves you. Place it in the mail and wait to see what happens.

Psst!

SecretsofMarriedMen.com

I make it a point to buy a card, then put it in a place where she can find it. Lay flowers on the bed. Write her a love letter periodically. The other day, I wrote her a note, which I taped to her computer: "Thank you for helping me find my heart." I have told her, "Without you, I would know nothing about oneness." Because I finally accepted her love, I was able to find out about love. I make it a point to tell her most mornings that "This is a much better way to live."

—Don, age 56, married 31 years

Be Thoughtful and Creative

Many men have learned to think outside the box in the workplace. In more and more occupations, innovation and creativity are highly rewarded. I encourage you to use this same kind of thinking to please your wife. What can you do for her that will knock her socks off?

I recently read a news article about J. Jackson, a sixty-seven-year-old Californian, who found a way to thrill his wife and show her just how much he loved her. The eye disease retinitis pigmentosa has been stealing Sonja Jackson's eyesight for more than thirty-five years. Eight years ago, she became blind in her right eye, and she had only limited vision in her left. When a specialist told the couple that bright colors would be easiest for her to see, Jackson got out his paintbrush. During the past seven years, he has transformed their home into a magical wonderland. People now come from far and wide to see the large, colorful butterflies that Jackson painted all over his house for his sweetheart to see, even with her limited vision. "He started this for me. It was a gift of love," Sonja said. "But I think now it's for everybody."[4]

That's tough to top, but see what you can do for your sweetheart. Here are some ideas for starters:

- Leave her a romantic voice mail.

- Bake her a cake.

- Celebrate her half-birthday.

- Clean out her car.

- Carve her name in a tree.

- Cut flowers from the side of the road on the way home from work.

- Paint her toenails.

- Run a bath for her with scented bath salts, take the phone off the hook, set up music and scented candles. Come in a few moments later to wash her back and then, despite your intimate instincts, offer to leave her alone. And for heaven's sake, make sure the kids don't interrupt her.

- Fill up her car with gasoline. This is something I especially like to do to show my wife I love her. When I fill it up, I also buy ice cream bars at the little food mart section of the gas station; she likes those Dove Bars. I buy a few and then put them in the freezer at home. The next day she says, "Oh, there are Dove Bars in the freezer." I say, "Yeah, I got them when I filled up the gas tank." Without this little lead-in, I don't think she'd ever notice the gas in her tank. It's the small things. (As a side note: I actually save money this way because my wife fills up at a more expensive full-serve station.)

Make Time to Play

When was the last time you and your wife had a play date? If playing is not part of your relationship, adding this dimension can be a great way to strengthen your marriage as you aim to please.

In the book *The Play Solution: How to Put the Fun and Excitement Back into Your Relationship*, authors Jeanette and Robert Laurer report their findings about play and marriage. They studied three hundred couples who had been married between fifteen and sixty-one years, and they found that the happiest of them agreed on the importance of play and humor in their relationships. In fact, both husbands and wives ranked play above sex as being a vital aspect to a successful marriage.[5] I'm not surprised. I often suggest that couples who play together feel better about themselves and the relationship.

What happens when children play? They become free from routine life. They spontaneously create their own joy. They laugh out loud. Imagine how good it would feel to experience these things again with your wife. Play lets even adults be spontaneous, free, and happy—and all these things are good for a marriage.

If you're not in the habit of playing with your wife, take time to brainstorm a list of activities you'll both enjoy. I suggest you consider these types of play:

Indoors. Take out your board games, play hide-and-seek, do a puzzle together. Watch sitcoms side by side on the couch.

Outdoors. Play a game of hoops, softball, whiffle ball, or basketball, or throw the football with each other. You don't have to coach her about how to do it better, just have fun with lateral passes followed by a loving tackle.

In nature. Go camping or hiking, cross-country skiing, or ski shoeing. Find something she loves and make doing it a priority, even if it's only going out to your backyard to make s'mores on the grill.

In public. Take her to the park or the museum, someplace where you can simply hold hands together and solve the problems of the world.

In private. Even if you don't have a surround-sound home theater, you can still take your wife to the movies in your own home. Rent a good chick-flick, order out Chinese food. (No, pizza and beer won't cut it.)

In culture. Go to live theater. Take her to an artsy movie in a foreign language. Excuse yourself before the movie begins and come back to the seat with a giant bag of popcorn and a large soda. Read her poetry as she falls asleep at night.

In romance. Hold hands, skip together, kiss in public, or write each other love letters and poetry.

In intimacy. There's lots of room for play in your romantic life. Drag a bear rug (or at least a couple beach towels) in front of the fireplace or wood stove and make out. Place ads for each other in the local paper's personal ads and try to figure out who's who. Or read other people's ads, have her find the most scintillating, then play-act for the night!

Our lives are all so hectic. We rush around each day trying to meet our responsibilities, and forget all about having fun. Well, one of our new responsibilities is to play. So starting today, be sure to make time for a play date with your wife.

SecretsofMarriedMen.com

My wife and I play a game called tag. One person is "it," and must do something nice for the other. When they do, that person becomes "it." (Not being "it" does not make one spouse immune from doing something nice, however.) One night before bed I found a mess on the floor. It was a bunch of Hershey's kisses with a note that said, "I worship the ground that you walk on." What a hit! I was smitten. I fell in love again, and I was "it."

—Gary, age 35, married 14 years

DOING IT FOR LOVE

After one lecture, a woman said to me, "I think this Aim to Please business is contrived and patronizing. I'm a little offended."

"You are absolutely half right," I said.

I then explained that deploying the Aim to Please strategy *is* contrived—in the sense that I am asking husbands to make a transition from being oblivious and unappreciative to being conscientious and generous. You can't just flip a switch to change behavior. But you can get started by planning out things you will do and say. If that's contrived, I can live with that.

But it's not patronizing when the husband is doing it out of love. And here's the best part: after a husband puts Aim to Please into play, it automatically displaces an enormous amount of negativity. As the magic 5:1 ratio becomes a more consistent reality, wives respond—usually warmly and sometimes passionately. In time, Aim to Please becomes natural, making husbands and wives happier and marriages stronger.

The point is women shouldn't feel indignant if their husbands choose to put aside their own pride and do these little extra things that make their wives happy. The effort is what makes a man succeed at the job of being a good husband.

TO DO LIST

- Use the people-pleasing skills you have honed so well at work to make your wife feel special.

- Increase the number of times you give your wife positive feedback each day.

- Pay attention to the things that please your wife and use that knowledge as a template for ideas to express your love in ways she'll appreciate.

- Celebrate the universal holidays by recognizing your wife for the contributions she has made to your life.

- Give cards and gifts in creative ways on nonholidays to show your wife the side of you that she thinks died after you said "I do."

- Arrange a play date that gives you and your wife time to be spontaneous, free, and happy together.

9

The Seventh Way

Understand the Truth About Sex

You may be reading this book with the hope that if you follow all the advice I have to offer, you'll be guaranteed more frequent and passionate sex with your wife. After all, up to this point, you've made such an outstanding effort to improve your marriage—applying your work skills to your relationship, carefully trying to get to know your wife, staying home more often, dealing with conflict, and aiming to please—that you figure you have a right to expect the big payoff in the end. Right?

Well . . . no . . . not exactly. If I had set out to write a book with that kind of guarantee, I would have tried to come up with a catchier subtitle. It would be something scrupulously tasteful, of course, but a little more self-evident, such as *Eight Ways to Get Your Wife Hot and Bothered and Enjoy Endless Monkey-Love*.

But no. That's a book for someone else to write.

FOR MEN WHO WANT MORE SEX

Let's begin with what may be a very surprising fact for many men. Contrary to popular belief, sex is *not* the overriding factor in either marital happiness or marital distress. That's right, guys. Sex is not necessarily the most important aspect of a good marriage, not the first thing to work on if you want to be happier with your wife, not the entire core of the relationship. It may be a barometer of how things are going, and it certainly can be emotionally and physically satisfying, fun, thrilling even—but it's not where we need to put our energy right now.

REMEMBER THIS
Sex Is More of an Issue When the Marriage Is Already in Trouble

Research has shown that when marriage is going well, sex contributes only 15 to 20 percent toward making the relationship satisfying. But when people in unhappy marriages weigh in, they say their sex life is responsible for 50 to 75 percent of their unhappiness.[1] This tells us that although sex is but one of many factors in a relationship, if you've got problems in your marriage, then you've probably got problems with sex.

It's also difficult to discuss sex in a book like this because in the bedroom no two couples are alike. It's possible that your sex life is the best part of your marriage. Or it may be that tension and bickering in every other room of the house have made performing in the bedroom impossible. Then again, it may be that sex is a very minor part of your marriage, and that suits both you and your wife just fine. Maybe your wife seems to use sex as a reward for good deeds. Or better yet, she craves your body because she loves and desires passion and intimacy, you lucky fellow. Or maybe she complains that it's all you think about. Maybe you're satisfied with quality, but discouraged by the quantity. Or maybe you'd rather have cybersex anonymously in a chat room than talk to anyone, anywhere, any time about your sexual needs. See what I mean? To cover all the scenarios, I figure the *Monkey-Love* book would run about ten thousand pages.

But leaving sex out of a self-help book aimed at married men would be like leaving Monica Lewinsky out of a book titled

Bill Clinton: The Man. So I've decided to go with the odds and address the most common complaint that men have about their sex lives.

Based on a profound and exhaustive statistical analysis of the contributions to my SecretsofMarriedMen.com Web site (well, I counted them up and divided), I found that 77 percent of men see themselves as having a higher sex drive than their wives. Many experts in the field have reported similar findings. Here's a typical comment from Austin, a forty-eight-year-old man describing his marriage of twenty-three years:

> My sex drive and my needs are much higher than hers. She goes through periods where her interests increase, but for the most part, she is more than satisfied with sex twice a month. Of course, there are times when she is in the mood for sex and I'm not so inclined, but I'm easily convinced if she makes any effort at all. Unfortunately, she turns away too easily.

Because I can't cover in one chapter all the possible sex problems out there, I'm putting my money on this one problem that affects most married men: they want more or better sex in their marriages.

Throughout the chapter, I will plant little hints so that if your wife picks up the book, she'll learn that having sex will improve your emotional connection to her (something she would really like) and that she can play an active role in making that connection happen. But unless she does peek in these pages, your wife probably won't understand that you and she often experience sex in different ways and that your manhood, your sex drive, is to be treasured, not scorned simply because it is different than hers.

So *I'm* telling you. Your needs are worthwhile, and not just because they provide a biological release. Sex is one of the most profound ways you can express your emotional connection to your wife. If you follow the recommendations in this chapter and throughout the book, you will certainly improve the quality of your marriage, and that's bound to lead to better and more sex.

However, throwing yourself into the To Do list at the end of this chapter will not produce a "perfect" marriage any more than working around the clock will result in a "perfectly" run business. Moreover, reading this book probably will not result in your getting great sex Saturday night *and* Sunday, at least not right away. But I do know that it will improve your marriage. In the first days of applying the Eight Ways, you may find dinner more pleasant. In the weeks that follow, perhaps you'll enjoy more time together without bickering. As you learn how to win her heart, her passion will grow. All your interactions—even the semiannual argument about whether the dishwasher is loaded the right way—will be more manageable. You'll master husbanding, and your wife will notice. And that's a big step in getting your emotional—and sexual—needs met.

REMEMBER THIS
Not All Men Have High Sex Drives

This chapter is written for men who feel they have higher sex drives than their mates. But of course there are men who have lower sex drives. This can happen because they have simply shut down after suffering rejection after rejection. Or, for biological or genetic reasons, they just have a less obsessive 24/7 need for sex. If this sounds like you, don't despair. Use the advice here to help you feel more hopeful about the positive effects that learning to understand your wife can have in your life. Lower sex drive can also be caused by physical problems, particularly if you are on medication or moving past middle age. In that case, this chapter may be helpful in general, but it probably won't be enough to make any significant changes without the help of a medical doctor.

So, with that caveat out of the way, I can say that in this chapter you'll learn at the very least these two things: (1) men and women think about sex in different ways, and (2) you can use that information to improve your marriage and maybe even your sex life.

WOMEN ARE PROGRAMMED FOR SEX DIFFERENTLY THAN MEN

We all know that men and women have different levels of hormones and brain chemicals coursing through their bodies. But did you know that these differences are among the most likely reasons she often isn't in the mood?

The Testosterone Difference

For starters, testosterone levels are higher in men. This is the chemical that allows us to build larger muscles than women and makes us more aggressive. It is the fuel that drives our search for social power, ambition, and independence, and it is responsible for giving us a much higher sex drive than our wives have.

So on a strictly biological level, your wife doesn't have the uncontrollable sexual appetite that you have because her testosterone level is only 10 percent of yours. For those who need proof, researchers found that women who were experimentally supplemented with testosterone became both more aggressive and more sexual in the bedroom.[2] And if you're looking back at your courting days thinking that she *used* to fall into that "sexually aggressive" category, you're probably right. Testosterone levels drop as women get older, particularly after they have children.

During their menstrual cycles, women do have a brief period of time when their level of testosterone surges a bit and increases their desire for sex. That happens once a month when they ovulate (release an egg) over a period of about forty hours. In fact, the rate of intercourse in women increases 24 percent the six days around ovulation.[3]

Let's stop for a moment and consider that interesting factoid, fellow men. Once a month there's a 24 percent increase in sex among all women. Hmmm . . . Good news, but at the same time, if women have this compulsion to have sex to reproduce less than one week a month, and men feel that compulsion all the time, there's going to be some tension in the sex department.

So here's a tip. If you're looking to get more sex, start by adding one more thing to your "get to know your wife" list from Chapter Four: pay attention to her menstrual cycle. About fourteen days after the first day of her monthly period, she will ovulate, and her sex drive will increase. Before you jump to the rescue, you should know that this is also when she is most likely to become pregnant as the unsuspecting egg awaits a sperm to fertilize it. So unless you are at the point where you want a child, watch out and plan ahead. Take responsibility, too; don't count on your wife to work out the details. Mobilize your skills as an organizer and leader in the contraception department.

REMEMBER THIS
Your Grandpa Was a Lucky Guy

A study conducted by *Prima* magazine of four generations of married women found that wives today have less sex than their grandmothers did. The magazine survey found that women in the 1950s had sex an average of twice a week. But two-thirds of today's young wives said they were too tired to match that level of sexual activity.

The root cause may lie in the fact that the one available TV station fifty years ago shut off at 10 P.M. But features editor Ruth Tierney says, "Since then we have started working and often still have to run the home and look after the kids. It's hard to find the time for sex, and when we go to bed we are too tired to do anything but sleep."[4]

Oxytocin: The Bonding Agent

Even when testosterone rises, women still are not usually willing or able to perform on demand, as most men are. That's because women have what can be described as an intimacy imperative, whereas men have a performance imperative. Again, it's the way women are made—blame it on oxytocin. This is the brain chemical that controls maternal nurturance, verbal-emotive connection, and empathic bonding. A woman's level of this brain chemical is ten times higher than a man's. Whereas testosterone pushes a man to desire the rush of physical contact, oxytocin puts emotional connection at a premium for your wife. That's the kind of closeness she desires above anything else.

Oddly enough, a man's level of oxytocin (the bonding hormone) rises to the same level as a woman's at only one point in the relationship—when he reaches orgasm. After the deed is done—then we're ready to feel connected!

WOMEN NEED HELP TO BE IN THE MOOD

Here's a statistic that might surprise you: a *Redbook* survey of five thousand couples found that 55 percent of wives said they desired their husbands sexually as much at that moment as when they first met. An amazing 24 percent said they desired their husbands more![5] Yet most polls show that well over 60 percent of men say they would like more sex with their wives. At a glance, the numbers don't add up. A majority of women seem to desire their husbands. A majority of men say they aren't getting enough sex. What's up with that?

Ah, to unravel the puzzle, we have to pay closer attention to the subtle meanings in the words they use. The women in that survey didn't say they desired sex. They said they desired their husbands sexually. To you and me that may sound like the same thing, but to women it's not. To crave sex, they first have to feel sexual. They may be saying, "I'm not in the mood" or "I have a headache," but what they probably mean is, "I don't want sex. I want to snuggle with you. I want to feel your arms around me. I want you to kiss me like you mean it and then, when I'm turned on, I want to make love." When men think *sex*, they mean *intercourse*. When women think *sex*, they mean intimacy, closeness, romance, *relationship*.

A marvelous bit of research from the Pfizer labs confirmed an important factor in why the word *sex* does not mean the same thing to men and women. Researchers testing Viagra for impaired female sexual response found that, as expected, Viagra increased blood flow to a woman's genital area, just as it did for a man.

But after eight years of research involving three thousand women, scientists stopped the experiments. Why? Dr. Mitra Boolel, the principal investigator at Pfizer, has said, "There's a disconnect in many women between genital changes and mental changes. This disconnect does not exist in men. Men consistently get erections in the presence of naked women and want to have sex. With women, things depend on myriad factors." Dr. Joe Feczko, the president of Pfizer's worldwide development, adds, "Diagnosing female sexual arousal disorder involves assessing physical, emotional and relationship factors, and these complex and interdependent factors make measuring a medicine's effect very difficult."[6] Apparently, for women, good sex is as much emotional as physical.

Perhaps a more telling statistic is one gathered by the advice columnist "Dear Abby." She once polled her female readers on this question: "Would you rather have intercourse with the man you love, or sit on a couch and have a meaningful conversation with him?" More than 80 percent of her respondents said they would rather talk than have sex![7] To a guy, this sounds ridiculous, but it's all a matter of timing. Unlike men, women feel the need to be connected *before* orgasm.

Talk About It

If it's talk she wants, give it to her. One important meaningful conversation you might have is about the subject that is so often on your mind—sex. Use the conversation to learn about *her* needs. If you open the door on the subject, you may find that she wants you to understand her lack of sex drive and will probably try to give you an explanation by blaming her job or the children or even you.

Now here's the hard part: don't get defensive and don't correct or criticize what she's saying. Just let her know that you want to understand her feelings about sex. And, unless she invites you to bed after this little talk, don't, I repeat, *don't* try to seduce her after this discussion. That would give her the message that you want to have these talks just to get in her pants. (Read Chapter Seven for more about hearing your wife.)

Psst!

SecretsofMarriedMen.com

Take the time to understand what is going on in your mate's head as well as her body. If she needs to vent some feelings, let her. She will benefit from it emotionally and then you will more than likely benefit from it sexually. She will feel like she is important enough to have your attention and concern as well as your physical presence. If she has worked through her problems before you begin to get intimate physically, she will definitely be more receptive to you.

—Rebecca, age 31, second marriage of 7 years

Take Action

In the meantime, while you're talking about sex and learning about your wife's sexual needs, your own sexual longings will build up, and you know very well that talking about sex won't satisfy these urges. This can become very uncomfortable for you, and if the yearning gets too strong with no hope of release, it'll make your relationship with your wife more strained. Your best manly skills that help you keep your marriage on track—strategizing, long-range planning, and inventing solutions—are all thwarted when you haven't ejaculated for a while.

In an ideal world, the ejaculation would take place inside your wife, but until your wife is ready, there's no shame in taking matters into your own hands. There are definitely times when it's appropriate to masturbate—those strong urges are part of the defining

---

Psst!

SecretsofMarriedMen.com

From the moment we said "I do" one thing has become obvious: I have a greater sex drive than my wife. Still, the first years of marriage were great. We didn't do it with the frequency I would have preferred (daily or several times a week), but I couldn't complain. As time wore on, and as responsibilities increased, frequency decreased and quality went through the floor. Since having a baby, it is worse. We are only now recognizing the problem, but the lack of desire (mainly on her part) and the lack of passion (on both of our parts) have really killed things in the bedroom.

Honestly, I feel sexually dead most of the time. That part of me has simply atrophied from disuse. If my wife doesn't instigate it, we don't do it. I've just grown tired of rejection (too tired . . . not in the mood . . . we've heard it all, haven't we?). And then once the act is initiated, there's the lack of practice and familiarity, the pressure to perform, desire to satisfy, lack of variety, and all that. All of it results in unsatisfactory sex for both of us. Frankly, if I didn't "take matters into my own hands" sometimes I feel like there would be little difference between myself and a monk.

—Jeff, age 33, married 10 years

characteristics of a man. But remember, timing is crucial. In some instances, it's more appropriate to be patient, wait, live with the tension and desire, and be prepared, not "tapped out" just at the worst moment, as Larry David once famously confessed in an episode of *Curb Your Enthusiasm*.

A WOMAN'S SEX DRIVE IS DISTRACTABLE

So the stereotype that feeds TV sitcoms is true: men want sex, and women want a romantic experience—the whole package.

This difference isn't just a matter of personal preference or even sex hormones: it's rooted in the way the male and female brain experience life activities. Men, more than women, have a tendency to compartmentalize. This sounds like a psychobabble term that shrinks invent to keep patients confused. But it's a useful word that probably originated from a fisherman's tackle box. Think about how the different sections keep everything in place. If your bag of sinker weights opens up accidentally, the weights still stay in the sinker section. Your hooks don't get tangled up in your power-bait. Each compartment holds something separate and operates independently of the other.

A man's brain works in much the same way. He is more apt than a woman to put each section of his life into a separate mental compartment of his brain and focus all his attention on the task at hand. A man's strong sex drive is one of these compartments. He doesn't need the whole romantic experience to get aroused. He can have a difficult business call, a kid with a scraped knee, even a feeling of annoyance with his wife—and quickly forget all about it if something in his environment becomes sexually arousing. His always-at-the-ready physical response generated by the bat of an eyelash or the flash of thigh allows him to block out all other distractions. But a female's brain is quite different.

An enormous amount of neuropsychological testing has shown how women, unlike men, will piece together events into a whole experience. We've talked earlier about the corpus collosum, the communication strip between the two cerebral hemispheres that allows women to better integrate all the data that enter their brain. To women, therefore, subtleties are important. They definitely see more shades of color. They hear more acutely, and their skin's touch and pain receptors are more sensitive. They see the big picture and sense a forest long before they are able to point out any specific tree. No doubt the idea of women's intuition emerged from this perceptual skill. Men, in contrast, with their less-developed corpus collosum, attend to specific details one at a time. They see every tree, but will take much longer to realize they are looking at a forest.

This difference in perception allows men to keep their thoughts in those little compartments where they don't overlap, whereas a woman's thoughts on one subject spill over and color her feelings about other subjects.

Perception Disconnects

Here's an example of how the thoughts on similar subjects in a male and female brain influence their feelings about sex:

A man may be thinking, "We agree on how we discipline our children most of the time. I do get angry when she runs up big credit card bills like she did today, but the fact is that she's not going to spend less anytime soon. Unless I lose my job. But I'm about 90 percent sure our department won't get hit with layoffs. I don't think she knows how much it bothers me when she jokes with our friends about my hair loss. Sometimes I come home from work in a bad mood, and yeah, I can be a real bastard when I'm like that. She's great about putting up with my mother's meddling, and she did bite her tongue when I loaned my brother $5,000. Guess I shouldn't gripe about her inviting the Steinbergs for dinner. Hey, my life is pretty good. Well, the kids are in bed, and it's only 9:20. It's been a pretty calm Saturday. Surely tonight's the night."

His wife may be thinking, "We agree on how we discipline our children most of the time. He is so unreasonable when he thinks I run up big credit card bills. I understand when he comes home from work in a bad mood, and it's really not that often. I wish his mother would get on her broom and fly back to Oz. What am I going to serve for dinner next weekend when Shelly Steinberg and her husband come over? Shelly has had such a terrible time with her mother in the hospital and all. I should call her. A nice rib roast, if I can find time to get to the butcher shop. He's got that look in his eye, but after just fighting over the credit cards and with the party for the Steinbergs on my mind, how can he even think about making love right now? I think I'll call Shelly."

Note the husband's compartmental thinking—his concern about his wife's credit card spending, the possibility of layoffs at work, and his hair loss don't leak into his sex-drive compartment. See how differently he views his individual stresses compared to his wife's perceptions of the "whole" of her life. Notice how each scenario ends up in a totally different place? Chances are, this guy would never dream in a million years that this difference in thought processes is the reason his wife isn't "in the mood."

Why She Turns Down Sex If She Has a Headache

Of course, you can't hear your wife's mental thoughts, so you can't even try to follow her line of reasoning, but you get a clear picture of how this overlap works if she's ever said something like, "I've been working nonstop all day, and I'm taking care of the kids. It's insulting and selfish for you to think I'd feel like having sex."

At the same time, I can't imagine a husband saying, "Of course I'm not going to be romantic with you. I just spent the whole day working. It's now six o'clock, and even though I'm exhausted, the first thing you do when I get home is drop a kid in my lap and ask me to help prepare a meal. I hope you don't expect me to make love to you, too."

We *don't* say that because we compartmentalize. Short of a serious and ongoing crisis, we don't ordinarily let what happens in other parts of our life put us out of the mood for sex at home. But women bring every part of their day and all their feelings about those events with them into the bedroom at night.

This way of either separating or mixing the day's events with sexual desire is a major difference between men and women and a persistent cause of marital problems. If you ever hope to have a great sex life, this is one aspect of your wife's brain that you need to recognize, accept, and deal with.

It's not that hard to reduce the cluttered compartments of a woman's angst to free up her mind for other things (like sex). One study, for instance, shows that men who do more housework have more active sex lives.[8] The man who vacuums the living-room rug, cooks an occasional dinner or arrives home with some terrific take-out food, walks the dog, or changes the baby's diapers actually reduces the probability that the stress in his wife's day will build up and then spill over, dampening her sex drive. Anything you can do to give your wife some peace of mind will help her more easily turn her thoughts to your needs under the covers.

Lights Off!

Lots of couples have the same argument when it's time for sex: Should the lights stay on or be turned off? Believe it or not, this preference often depends on one's gender. A startling 76 percent of men want sex with lights on versus 36 percent of women.[9] This may be because females see better in lower light, and males see better in brighter light. But I think it's something more sexual. I think it's directly related to what turns men and women on.

Surveys show that men get turned on by concrete things they can see (and therefore need light for), such as female nudity and lingerie. Women, in contrast, get turned on by abstract, emotional things they can't necessarily see but definitely feel inside—emotions and sentiments that can be more easily accessed in the dark, such as romance, commitment, and intimacy.[10]

The lights-on versus lights-off controversy is the kind of argument that can be especially irritating to married couples because it seems like a question of stubbornness. She wants them off. I want them on. Who's going to win? But like so many other seemingly simple disagreements that escalate into major sources of resentment, differences in male and female biology once again are at the core of the problem.

WOMEN DON'T WANT A QUICK FIX

The way a man typically responds to a woman's complaint of being unromantic usually makes the problem worse. In my practice, I've noticed that when a husband hears his wife say, "If you were more romantic, I'd feel like having more sex," he jumps to the conclusion that he now knows how to quickly fix the problem. His brain is hard-wired to take a very specific, task-oriented approach to problem solving. See the problem—fix it.

But he forgets that what women say isn't exactly what they mean. So the next day he comes home with a bouquet of flowers. He kisses his wife on the cheek and then wears a grin all evening that says, "Now how about some wonderful sex?" Before that happens, his wife is likely to ditch the flowers and accuse him of being romantic only to get laid. And of course she's totally correct.

Here's the problem. When she asked him to be more romantic, she meant in general—not just when he wants sex. The problem is, the male's what-you-say-is-what-you-mean mind causes him to keep missing the underlying message. He tries again and gets turned down again. Time after time, he just can't seem to get it right. Tired of rejection, he eventually stops asking. The wife breathes a sigh of relief as her husband just tunes out and gives up. This is not how marriage is supposed to be.

The Problem with Trite Advice

Some of these disillusioned couples will try marriage counseling in hopes of revitalizing their love life. The reasons why this can be a disaster in general were explained in Chapter Two, but it can also be especially detrimental in the sex department. Too many therapists and talk-show psychologists try to simplify a complex problem with simplistic advice: cater to your wife and eventually she'll come around to desiring sex with you.

Women love this advice. When they hear it on the tube, they point at the TV and say to their guy, "See! See! That's all you have to do." So you try and try. You fawn over your wife, you buy gifts, and you listen intently to the complete description of the day's events, all in an effort to meet some undefined and seemingly unattainable standard that will make your wife begin to get horny. If you do succeed with this approach, I'll bet you anything that the day she does get turned on will be the fourteenth day of her cycle!

And even when it works, what are the odds that all this fawning will result in continued bouts of sexual ecstasy? Will you have to act this way for the rest of your life every time you want to get some? I've heard countless men tell me that they're tired of sucking up to their wives just so they can get them into bed. Jack, age thirty-nine and married ten years, is a guy who seems romantic and keeps trying but is still far from monkey-sex heaven:

> I have to hint for three to seven days in advance before I get anything. I am always the one to set a romantic scene and initiate sex. Once I light the fire then it's pretty good. But I just wish she would come on to me sometimes without me having to jump through hoops.

The therapist's trite advice to improve your love life by being more romantic doesn't work automatically because it lumps together intimacy (a feeling of closeness) with eroticism (a sense of sexual titillation). Both are important for great sex in marriage, but they are horses of entirely different colors.

Let's examine the premise that establishing a closer emotional bond will automatically improve sex. That's false. Studies on sexual behavior demonstrate that couples who focus solely on connecting emotionally become stronger friends, but they become weaker lovers.[11] Hey, I've got nothing against intimacy; you must ultimately feel close enough to each other to be able to initiate sex. But if you're too much like brother and sister and not enough focused on lighting each other's fire, your love life is likely to burn out.

That's why being romantic is so important, not necessarily because it will make you connect more—as your wife would like to think—but because bringing gifts, helping around the house more, and spending time just listening can be very erotic to your wife. But I also said right from the start that these things won't automatically improve your sex life.

Another error in the romance-is-the-answer advice is that it may encourage the woman to withhold sex until her husband meets her romantic expectations. On the face of it, this seems reasonable: in order to clear out the negative feelings that have built up, a woman expects her husband to make an effort to make her feel better. In fact, much of this book is devoted to just that: helping husbands make things better for their wives. But if a woman withdraws from engaging in sex and romance until things are just right, the couple's intimacy issues won't get better when they finally do start again. Studies prove that the longer married couples avoid sex, the more difficult it is to generate a positive sexual relationship when they start up again. Regularly refusing sex creates one of the most problematic roadblocks to a good sex life: chronic avoidance. Many couples who avoid sex find it easier to go the lawyer's office than to go back to bed together. Does that mean I advise couples to keep having sex even if they're not necessarily feeling "emotionally connected" at the moment? You bet it does.

Your wife might ask, "How can you say that? Isn't it at the very least a bit difficult to have sex without emotional connection, and awfully glib to suggest doing so?" Perhaps, but there may be many things in your life that you both do even when you don't want to. Ever go to your second grader's poetry reading and listen to twenty-two other children recite their verses? Is that really what you wanted to do? And how about that soccer game in the rain, when you know your five-year-old barely knows which way to run? I don't think it's unreasonable to ask someone who loves another to invest something of himself or herself, even when that person doesn't have a desire to do it. And . . . even when you're not in the mood at first, it's very likely that you'll be enjoying yourself by the end. There is sound research that debunks the myth that "unless you each feel like doing it equally, then it shouldn't happen."[12]

Let's be clear. I'm not suggesting sexual coercion here. I am recommending a regular rhythm of sexual attachment with the understanding that some sexual experiences will be better for him than her and some better for her than him, but that the best sexuality does integrate intimacy, pleasuring, and eroticism for both people. You want to be both positive and realistic about joining together as a couple. For many, this attitude is a critical means of regaining the connection.

A Five-Stage Plan

One thing that almost all therapists do agree on is that if your wife is a reluctant lover, there is no ten-minute fix for the problem. However, that doesn't mean you have to throw up your hands in disgust, claiming there's just no pleasing her. Keeping in mind that your wife's sexual response involves all her senses and her emotions, you can learn to enjoy the bigger picture of your sexual relationship by expanding your definition of sex.

You can be do this through five different stages that we'll call "gears."[13] Each gear offers its own complete and satisfying form of sex—if you can make yourself let go of the idea that sex must include intercourse and nothing else will do. In this broader view of sex, each gear, as in a manual shift car, may lead to the next, but each can also get the job done alone.

The First Gear—G-Rated

Driving in this gear allows you to get as far as you did when you first met and fell in love. These are the hands-on, clothes-on interactions: holding hands, kissing, and hugging. This may seem like tame stuff, but you'll be surprised to find that if you do it in front of your children, they'll tell you to "get a room." But don't, yet. Sometimes first gear is as far as you'll get. And that can be just fine.

First gear is far different than typical foreplay, which usually rushes through a few kisses and body rubs, moving quickly on to intercourse. This is an opportunity to take your time. Knowing that you may not move out of this gear at all allows you to slow down and enjoy the ride.

Second Gear—Sensual

Speeding up a bit, second gear leads you to please each other without touching the genitals. This gives you time for connecting emotionally, perhaps by candlelight, while you explore each other's body. Without rushing forward to the goal of intercourse, you can enjoy simple cuddling, spooning, or body massaging while you lie together on the couch or in bed. In this gear, you can be clothed, semiclothed, or nude—whatever makes you both comfortable yet eliminates performance expectations.

In the sex therapy world, we call this gear nondemand pleasuring. It's pretty basic. It means: "I give you pleasure but expect nothing more in return than the good feelings I get from seeing you happy. And if you want to do the same, I'm open to it but not expecting or demanding it." Try it some time, because giving is the best kind of getting.

The Third Gear—Playful

Here is a chance to intermix nongenital with genital touch. The sky's the limit with this gear because it's a transition between holding back and going full steam ahead. This gear doesn't involve "sex" in the same way that climbing into bed does, but can be much more fun and fulfilling if you allow it to be.

Don't lose a chance to enjoy this gear for exactly what it is—playtime. Yet it also serves a very serious role in giving you a chance to enjoy each other as sexual beings. In this gear, you may choose bathing or showering together, dancing semiclothed, or playing strip poker. This is where you pull out that silly sex game you got at your wife's bridal shower or read to each other from D. H. Lawrence. Nowhere else is it truer that it's not whether you win or lose but how you play the game!

The Fourth Gear—Erotic

We're not playing games any more! Once the clothes come off and before intercourse takes place, a world of opportunities is open to you. Don't lose a chance to make the most of fourth gear—even if intercourse doesn't happen. It can still be your greatest night of sex ever.

When I talk to couples about their sexual liaisons, they tell me that this gear is often the most challenging. In this phase, sexual dynamics usually involve nudity with manual, oral, vibrator, or skin-to-skin stimulation that stops short of intercourse but ends in high arousal or orgasm for one or both partners.

For some couples, these activities seem shocking, and inhibitions make it difficult to enjoy this gear as much as they might. But if your wife seems reluctant to have intercourse as frequently as you would like, give fourth gear a try. She may find its lower expectations much more enjoyable than traditional sex.

Fifth Gear—Climactic

This is the gear you're most accustomed to—intercourse. Some men strip through the earlier gears in a race to this point. If your wife likes a fast ride herself, you both may be very happy with your high-gear relationship. But most women (and most men who slow down long enough to admit it) find sex more personally fulfilling when they learn to view intercourse as just one sex gear among others.

When I went to high school, we used to call these "bases." But I differentiate gears from bases, because if a runner got all the way to third base but didn't score, it didn't count for anything. The idea that the only goal is a home run has no place in good marital sex. When you and your wife let your sexual life evolve from intimacy, to pleasuring, on to erotic flow, and then finally to intercourse, you remove the stigma that makes sex a pass-fail competition. Considering the broader definition of sex allows you to "pass" if you have intercourse and "pass" if you don't. In any gear, you and your partner always win.

BRAIN CELLS AND PORNOGRAPHY

Yes, pornography. Uh-oh, you may be thinking. That's off-limits. Too personal, too shameful, too politically incorrect. But hey, let's be real. Pornography is a multibillion-dollar business because most men are familiar with it, and many seek it out.

So let's talk about it. From my perspective, pornography includes a very broad spectrum of usually graphic material that ranges from tastefully constructed, even artsy (or with pretension of art at least) depictions of erotic love to the totally disgusting, sadistic, perverted, and evil. My own position is that the disgusting stuff degrades sex, men, and women to the point where it precludes any serious human relationships. That crap might as well be about goats or grasshoppers. It has nothing to do with reality. The more thoughtful material, sometimes created by women directors, is less objectionable and, in some circumstances, can even be useful.

Useful Versus Harmful

Remember the scene in *Something About Mary* when Ben Stiller's character decides to masturbate before dating Mary for the first time? His friend recommends it so that he won't be obsessed with sex. (It's right before that funny scene when he gets ejaculate on his earlobe—and she uses it as hair mousse.) The character's jerking off into the lingerie section of the newspaper before his date is an example of how a man might use sexualized images now in order to be less obsessively aroused later. I believe it's an example of a useful and healthy use of porn.

But I don't want to suggest that porn is always completely harmless. Even soft porn can be destructive to a marriage if the viewer of porn puts more emphasis on artificial relationships with magazine or Internet bunnies than on his real relationship with his spouse. Obsessive preoccupation with porn is a growing problem with the advent of the World Wide Web. There's no clear-cut definition of pornography addiction, but if you're spending hours every week looking at porn, spending money every month, or finding yourself hotly anticipating an Internet porn "date" when you're supposed to be involved in work or family activities, there's a good chance you're hooked—and you need to get help.

As an interesting aside, the fact that men more than women are aroused by concrete things they can see accounts for the higher male interest in pornography. As the Viagra researcher points out, most men are immediately turned on by a picture of a nude woman. Most women don't react the same way to a picture of male genitals alone. A woman may respond to a scene of couples having sex, but that's because she's watching a *relationship* in action. Also, women are less visually stimulated, but may be more prone to be aroused by the touch of satin sheets, the sound of your voice, or the smell of your aftershave.

Differences in Reaction

Because women do not respond to pornography in the same way that men do, they usually complain (and often cry) if they find their husbands enjoying a little printed peep show. Because all experiences overlap in a woman's brain, she has a hard time understanding that a man can enjoy the sensation of arousal without any emotional involvement. But a man, with his orderly brain compartments, can easily put his enjoyment of pornography in one compartment and his love for his wife in another and be completely baffled as to why this would upset her.[14]

The point is: it does. So although you may enjoy porn and feel it is an innocent way to spice up your sex life, be sensitive to the possibility that your wife may not understand why you like it and may even feel that it's a form of infidelity. This is the kind of differing viewpoint that you will better recognize and deal with as you follow the guidelines in this book; as you get to know your wife better, you will learn how to ask her for exactly what you need in a way that will appeal to her innate need to nurture and love. That's the secret of a great sex life.

YOUR BEST BET FOR GREAT SEX

We sure work hard to get good sex, and even then there are no promises. But I *can* promise you this: if you work hard to win your wife's heart as you once did when she said "I do," her emotional need for closeness, connection, and love will bring her back into your arms. There your chance of sparking a fire is most promising.

Psst! ─────────────────────────────

SecretsofMarriedMen.com

I have matured in our marriage; my sex behavior is now focused on her pleasure and the emotional sharing that we derive from really great sex. And we have really great sex. While it takes my wife longer to get aroused, I am content to help and enjoy the pleasuring I get along the way. For us, a great day leads to great sex. I am sure to touch my wife, embrace her when I come home from work, engage her in my decision-making and do other things that reinforce for her that she is a vital part of my life.

—Mickey, age 41, married 15 years

TO DO LIST

- Keep in mind that sexual energies differ based on biology and social expectations.

- Don't take it personally if your wife isn't always supercharged for sex.

- Remember that your passionate cravings are not perverted or sick. They are one of the healthiest ways you have of getting close to your wife. Don't be ashamed of loving sex.

- Be proactive about getting your sex life back on track, including having your wife read this chapter. Avoidance can worsen the quality of sex over time.

- Don't stop being romantic, but recognize that there's not necessarily a quick solution to the problem of a female's decreased sex drive. She needs to know that you love her, from deep within yourself.

- Pitch in to help around the house. That will help her clean out her emotional closet and make more room for you.

- Take time to talk to your wife about what sex means to her.

- Rethink your definition of sex and enjoy all the sensual levels of intimacy.

- Be patient. Rewards won't come all at once. But as you begin to convince her she's number one, don't be surprised if, in response, she bats an eyelash or shows you more thigh.

10

The Eighth Way
Introduce Yourself

In case you haven't noticed, the major theme of this book so far is that your main mind-set ought to be one of understanding your wife, and your main actions must focus on making her happy. By this point, you've certainly understood that the greatest way to elevate your own sense of well-being is to promote the well-being of those around you. More specifically, if you've started to make your wife happier, you've already gained tremendously. If your wife knows that you care about her happiness, she's likely to display less tension, describe herself as more fulfilled, and have more meaning in her life. Living with a woman like that sure beats struggling against a person who feels inadequate, unappreciated, and overwhelmed.

But I know you didn't buy this book because you were looking for secrets of men who solely and exclusively slave for their wives without getting their needs met. No. You want the secrets of the guy who gets what he wants out of his marriage—the guy who you see at the theater, the museum, or the ball game with his arm draped casually over his wife's shoulder as they laugh together at a private joke, obviously enjoying each other's company and showing an enviable level of comfort and commitment.

Men who have this kind of marriage have wives who know who their husbands are, understand what they need, and want to give them what they want. To get your wife to that level, you need to make her feel secure in your love and make her trust you and your intentions. That's what you've been doing through each chapter of this book so far. Now for step two. You need to introduce yourself: "Honey, this is who I am, and this is what I need."

WHO ARE YOU?

To prepare for this formal introduction, it's time to step back and ask yourself, "Who am I?" Who is this person that I want my wife to know and understand? Are you the same man your wife married? Older but wiser? Fit as a fiddle? Or struggling to maintain, worrying about slowing down a step, slipping down that ladder, being less powerful or attractive?

Let's take a good hard look at you. My intent is not to be critical or harsh. Remember, I'm on your side—even if your wife bought you this book. But if you're wondering why your wife isn't as close to you as you remember, it's worth asking whether there's anything about *you* that could be causing the distance.

The Physical You

Your first test before introducing yourself to your wife is to strip down, stand in front of the mirror, and take an honest appraisal of what you see. What kind of shape are you in? The average adult American man gains about a pound a year; moreover, the muscle-to-fat ratio declines every year, so that even men who maintain the same weight generally have less muscle mass.

Back in high school, we all thought that jocks were naturally separated from the nerds. Even though we assumed that those labels would apply for life, things may have turned out differently from how we thought. Many of the doctors in my town are among the most athletic people I know, and they were nerds in high school. By contrast, I was taken aback at my twenty-fifth high school reunion, where many of the jocks who in my teenage mind were destined for Herculean greatness appeared to have ended up as out-of-shape guys who were barely scraping by.

The fact is, you can't rely on the stereotypical slot that you fell into in your teens or early adulthood. You are constantly changing, and, like it or not, your physical body represents to the outside world how you feel about yourself and what's inside you. You must take care of it.

My friend Michael is a good example of someone who looked at himself in the mirror and got a bit worried about what he saw. As a very physical youth and young man, he served active duty in the Israeli army. Afterwards, he married and settled down. In less than two decades he ballooned to 413 pounds. Then, in fall 2003, he decided that if he wanted to live long enough to see his daughters grow to adulthood, he needed to do something different, and fast. In a year, Michael brought his weight down to 240 pounds. He doesn't feel as though he's lost anything (except body mass) by giving up unhealthy habits—quite the contrary. He's never felt more in control of his life.

How do you think his wife, Judy, feels about him now? Although she has always deeply cared about Michael, she now has developed a profound respect for him. In fact, she has adopted improved health habits for herself and her family. I haven't had the nerve to ask about changes in their sex life, but I can only imagine that things have improved in that department as well.

There's no doubt that your body is intimately linked to your emotional state and your relationships. I know it's politically correct to say that we shouldn't judge others by physical appearance. But as a physician I can truly say that being in poor physical condition leads to increased risk of experiencing many medical ills and cannot be justified as a lifestyle choice any more than can exposing yourself to radioactive isotopes—not to mention the impact on your self-respect.

If you're out of shape, it's your responsibility to do something to fix it. You cannot ignore the critical role of exercise in improving your health. For my patients who are out of shape, I usually recommend that they begin slowly, working up to forty-five minutes of aerobic exercise daily over two months. Walking or biking (no, not on a Harley), especially out of doors, is a good way to combine fresh air with exercise. But even treadmills or stationary bikes work. These low-impact exercises damage the body less than jogging or running on hard surfaces. I'm also a big advocate of swimming—it's a great way to get in shape without excessive strain on your joints.

In addition to cardiovascular routines, you may want to firm up a bit in the muscle department by doing some isometric exercise with free weights or those sleek new training machines. Face it, your wife wouldn't mind. It may be worthwhile investing in a gym membership, particularly if your wife wants to join with you. I tell all my clients to eat in moderation and make a few simple changes in their choice of foods; switch to fresh vegetables and eat whole-grain foods: wheat bread, whole-wheat pasta, and brown rice. When you eat complex carbohydrates high in fiber, the slower release of sugars into the bloodstream results in a more gradual absorption of calories and better blood insulin levels. You don't get hungry so quickly after a meal, and thus you are able to eat fewer calories during the day. That's not so hard, really. Just think about what you put in your mouth and ask yourself whether what—and how much— you eat will help you stay physically fit.

Your goal here (besides improving your health and boosting your self-esteem), achieved through improved exercise routines and diet changes, is to make sure that when you introduce yourself and your needs to your wife, you do it from a position of strength—from the position of a man who shows that he cares about keeping himself in shape to be more healthy, energetic, and attractive to his wife.

The Hygienic You

I recall a story a client told me. A divorced man, in his seventh decade of life, went to a singles event. There he met an extremely attractive woman, who asked him to dance. As they began to move across the dance floor, he was so overpowered by the smell of garlic on her breath that he politely extracted himself from the dance as soon as the song ended. Needless to say, he didn't take her home that night.

Granted, it's hard to know exactly whether we suffer from bad breath from day to day, but there are many hygiene issues that we paid more attention to before we got married. And even then, whether you turned to Brylcreem or breath mints before you met your wife, you probably didn't spend nearly as much time primping as she did. You probably still don't. And that's a shame. I've spoken to women who tell me that they spend a good part of the day getting themselves ready for their husbands with such thankless activities as shaving their legs, plucking their eyebrows, and pushing back their cuticles, only to get into bed with a guy who hasn't showered for three days.

Okay, so maybe it's not that bad for you. But it's a good bet your wife puts more time into her personal hygiene than you do. I'm sure you've come to appreciate how long it takes your wife to get ready to go out to a dinner party, but she often spends just as long getting ready for *you*, only you don't know it because you don't notice. Would it be so bad to do a bit more of the same for her?

Beside the obvious need to shower and use deodorant after physical activities, you have the additional burden of managing your facial hair correctly. If your wife has a sensitive face and you are planning a night of nookie, then you ought to shave beforehand so that the next morning she doesn't look like she underwent a chemical peel. If you keep a beard, you may like that ZZ Top look, but does it really appeal to your wife? Even if it does, you should keep your beard and hair trimmed and neat—for her.

I've also heard from men who contributed to my Web community report that they occasionally trim their pubic hair and chest hair. There's no rule saying that if you're covered in body hair you can't do anything about it. Just remember to put all the clippings in a garbage can where your wife won't have to see them.

I don't think husbands should have to go to a spa to look good for themselves or their wives; they don't need body waxings or manicures. But I do say that you should keep yourself well groomed and smelling okay—the way you did when dating—if you really want to keep your wife closer.

The Healthy You

Men historically don't take care of their own medical health; they visit the doctor less than women do and are less likely to seek medical attention for problems,[1] yet they are vulnerable to dying at an earlier age from almost all of the top ten disease types.[2] Women insist that men visit their doctors, but most of us guys put it off. For me, it's gotten to the point that when I go for my yearly physical, my doctor looks at me and says, "So, you're here for Susan again, right?"

Women shouldn't have to nag on this one. Get real. Be an adult. Get to the doctor, get your prostate checked, get your blood pressure and cholesterol checked . . . take care of yourself. Part of being happily married is being able to enjoy your physical health. Don't take it for granted.

Keeping your head healthy is as important as taking care of your heart or lungs. A careful review of mental health issues demonstrates that nearly 25 percent of Americans suffer from some diagnosable mental condition. These conditions often impair a man's ability to work or function successfully in social interactions.

Depression is perhaps the most underrecognized psychiatric condition, affecting approximately one in six people.[3] Depression is a medical illness characterized by at least two weeks of a persistently low or down mood. But some of the typical symptoms of depression, such as crying or feelings of sadness, may be absent when men suffer from this syndrome. Males may be more likely to demonstrate irritability, distractibility, fatigue, boredom, or loss of enthusiasm. Although men experience depression half as frequently as women, a man is three times more likely to kill himself.

By *depression* I don't mean a day or two of feeling bummed out. But if you have episodes that last two weeks or more and you notice changes in your energy level, concentration, or sleep or appetite habits, or if you experience guilt, feelings of worthlessness, loss of interest in usual activities, or thoughts of suicide, don't assume that these feelings will correct themselves on their own. You may be suffering from depression, and treatment and relief are as close as a visit to your doctor.

The Moderate You

Substance abuse is one of the greatest impairments to successful relationships. Many couples I treat met originally at a time in their life when they were both partying. In your late teens and early twenties, it may have been fun to hang with other friends who enjoyed drinking or doing drugs. It may still be fun, but before you pick up your next drink or roll your next joint, ask yourself whether your decision to use mind-altering drugs is affecting your marriage.

Lifetime rates of drug and alcohol abuse approach 25 percent, with rates higher in men than women. You may read this statistic and tell yourself that you're not one of those people. The problem is that most people who use alcohol or drugs tell themselves that *they* don't have a problem—it's just the others around them! The purpose of this book is not to tell you whether you have a problem, but you can ask yourself these questions to gain some insight into whether or not you need to get help:

1. Has your wife or have others close to you asked you to cut back on your substance use?

2. Do you hide from your wife the fact that you are using?

3. Are you siphoning off money earmarked for other things to pay for your substance use?

4. Are you unable to go for more than a day without your substance of use? (In the case of cocaine and crack abuse, chronic daily use is not typical; people addicted to cocaine

frequently binge and then go days with no interest in the drug at all.)

5. Do you spend time thinking about or craving your substance when you're not using? Do you use primarily alone, when no one else is watching?

A "yes" answer to any one of these questions may indicate a problem with addiction or dependence. If you responded with "yes" to two or more, it's more likely than not that you're hooked.

Let's face it, if you're buying heroin off the streets, you know you have a problem. But alcohol of any kind, marijuana, cocaine, Valium, Vicodin, and other drugs have the potential to be just as addictive, even if they seem more sociably acceptable. Folks tend to justify their drug use because they see it as helping them deal with stress or improving their creativity. These pharmaceuticals can alleviate mood swings and reduce stress and anxiety temporarily. But over the long haul the use of such drugs is irresponsible and dangerous. They can start to run your whole life: your day consists of waiting for the next ingestion. They interfere with relationships, creating a cloud, a barrier between you and other people. They lead to secrecy, deceit, financial waste, and alienation. They ruin your health.

If you aren't able to cut out the drugs or the excessive use of alcohol, you're going to do some serious damage to your marriage. From the beginning of this book I've pointed out that, as a man, you've got excellent problem-solving skills—the temperament and the brainpower to think out problems and focus on looking for creative ways to improve how you do things. Now, remember to think of the First Way: make marriage your job. How many jobs do you know where employers encourage people to do their work "under the influence"? I don't care how well a few drinks loosen you up: your boss does not expect you to spike your morning coffee with bourbon, and you're not supposed to use your coffee breaks to go out and smoke weed. You'd be fired on the spot.

Similarly, you can't do a good job of making marriage your job if your judgment is impaired. You can't learn about your wife when you're soused. I think you get the idea: in my clinical experience, mastering conflict, applying listening skills, and aiming to please aren't worth a damn if you're under the influence of drugs or alcohol.

If you've got a substance abuse problem—including alcohol abuse—you need help, and you need it now. Call your physician. Check your phone book for the number of your local Alcoholics Anonymous chapter and call to find out where there's a meeting. Consider every resource available to you, from the Yellow Pages to your parish priest. But get help before it destroys your marriage and your life.

The Faithful You

I've addressed unfaithfulness briefly in Chapter Five, and the bottom line hasn't changed: you can't play the field and be a good husband at the same time. Impossible. Can't be done. Forget it. Such ideas are just immature escapism, self-indulgent and childish fantasies.

Accurate estimates of rates of extramarital affairs are hard to come by. Most experts agree that up to 40 percent of men will have affairs, with about 25 percent of women sneaking around. Some studies have suggested an infidelity rate of 70 percent. One reason it's hard to state accurate statistics is because unfaithfulness is so hard to define. Fidelity does not merely apply to the promise to restrict sexual intercourse to your wife. Faithfulness is a more complicated set of etiquette and moral rules you may not be aware of.

For instance, having lunch with another woman and keeping it from your wife is a form of infidelity. Why? Well, consider this: Why is it that when you take this person to lunch you *don't* tell your wife? Are you concerned that she would be upset if she found out? If your wife feels threatened, she may have a realistic concern. Perhaps you're simply meeting with the gal up the street to discuss the upcoming block party. But if so, why *don't* you tell your wife? Are you keeping your options open, playing it close to the vest in case you want to make your move later on? Being truly faithful to your wife requires that she know about all the other women with whom you have contact.

The most likely place to begin a casual affair is at work. Most people enjoy the reassurance of being able to share themselves with the person sitting down the hall. Telling each other your stories can generate a sense of interpersonal closeness. That bond can evolve, very gradually, into an emotional connection. This may not be an affair yet, but have you stopped mentioning your coworker to your wife? Over time you might find yourself sharing things about your home life to your office mate that your wife "wouldn't understand."

If you can't share something with your wife, you shouldn't be sharing it with anyone else, especially when there is even the remotest possibility that you could have an attraction to that person. Every person you spend time with, every phone call you make, every email you send should be open and available for your wife to see. Every person you connect with should be a friend of the marriage, not just a friend of yours.

Trust me on this one. Your wife has better instincts about when women are moving in on you than you do. If she wants you to stay away from your kid's new kindergarten teacher (who happens to have a striking resemblance to Jessica Rabbit), stay away!

I've also treated a number of patients whose spouses have begun relationships with an Internet friend—relationships with a degree of intimacy rivaling any "real" friendship. Internet relationships allow for a more intense idealization of another person; every thought can be modified by a touch of the backspace or delete key, so the "real" you is an edited you. In my clinical experience, I find that Internet relationships are fraught with peril. I'm not saying that electronic relationships can't be real—I know many people who are now married after meeting on the World Wide Web. But to meet someone when you're already married, or even to continue a computer relationship, clearly enters the official territory of infidelity. If you wish to introduce yourself to your wife, she needs to be introduced to all of you. Harboring thoughts of infidelity robs your wife of *you*, and gets in the way of achieving your relationship goals.

The Metaphysical You

With all the demands involved in caring for a family, succeeding at work, and maintaining our physical health, it seems as though there's not much room for anything else in life. But if all we have is what we can see, then there may be something missing from our oh-so-hectic lives.

Almost all Americans hold some kind of belief in a higher power. How you integrate this belief into your family can have profoundly beneficial effects on the quality of your marriage. How do you let your wife and kids know how you incorporate these beliefs in your everyday life? Whether you attain spiritual fulfillment through prayer, meditation, services in a house of worship, or giving to others, you can strengthen the bonds of your marriage by strengthening your connection to a higher power.

Robert, a thirty-seven-year-old who has been married for fifteen years, wrote to SecretsofMarriedMen.com to remind me that the guidelines we need for a good marriage were written down long ago: "A successful marriage is one where God is the center. The Bible tells us that love is: 'patient and kind; not jealous or conceited or proud; love is not ill-mannered or selfish or irritable; love does not keep a record of wrongs, love is not happy with evil, but is happy with the truth. Love never gives up; and its faith, hope, and patience never fail.' Even if you don't read the Bible, this is sage advice for a successful marriage whose love transcends time."

So now we've reviewed the complete you: the healthy, moderate, faithful, and spiritual you that your wife must know and understand so that she in turn can give you what you need, and the two of you can have a true and devoted partnership.

TIME TO PUT YOURSELF FIRST

When I present Secrets of Happily Married Men workshops, there are usually two or three men who show increasing signs of restlessness as I march through the first seven ways that encourage husbands to better understand and even pamper their wives. Sooner or later a hand shoots up, and the man asks, "Hey! What about *my* needs?" If you're anything like the guys who go to my talks, I hear you. This chapter is about you, your needs, and how to communicate these needs to the woman in your life.

"Finally!" you say, and then wonder, *Was it really necessary to put this section that acknowledges my needs way back here toward the end of the book?* If all I hoped to do in this book was to make you happy with the status quo, I certainly could have pumped you up with encouraging truisms in the very first chapter. I would have elevated your self-esteem (telling you to love yourself more), stroked your ego (telling you that you are perfect just the way you are), and empowered you to "Go get 'em, Tiger" (telling you to trust your own judgment and press ahead with your beliefs no matter how that affects others).

This kind of advice, which you might get from pop psychologists, can provide great short-term gains, but with devastating long-term consequences. I've held this chapter until the end because I honestly believe that the key to getting what you want in your marriage depends first on showing your wife that she can trust you and depend on you. Until your wife knows this with every fiber of her being, until she has examined your trustworthiness from every angle and still knows you stand by her 100 percent in all situations, until she can look you in the eye and know she'll always be safe with you, you won't begin to cash in on your essential needs.

Okay, maybe I exaggerate a bit. Maybe she needs to trust you only 99.9 percent of the time. But don't lose the thrust of my point—if you seek to meet your personal needs before your wife sees her needs met in the marriage, she will feel betrayed and abandoned every time you hunker down in front of the TV or computer. No, not all wives, not all the time. But if you've been running into roadblocks whenever you try to sit through a Cowboys' game or spend an afternoon at the club, maybe you haven't first convinced your wife that she's the center of your life.

But all that's changed, right? After going through each of the "ways" to improve your relationship with your wife, she now trusts you. And that's why this chapter comes now, not at the beginning of the book. By now your sweetheart has gotten the message that you've given highest priority to your relationship with her—so getting your own needs met won't conflict with what she thinks ought to be your first goal—to be a good husband. She may be thinking, *first and only goal*, but this is the time to let her know that you have personal needs that extend beyond the marriage but don't conflict with it.

Psst!
SecretsofMarriedMen.com

What about me? I hug her when I get home from work and ask how her day was. What about me? I kiss and hold her, telling her how much I adore her. What about me? I write her poems and bring her gifts. What about me? I promise to love and cherish my bride. What about me?

—Carl, age 34, married 7 years

IT'S ALL ABOUT VALUES

I did an interview on a radio show around Valentine's Day. The interviewer asked, "What do most husbands want for Valentine's Day?" I explained that for most husbands, their number one objective on this day is for their wives to be happy. The host, a married man, nodded in agreement. Just as he clicked off the microphone to go to a commercial, an addendum to my comments leaped into my mind: ". . . but if we can't have that, a new plasma HDTV wouldn't be so bad."

I don't think the interviewer knew it, but he was asking about a man's values. I defined those primary values as "wife's happiness," with "recreation" ranking a close second. I've studied lots of men, and I do believe that these two priorities are high ranking for many of us. But, obviously, I haven't studied you personally. So you've got to figure out for yourself what you deem important: what's worth fighting for and what's not. Don't feel bad if you find yourself more in tune with the men who responded to a CNET survey at Christmastime in 2004. When asked what they wanted most, the number one answer among men was "big-screen TV"; the top answer among women was "peace and happiness." It's these kinds of differences in values that set men up for conflict in their marriages if they don't recognize and deal with them.

In Chapter Six, when the focus was on resolving conflict, I asked you to invite your wife to explore her value system, to help you get a clear idea of what's important to her and what's second tier . . . I also promised you that you'd get your chance to do the same. Now is that chance. Here's a copy of the list of values that we originally reviewed back in the money section of Chapter Six. You asked your wife to define the three values that are most important to her. Now it's your turn. In order for you to proceed with getting your needs met, you have to understand what's really important to *you*. Using the same list you used to get to know your wife, ask yourself, "How do I feel about these core values?"

Financial security	Generosity
Possessions	Productivity
Health	Justice
Family	Friends
Learning	Lifestyle

Personal growth	Contribution to society
Personal appearance	Spiritual fulfillment
Peace of mind	Work
Home comfort	Entertainment
Education	Children

To help you decide what's really important to you, imagine what you'd like people to say about you at your celebrity roast: Who would be on the stage, and, after the jokes are passed along, what's the main message you'd want people to hear? How would you like the world to see you? What defines you at your best? In other words, what's important?

Just as you gave your wife freedom to be honest about what was truly important to her, don't interrupt your own evaluation with negative judgments about what appeals to you. We all know that truth, justice, and the American Way are supposed to be what we believe in, but maybe you're into something just a little different.

During the early 1990s, I worked with Al, a psychologist who had lived for his vacations to exotic lands. He knew what he liked and made no apologies for it. Over six months, he would accrue his vacation time and go for a two-week trip to the finest beaches and best restaurants on islands I've never heard of. It didn't matter to him how fancy his car was or whether he could play basketball in the over-forties league. Getting away is what he loved, and he could do it because he had the money and didn't have any children at that time.

But eventually he and his wife did produce offspring, a beautiful boy. And Al and his wife continued to go on lavish vacations as they always had, right? Wrong. Of course they had to slow down and change their life, but Al's core values never changed—they were just put on hold for a while. Now his son is elementary school age, and when I last saw Al, he was planning a trip to yet another exclusive beach—his first since the birth of his son.

Al knows what he loves, and he invests his energies and time into realizing that dream. But he juggles it with other things that are important to him also, like family and financial security. Al's story illustrates that you can't have it all, all of the time—but if you know what's important to you and you recognize it, at least it's more likely you'll get what you want out of life. The rest of this chapter will help you do that.

REMEMBER THIS
What's Good for You Is Good for the Marriage

One of the most important ways to engage your wife is by defining your goals and aspirations as being good for the marriage, not just good for yourself. In other words, if it's been your life's dream to compete in a triathlon, then your efforts to achieve this will be a source of enrichment to you. It's an investment in time, yes. But the payoff is better physical well-being, a more complete sense of self, and healthy competition with other men. In other words, your wife will now live with a guy who's better looking, has a greater sense of self-worth, and is less prone to argue in the home. What a deal!

ASKING FOR WHAT YOU WANT

I'm going to venture a guess: at least one or two of your core values have already been addressed in this book. If you've been following the recommendations in *The Secrets of Happily Married Men*, then you're finding that your wife is happier, which is probably one of your core values. If your wife is happier, there's more peace in the household, less criticism, and more fun. These attributes may also be at the top of your list. That may be all you were looking for, and they encompass values as defined by an intimate team—you and your wife. But it's time to talk about the things you desire for yourself that are yours only.

Let's say, for example, that one of your core values centers on recreational or social activities (that do not include your wife). Maybe you want more time to play golf or to meet with your friends or colleagues for a few drinks, or you really want to get to the next round in "Grand Theft Auto." Surprisingly, you can use the strength of your relationship with your wife as a foundation for realizing these wishes. Here's how.

Boys at Play

Recreation ranks as one of the greatest needs among men. Educational experts have long examined classrooms and schoolyards and discovered that boys engage in more physical activity than girls. The level of activity tapers off as we men age, but the need to move and engage in competitive play still brews within us. Whether going to the gym, shooting pool, or watching golf, a man needs to be engaged directly or indirectly in moving through space. For most men, nurturing a relationship isn't quite fulfilling enough.

So, you ask, how do you get a "hall pass" from your wife to be excused from folding the laundry to go out and play? You first give your wife what *she* wants. My area of expertise is in understanding husbands, but I've also talked to a lot of wives, and I know that they truly want (1) happy marriages and (2) happy husbands—usually in that order. Once she's grown to trust you, you can help her understand (if it's not already clear to her) why a critical way to achieve the first goal is to permit the second to occur.

Yes, permit. As in *permission*. Despite how wildly you've struggled for self-actualization in life, despite your need to be your own boss in the workplace or your passion for fierce independence in political debate, a good, strong, and loving relationship with your wife requires that she give the thumbs-up to who you want to be and what you want to do.

Before you throw this book in the garbage, hear me out. I have a friend, Azriela Jaffe, who wrote a marvelous book called *Permission to Prosper: What Working Wives Crave from Their Husbands and How to Get It.* Azriela told me that when she wrote an article of a similar title in a popular business magazine, it generated more mail than any other article that year. Women from all over the world were outraged at Azriela's suggestion that they should *ask* for what they want. After all, they had not come this far in the woman's movement just to await some man to give the green light to their success. But in this article, and later in her book, Azriela shares my philosophy: you didn't marry to be a pair of "ones"—you married to form a partnership. If you cannot get your significant other on board to accept an idea of yours, there's a good chance you will be undermined, backstabbed, put down, or discouraged. Every time you seek advancement of your needs, your partner may respond by retreating from you. If you choose not to collaborate, either by hiding your actions from your wife or by adopting a "Damn the torpedoes—full speed ahead!" attitude, you'll regret it.

I don't mean to imply that if you want to watch two back-to-back football games or go for a ten-mile hike with your best friend this weekend, your wife has to exclaim, "Why, that's the best idea you've ever had!" What I do mean is that your wife has to agree, at minimum, that in the grand scale of things, she's okay with it. You can imagine, now that you've done such a good job of getting to know your wife, that there are good and bad ways to approach asking for permission. Your wife values verbal expression; she looks for signs that you care about her; she needs to feel connected to you. Keeping this in mind, you might take the following approach:

> Hey, pumpkin! This morning I vacuumed your car before I brought you your coffee. I'm really looking forward to grilling some steaks tonight so we can have a nice dinner, but this afternoon I'd really like to put aside some

time for a hike with Jeffrey. If it will help out, I'll set up your drawing table before I leave. But I'm really excited about this hike, the weather's supposed to be great, and it's important to me that I get some fresh air.

Her response: "Oh, Scott, don't you remember? It's my mother's birthday party today!"

Oh well. My point isn't that you'll always be able to get everything you're looking for in marriage. If you wanted to do everything your own way all the time, you never would have gotten married. But you do have the right to ask for what you want, and if you do it correctly, everyone ends up a winner.

When it comes to introducing your dreams to your wife, it helps if she can understand that your goals aren't strictly selfish. You can go too far: "Honey, I'd really like to do some marriage boosting by going fishing all morning." But you can say, "This will really give me

REMEMBER THIS
Sometimes You Just Have to Do It

Things like an occasional night out with the guys or good workout session at the gym may be important for keeping your sanity. If you can't get your wife to give you permission, try to understand why not. But if an opportunity opens for you to do something you think is important, sometimes you just have to dive in and deal with the fallout later. Your wife will respect you for your backbone. For fifteen years now, I've belonged to a tennis league, and when Wednesday calls, I am out the door. There were times in the past when my wife practically begged me to stay at home, but I knew it was essential for me, even though she didn't know that my having that time was good for *her*. Today she looks back and agrees that my commitment to tennis has been a good thing, and she respects me for holding my ground.

a great chance to unwind and reenergize. When I get home, I'll shower up and take you and the kids out to dinner." There really is an opportunity for win-win. You just have to help her see it that way. Like any good salesman, you have to believe in the product yourself if you're going to sell it. So take it from me, this isn't B. S.—you *will* be a better husband if you take care of yourself. But not all the time, not to the exclusion of your family, and not if it means missing your mother-in-law's birthday party.

Boys and Their Toys

Now that we've covered football and triathlons and the rest of your competitive needs, it's time to talk about that plasma HDTV you've been eyeing. If they were giving them out free on the street corner, there wouldn't be much debate on the issue. But technology costs bucks. This isn't the first time we've talked about money issues in this book. In Chapter Six we addressed understanding the important goals that your wife has and how to use those goals to create a reasonable and realistic budget. Now it's time to look at the toys *you* want.

Despite the statistics about women spending most of the household income, I've heard plenty of stories in my practice about households that are near bankruptcy, yet still the husband insists on buying a new sports car and contracting for high-end digital cable. If that's you, then you've got some work to do. You've got to earn the money you need for all the toys you want.

Look back at your list of values, review what's at the core of what it means to be you, and figure out how to balance your purchases against what really matters.

Let's say you have determined that one of your top core values is "enjoying sports" or "watching great old films on DVD." In that case you can set your sights on that HDTV and with a clear conscience set aside money each week to save for this purchase, but you will have to forgo the tropical island vacation, the new car, and the hottest electronic gizmos. But if the core values on the top of your list are "financial security" and "spiritual fulfillment," the HDTV is out. Remember that my friend Al had to give up fancy cars and electronics because "getting away from it all and being pampered" was at the top of his values list.

In the same way you've asked your wife to create a budget that focuses on her true life needs, you must now do the same. You're being childish if you think running up credit cards is a problem that will take care if itself. It won't, and you need to accept your role as the man of the house and take responsibility.

If you're not filing for Chapter 11 yet, and, in your opinion, too much is going toward your wife's spa membership and not enough toward you, then it's time to talk to your wife about what you'd like to buy for yourself. First, a word of encouragement: you work hard for your money, even if you're a stay-at-home dad. You make real contributions to your household, and you have the right to enjoy material things if that's what you want. But balancing your personal desire for new toys against your family's need for security may leave you feeling damned if you do and damned if you don't.

To get what you want without feeling guilty, I suggest that you proceed as you did when you wished for time for yourself: ask for what you need or want. Now, you know the drill. You have to ask in a way that is respectful, that is considerate of your wife's needs and of the impact your decision will make on her, and that lets her know that taking care of yourself can be a powerful way of taking care of your relationship.

Brian was a salesman I treated who had his eye on a classic Triumph Spitfire that one of his coworkers had up for sale. Rather than dish out the money and pull into the driveway with his new toy, he followed my recommendations and first sat down and talked to Ellen, his wife, about his dream-mobile. Ellen's first reaction was to ask him why he needed it, and Brian began to feel himself get defensive—after all, he didn't needle her when she had to have a new car last year. But he followed my advice, and instead of snapping back, he reassured her that his most important need was for the safety and security of the household. He listened to her concerns about the costs of this dream car; he let her know that part of the expense would be offset by using his coffee-break budget, having calculated that by not spending $4 daily at work, he would be putting aside more than a thousand dollars a year. Of course there are still the insurance and maintenance costs. But Brian recognized that ultimately he couldn't justify all this as a "need" and took the time to let his wife know that it was a "want," but one that would bring him great joy. As he drew a picture for Ellen of how happy he would be seeing her in the passenger's seat, hair flying in the wind, looking upward at the sky as her scarf fluttered in the wind (you get the idea), she was sold.

Sex

Sex is the one thing that you may want more of in your marriage that will have no effect on the pocketbook and won't take you away from your wife's company. So you would think that women would value this activity for its intrinsic marriage-building properties.

You would think! Yet many men have told me that their efforts to meet their sexual needs frustrate and irritate their wives. And the fact is, although you may be able to watch back-to-back gridiron games or buy a new iPod without your wife's permission, you cannot engage in marital sex without her consent.

I talked about sex in great detail in Chapter Nine—primarily to help you better understand your wife's point of view. Females and males do not have the same feelings and attitudes about sex; their urges and needs don't always match. But I return to this subject as part of the Eighth Way because introducing your sexual needs to your wife does not differ dramatically from making her aware of your other needs for play and for toys. If you have worked hard to make sure that your wife knows you respect her, if you've treated her with dignity, if you've recognized and honored the differences between you, if you've listened to her and made her feel important . . . then there's a good chance that she's caught on that you have put her number one. Once you've reached that 99.9 percent trust threshold, she won't perceive concerns about your sexual needs as strictly selfish on your part. It's time to start asking for what you want.

There is no cookie-cutter formula for determining how much sex is reasonable and how much is too much to ask for. It may help you to know that according to the best studies, the average married couple has sex approximately 68 times a year;[4] that averages to just over once a week—and includes newlyweds!

It's true that she is tired, and so are you. It's true that she has other things on her mind, and so do you. So if she puts up road-blocks when you start to engage in a little foreplay, it may not make a lot of sense from your point of view. But if your sex drive is higher than hers, you must let her know about your desires so that she can be involved in meeting them. In some cases, your wife may be waiting for you to ask—at other times, she may be hiding in some part of the house waiting for you to fall asleep because she fears you *will* ask. You won't know until you talk about it.

So . . . how do you ask? It's all about communication. Go back to Chapter Four, "Know Your Wife," and *you tell me* the best way to communicate with her. Is your wife the kind of person who wants to learn from you how you feel about things? Does she enjoy light-hearted banter? Does she like to tease you and make you work for your rewards? Think about the best way to reach her. Here's one way I recommend approaching this issue:

First, set aside a place and time to talk to your wife. Preferably a time when she's not wiped out and exhausted for the day. The setting need not be one in which the sex will happen imminently. Let your wife know that you want to talk about important things that are on your mind.

Next, begin the conversation by letting your wife know that you have strong feelings about your emotional connection. Letting her know you wish to address the "feeling" rather than the "thinking" nature of your relationship will help her better tune into your concerns. Focusing on the quality of your connection is a lot better than saying you want to relieve an internal urge. *Important note:* the approach I discuss is not meant to mislead or control your wife with anything that isn't true. If you don't think that having sex has to do with your emotional connection with your wife, then don't say it. It may be true, however, that you both desire an emotional connection *and* have an internal urge. What I'm saying is that there are some things you should say because they will be helpful and others you should avoid saying. That's not being manipulative; it's being smart.

After you have settled down into a discussion mode and have her attention, you next need to state what the problem is. Don't say it in a way that will make her defensive: don't blame, and don't make the problem hers. It's yours, and by extension, it's the marriage's.

You might say something like this: "I really enjoy the connection I feel with you when we're together sexually. I think it's an important part of our relationship."

You should also be sure to add that she turns you on so much, more than ever, even after all these years—after all, that is a real compliment and a real support of your cause. But don't go overboard on this. In the years I've treated couples, I've frequently found a deep-rooted ambivalence in women. On one hand, it's very important to women to feel sexually attractive; the cosmetics industry, apparel designers, and women's magazines all give women the message that they should aspire to sexual attractiveness. On the other hand, when husbands tell their wives they feel turned on, their wives may express disgust that "all you think about is sex," leaving the husband confused. Chalk it up to the mystery of women. Although it's important to let her know that she still stirs up your passion, you may not want to focus too intently on this.

Now remember, if you want your wife to hear what you have to say about things, you won't get anywhere unless she feels heard first. Make sure you reflect back what she says, and let her know that you are paying attention to her needs. If she says "I'm just not interested in sex lately," ask her more about that, why she thinks that is, and how she feels about it. *Don't* jump in and say, "Well, you were plenty interested when we were dating." (If you're not sure why this isn't the best response, reread Chapter Seven, "Learn to Listen.")

When you ask her to explain, she may give reasons that make no sense to you and that may not stand the test of the scientific method, but they're important to her. She may say she has something else on her mind at this moment, that she's worried about one of the kids or her best friend or her job. She may say she's not feeling well and may really have some symptoms. She may blame you for not being romantic. She may say she was abused as a child. She may say she is in perimenopause. She may state she is overworked or bored at home. Because women look to attach emotional meaning to activities, the odds are she'll have some reason, and just getting that reason out in the open will help you begin to understand what's happened to your sex life.

Psst!

SecretsofMarriedMen.com

When my wife and I were dating sex was great. She wore sexy outfits, let me tie her up, oral sex, the works. Frequency was great too; we did it 7 times in one day. Five years later and 2½ years after the birth of a child, things are different. Frequency is good, twice a week, but very scheduled due to two kids in the house. However the passion and intensity of sex has declined. It depressed me and led to thoughts of having an affair, but I love my wife and wanted to work things out. So I did something men rarely do, I communicated with her. I asked her why things were different. I found out that from her point of view the problem was the way that I treat her. So I have resolved to become more romantic and treat her the way I treated her when we were dating, and hopefully she will treat me the way she treated me when we were dating.

—Todd, age 34, second marriage of 4 years

Once you've established the problem, it's time to ask for what you need. You may want good old sex, different sex, more experimental sex, or just more frequent sex. Let's suppose it's more sex that you'd like. You might say, "I'd like to spend more intimate time together. What do you think?" This is big, so take your time and don't jump into explaining where, how often, or other details she may not be ready for. Be prepared to let her really reflect on this, and remember to use your enhanced listening skills and try to see it from her point of view. Remember, this issue doesn't have to be resolved the first time you set aside time to discuss it. It's a chance to open a dialogue, and you should be sure to let her know you want to understand.

Again, before you jump into solutions, take time to ask what she thinks might help the situation. You're moving gently from identifying problems to solving them, and you're letting your wife take an active role in the process. She might jump in and agree to be more open to experimentation. She might hold back and let her reasons for avoiding sex take precedence over the reasons to engage in sex. If she can't come up with a way to solve the problem, you can then make some suggestions.

First, remind her that sex doesn't have to be an all-or-nothing proposition. You learned the five gears in Chapter Nine; now is the time to teach your wife about your enlightened view of sexual fulfillment.

Next, agree to what a reasonable time frame is to start to work on this. Remind your wife about the important research that demonstrates how avoiding intimacy can harm efforts to reconnect later on.

In addition to finding a time to start, try to agree on how often you'd like to arrange sexual dates. Contributions to SecretsofMarriedMen.com show that men are more focused on the frequency aspect of sex, women more on the emotional aspect. So let your wife know that if you have a time frame in which to anticipate positive changes in your love life, you'll be better able to focus more on her emotional needs.

Support her need to reacquaint herself with the nymphomaniac within (well, the woman who had more of a sex drive, anyway). Once she knows you have her best interests in mind, she won't mind letting you help solve the problem of low sex drive. Some books may be helpful if she needs additional support, such as Pat Love's *Hot Monogamy* or Michelle Weiner-Davis's *The Sex-Starved Marriage*, both of which are written by women. But even checking out the local supermarket for *Cosmo* or *Redbook* articles may be enough to get the motors recharged. Usually these kinds of sources will encourage your wife to be romantic. But they will also offer your wife such suggestions as using fantasy or music to help get her get in the mood, projecting positive outcomes on intimate interactions, and thinking of sex as energizing, not depleting. Further, these books and articles frequently refer women to their gynecologists to make sure that there aren't any medical problems interfering with their sexual response. You may find these reading resources helpful for you as well. Just use your judgment about where you let yourself be seen with a copy of *Glamour!*

Finally, even though I don't believe that sexual romps simply materialize out of doting behavior from husbands, I do feel strongly that you should not stop being romantic. Keep your focus on making your wife feel loved, strong, smart, and sexy. It's an important part of the equation.

MAKING YOUR WISH LIST A REALITY

There are probably lots of things you put on your wish list every day, ranging from a juicy steak (despite your wife's new vegan menu) to an Outward Bound adventure in the Rockies. No, you can't have it all. But you can have *some* of it!

If you have been working hard at making your wife feel great, then you've set the stage for getting your own needs met. So introduce yourself. Let your wife know who you really are, what you value, and what you need to be happy. It's your turn to get what you want.

TO DO LIST

- Take a good look at the physical you: Are you proud of your appearance? Is your wife proud of you? If not, start yourself on an exercise and diet routine that will get you back into shape.

- Schedule a checkup with your doctor to keep yourself healthy.

- If you struggle with any type of addiction, seek help—now.

- Be faithful. Any form of infidelity undermines a strong marriage.

- Reconnect with a higher power to support your place in this world.

- Evaluate your core values so that you have a better idea of what's most important to you and of what your wife can do to help you attain these values.

- Don't hesitate to ask your wife's *permission* to do the things you want to do. Give your wife what she needs before asking for what you need.

- Learn how to ask for sex in a way that allows your wife to feel respected and loved and also enhances her understanding of you.

Epilogue

Celebrate Your Love

After all the hard work you've put into improving your marriage through each chapter of this book, you and your wife now deserve to celebrate the partnership you've created based on mutual respect and love. That's right—party hats, noisemakers, and all, to commemorate the best thing that's ever happened to you.

I know; I know. You may not think that celebrating your marriage is a particularly manly activity. After all, traditionally women arrange celebrations. They prepare parties, send out invitations, and fuss about every detail. Most men remain passive (or, as women might say, "aloof") about these festivities. But when I say celebrate your marriage, I don't mean throw a white-tie garden party. Instead, consider it as you would winning the division championship—you should rejoice like there's no tomorrow.

We've seen the scene a dozen times after the Super Bowl, the NCAA finals, and even at high school championships. As the clock ticks down, the excitement grows. At last the buzzer goes off in the final period, and the victors turn to each other in excitement. They hug. They huddle. The tense moments of the game melt away as they enthusiastically share their joy with each other. In a moment of delirium, they grab the Gatorade dispenser and dump the contents on the coach's head. In sports, winning is the goal. And once the victory is achieved, the winners celebrate—they literately bathe themselves in their success!

In this way, marriage is like sports: when things are going right in your marriage, you owe it to yourself and your spouse to make your success a joyous occasion.

CELEBRATE FOR MANLY REASONS

Having a good marriage makes you a winner—that's a big deal in the male kingdom. We've seen in earlier chapters how testosterone steers the male fetus toward developing distinctly male characteristics, everything from a penis to larger brain. Testosterone continues to influence men during the course of their lives; it is, after all, the hormone most associated with aggression and competitiveness. As long as the chemical surges through a man's body, it will feed an urge to beat out the other guy. In other words, testosterone makes you want to win.

When you do grab the prize, your male instincts for tribal behavior and ritual socialization will remind you that winning isn't a solo act. When a man is Numero Uno, he wants to stand on a mountaintop and bang his chest. Or howl. At the very least, he wants to share it with the world.

There's another very important reason for you to celebrate: it gives you positive reinforcement. You know the principle of positive feedback—especially if you have children. They're far more likely to get into bed if you promise to read their favorite bedtime story than if you yell at them. It also works with pets—even cats (not that they all really like a bedtime story). Psychologists have demonstrated that people best learn to modify behavior not through a fear of punishment but through a search for comfort or pleasure.

The experience of positive reinforcement acts on the thrill-seeking parts of the male brain. We've spoken about dopamine earlier in this book—it's the neurotransmitter associated with reward and pleasure. I believe dopamine plays a much more active role in men's brains than in the cerebrum of women. Any activity that generates a reward releases dopamine into the bloodstream and produces a kind of high. It's easy to see the power of a good, strong reinforcer—even when you give that reward to yourself. That's why your manly skills are exactly what are needed to mark the success of your union.

CELEBRATE HOW MARRIAGE HAS MADE YOU WHO YOU ARE

Your marriage has created a world, an environment, that encompasses the life you live. As you begin the celebration of your marriage, take some time to think about all the good that's come your way *because* of your marriage. Some advantages are overt; others are not so easy to see. Look at the following list and note the ways that having a strong union with your mate has enhanced the quality of your life:

- I live in a good community.

- I play an active role in my church, synagogue, temple, or mosque.

- I enjoy a sense of safety in my home.

- I have a feeling of purpose when I go to work every day.

- In discussions with my wife, I am introduced to new thoughts, ideas, and perspectives every day.

- I have an active sex life with a partner I love.

- I have a healthy diet that includes having meals with my family.

- I have children whose lives bring me joy.

- I have a companion for meaningful life experiences.

- I feel that my life is full.

- I am committed to being a better person—more self-less, more giving, more loving, more connected to my loved ones.

Okay, I'll admit that at first glance, these achievements may pale in comparison to winning the Super Bowl, but don't underestimate their impact on your life. I would bet that if you asked a Super Bowl champion whose marriage fell apart, "Which would you rather have, your marriage and family or your championship ring?" if he had a shred of integrity, he'd trade in his ring for a happy marriage any time. That's because among all your achievements in life, from sailing across the world to finishing a crossword puzzle in record time, no one thing has the potential to shape your life—your identity as a man—more than your marriage.

CELEBRATE YOUR PRIVATE TIMES

Your marriage has evolved over time because of what you and your wife bring to it. And much of that is the stuff that no one else will, or ought to, know. When you celebrate the achievement of your marriage, you have a chance to reflect on the moments that are yours alone. You may have brushed these moments aside in an effort to keep forging ahead in life, but I urge you, for the sake of appreciating what you've got, don't.

These are the moments that belong only to the two of you. The moments when you cried in your wife's arms over some terrible hurt, or the times when you slow-danced with her just as the babies drifted off to sleep. These are also the times of the infuriating arguments that challenged your best coping skills or that led to the most intense sex.

Your private times together are the ones that helped forge an identity that no one besides you and your wife can know. Don't forget them—celebrate them.

CELEBRATE ANY WAY YOU LIKE

Some people like cocktail parties. Some like walks alone on the beach or a long run through the neighborhood. You and your wife have evolved over time into the couple you are, with your unique idiosyncrasies, tastes, and style. That's why no one person can tell you exactly when or how to celebrate your love. The rejoicing may happen because you feel like taking your best girl out on the town tonight, or it may follow a particularly emotional event or revelation.

I remember a few years ago, during some of the darker days of my marriage, when my reason to celebrate came on me quite unexpectedly. I had begun to wonder if I had married the wrong person for all the wrong reasons. It happened when I was clearing out my office drawers, a ritual I engage in about every time the cicadas emerge from their pupae. I saw an old piece of paper for a religion course that Susan and I took prior to our wedding. There, scratched in the corner of a worksheet, were words *I had written to Susan* saying, I LOVE YOU SO MUCH. I wrote that. Me! In the years since we took the course together, I had gotten sucked into the belief that any positive feelings I may have had for Susan were illusions, that because I wasn't feeling wild about her at that moment in time, I must never have been really smitten.

This small note came out of the past a decade after we were married to remind me of how much we had loved each other—more to the point, of how much I loved her. History can repeat itself, if you let it. For me, it was an important lesson. I vowed to get back to the point where I could feel those words all over again, and I knew that this realization was reason for celebration. It was more than a high-five moment; it was a grab-my-wife-and-run-through-the-streets-shouting-out-in-joy opportunity.

Other times, celebrations can help us remember special moments. A doctor friend of mine met his wife-to-be on a disastrous blind date. Just before he was scheduled to fly off to a medical conference, they arranged to meet at a small burger joint near the city's airport. Now, after decades of marriage, Dick makes a point once a year to plan a "date" at this austere little restaurant as his way of celebrating his good fortune. He's not really a romantic guy. He would tell you he simply gets an urge for a burger with the works and a large order of fries. But his wife knows better. And to her, that night out each year beats dinner at the Four Seasons.

Of course you don't have to wait for some emotional revelation or special anniversary to push you into the winner's circle. Just being happy about waking up next to your wife this morning is reason enough to celebrate.

Scratching your head trying to think of a way to celebrate? Here are some suggestions to get you started:

- Renew your commitment: Why not get married again?

- Buy yourselves an anniversary present, even if it's anniversary number eight and five-twelfths.

- Take a bath together.

- Donate money to your favorite charity in honor of yourselves.

- Have sex.

- Get a couple's massage.

- Go away on a trip together.

- Take a sick day off from work and spend the stolen hours together.

- Go to the beach, on a merry-go-round, to the movies, to an amusement park.

- Place an ad in the local paper announcing your love for each other.

- Proclaim your love on a billboard or at a ball game.

- Write or read love poetry to each other.

- Look at your wedding album together and toast your past and your future.

- Write a love letter to your wife. Without telling her about the letter, take her to the shore, let her read the letter, then place it in a bottle and set it out to sea.

- Have a celebratory party at your house.

- Ask your friend to have a party for both of you at his house.

- Check into a motel room together.

- Mentor another couple to share your good fortune.

- Have a balloon-gram delivered to your house.

If you've used information from this book, from the secrets of other married men, to make your marriage better in even a small way, then you should definitely celebrate your love. Life's just too short to miss out on the opportunity to party, rejoice, and have an absolutely great time whenever possible with the one person in this world who has pledged to return your love forever and to build a loving relationship by your side.

When you finish this chapter and put down this book (for the time being), someone who has spied you reading it (perhaps your wife) may very well ask, "Okay, smarty-pants, you just read the whole book. So tell me, what *is* the 'secret'?"

Take your time as you answer and speak from your heart: "As a man, I have a deep sense of honor and commitment to my wife. I may not be able to verbalize the depths of my love for her, but my deeds speak louder than my words. And what deeds! Through the use of my problem-solving skills and specific marriage-boosting strategies, I have the ability to create a better world for my family. In so doing, I elevate the status of my wife and discover a deeper meaning to my own life. That's the secret of happily married men." Or, better yet, shrug nonchalantly and say, "*You* read the book!"

Notes

Introduction

1. Waite, L., Browning, D., Doherty, W., Gallagher, M., Luo, Y., & Stanley, S. (2002). *Does divorce make people happy? Findings from a study of unhappy marriages.* New York: Institute for American Values.

2. Brinig, M., & Douglas, A. (2000). These boots are made for walking: Why most divorce filers are women. *American Journal of Law and Economics, 2,* 126–169.

Chapter One

1. Kammer, J. (2002). *If men have all the power, how come women make the rules?* (2nd ed.) [e-book]. www.rulymob.com.

2. Condry, J., & Condry, S. (1976). Sex differences: A study of the eye of the beholder. *Child Development, 47,* 1417–1425.

3. Details about fetal brain growth in pregnancy can be found in Beal, C. (1994). *Boys and girls: The development of gender roles.* New York: McGraw-Hill.

   The twin study that shows uterine transfer of hormones is found in Kimura, D. (1999). *Sex and cognition.* Cambridge, MA: MIT Press.

   Evidence of differences in white and gray matter of the brain is demonstrated in Gur, R. C., Turetsky, B. I., Matsui, M., Yan, M., Bilker, W., Hughett, P., & Gur, R. E. (1999). Sex differences in brain gray and white matter in healthy young adults. *Journal of Neuroscience, 19,* 4065–4072.

Information on regional brain differences showing increased right visual-spatial skills can be found in Kimura, D. (1999). *Sex and cognition*. Cambridge, MA: MIT Press.

Studies on brain scans that show speech-processing differences are found in Gur, R. C., Alsop, D., Glahn, D., Petty, R., Swanson, C. L., Maldjian, J. A., Turetsky, B. I., Detre, J. A., Gee, J., & Gur, R. E. (2000). An fMRI study of sex differences in regional activation to a verbal and a spatial task. *Brain and Language, 74,* 157–170.

Women's relative verbal superiority is demonstrated in Barrett-Conner, E., & Kritz-Silverstein, D. (1999). Gender differences in cognitive function with age: The Rancho Bernardo study. *Journal of the American Geriatric Society, 47,* 159–164.

Some of the physiological differences in the size of the corpus callosum are explored in Hwang, S. J., Ji, E. K., Lee, E. K., Kim, Y. M., Shin da, Y., Cheon, Y. H., & Rhyu, I. J. (2004). Gender differences in the corpus callosum of neonates. *Neuroreport, 6,* 1029–1032. Also in Holloway, R. L., Anderson, P. J., Defendini, R., & Harper, C. (1993). Sexual dimorphism of the human corpus callosum from three independent samples: Relative size of the corpus callosum. *American Journal of Physical Anthropology, 4,* 481–498.

4. Dillon, S. (2005, January 18). Harvard chief defends his talk on women. *New York Times,* p. A16.

5. Mid-Atlantic Equity Consortium. (1993, September). Beyond Title IX: Beyond gender equity issues in school. *The Network.* www.maec.org/pdf/beyondIX.pdf.

6. Vecsey, G. (2005, January 30). Curiously, Belichick made it happen, but elsewhere. *New York Times,* pp. 8–11.

7. Blanton, R. E., Levitt, J. G., Peterson, J. F., Fadale, D., Sporty, M. L., Lee, M., To, D., Mormino, E. D., Thompson, P. M., McCracken, J. T., & Toga, A. W. (2004). Gender differences in the left inferior frontal gyrus in normal children. *NeuroImage, 22,* 626–636.

8. Killgore, W. D., & Yurgelun-Todd, D. A. (2004). Sex-related developmental differences in the lateralized activation of the prefrontal cortex and amygdala during perception of facial affect. *Perceptual and Motor Skills, 99,* 371–391.

Hall, J. A., & Matsumoto, D. (2004). Gender differences in judgments of multiple emotions from facial expressions. *Emotion, 4,* 201–206.

Thayer, J. F., & Johnsen, B. H. (2000). Sex differences in judgment of facial affect: A multivariate analysis of recognition errors. *Scandinavian Journal of Psychology, 41,* 243–246.

9. Tannen, B. (1991). *You just don't understand.* New York: Ballantine, p. 53.

10. Brain receptivity to social cues is covered in McClure, E. B., Monk, C. S., Nelson, E. E., Zarahn, E., Leibenluft, E., Bilder, R. M., Charney, D. S., Ernst, M., & Pine, D. S. (2004). A developmental examination of gender differences in brain engagement during evaluation of threat. *Biological Psychiatry, 55,* 1047–1055.

The brain reaction to sexual stimuli is studied in Hamann, S., Herman, R. A., Nolan, C. L., & Wallen, K. (2004). Men and women differ in amygdala response to visual sexual stimuli. *Nature Neuroscience, 4,* 411–416.

Men's abilities to shut down the amygdala were pointed out to me by Rego, M., personal communication regarding the National Institute of Mental Health Psychopharmacology course: From research to practice, update 2003 (Bethesda, MD), November 17, 2003.

Studies on blood flow and emotional memory is demonstrated in Bremner, J. D., Soufer, R., McCarthy, G., Delaney, R., Staib, L. H., Duncan, J. S., & Charney, D. S. (2001). Gender differences in cognitive and neural correlates of remembrance of emotional words. *Psychopharmacology Bulletin, 35,* 55–78.

Differences in the amygdala's response to sadness is researched in Schneider, F., Habel, U., Kessler, C., Salloum, J. B., & Posse, S. (2000). Gender differences in regional cerebral activity during sadness. *Human Brain Mapping, 9,* 226–238.

11. Gray, P. B., Kahlenberg, S. M., Barrett, E. S., Lipson, S. F., & Ellison, P. T. (2002). Marriage and fatherhood associated with lower levels of testosterone. *Evolution and Human Behavior, 23,* 193–201.

12. Barry, D. (1996). *Dave Barry's complete guide to guys.* New York: Ballantine, p. 65.

Chapter Two

1. Doherty, W. (2002). How therapists harm marriages and what we can do about it. *Journal of Couple and Relationship Therapy, 1*, 1–17.

2. Doherty, W. (2002, November–December). Bad couples therapy. *Psychotherapy Networker*, pp. 26–33.

3. Wilder, T. (2003). *The skin of our teeth*. New York: Perennial Classics, p. 79. (Original work published 1943.)

4. Amen, D. (2004, December 12). Male-female brain differences. *Brain SPECT Information and Resources*. www.brainplace.com/bp/malefemaledif/default.asp.

5. Rego, M., personal communication regarding the National Institute of Mental Health Psychopharmacology course: From research to practice, update 2003 (Bethesda, MD), November 17, 2003.

6. Ginzburg, K., Solomon, Z., & Bleich, A. (2002). Repressive coping style, acute stress disorder, and posttraumatic stress disorder after myocardial infarction. *Psychosomatic Medicine, 64*, 748–757; also Slater, L. (2003, February 23). Repress yourself. *New York Times*, 48, sec. 6.

7. Baron-Cohen, S. (2003, April 17). They just can't help it. *The Guardian*. www.guardian.co.uk/print/0,3858,4649492-111414,00.html.

8. See note 7 above.

9. See note 7 above.

10. Gottman, J., & Silver, N. (1999). *The seven principles for making marriage work*. New York: Crown.

Chapter Three

1. Chatzky, J. (2005). Why men and women keep money mysteries. *MSNBC*. www.msnbc.com/id/7148333.

Chapter Four

1. Russell, B. (1985). *Impact of science on society*. New York: Routledge. (Original work published 1951.)

2. Pease, A., & Pease, B. (2001). *Why men don't listen and women can't read maps: How we're different and what to do about it.* New York: Broadway.

3. Profiles in Shopping: Women vs. Men. (Spring/Summer 2000). Cotton Incorporated Lifestyle Monitor 2000. http://www.cottoninc.com/LifestyleMonitor/LSMSpringSummer00/?Pg=5.

Chapter Five

1. Beal, C. (1994). *Boys and girls: The development of gender roles.* New York: McGraw-Hill.

2. Waite, L. (2001, June 22). *How bad marriages go good: The case for waiting.* Orlando: Coalition for Marriage, Family and Couples Education.

3. Waite, L., & Gallagher, M. (2001). *The case for marriage: Why married people are happier, healthier and better off financially.* New York: Broadway Books.

4. National Center on Addiction and Substance Abuse. (2004, September 25). Family day—a day to eat dinner with your children. www.casafamilyday.org.

Chapter Six

1. Stout, H. (2004, November 5). The key to a lasting marriage: Combat. *The Wall Street Journal.* http://online.wsj.com/public/page.

2. Gottman, J., & Silver, N. (1999). *The seven principles for making marriage work.* New York: Crown.

3. The findings of an 80 percent rate of individuals considering divorce can be found in Tucker-Ladd, C. E. (2000). *Psychological self-help* [e-book]. Mental Health Net. http://mentalhelp.net/psyhelp/chap10/chap10n.htm; also the German study that looks at happiness after marriage is Lucas, R. E., Clark, A. E., Georgellis, Y., & Diener, E. (2003). Reexamining adaptation and the set point model of happiness: Reactions to changes in marital status. *Journal of Personality and Social Psychology, 84,* 527–539.

4. References to differences in body proportions and pain sensation can be found in Pease, A., & Pease, B. (2001). *Why men don't listen and women can't read maps: How we're different and what to do about it.* New York: Broadway.

5. Taylor, S. (2000). Biobehavioral responses to stress in females: Tend-and-befriend, not fight-or-flight. *Psychological Review, 107,* 411–429.

6. See note 2 above.

7. Arent, L. (1999). How women buy, and why. [Poll sponsored by Harris Poll, Woman.com, and Proctor & Gamble]. www.wired.com/news/women/0,1540,32483,00.html.

8. Austen, J. (1984). *Emma.* New York: Bantam Classics, p. 76. (Original work published 1816.)

9. Hours of work inside the home are researched in University of Michigan Institute for Social Research. (2002, March 2). U.S. husbands are doing more housework while wives are doing less. *University of Michigan News Service.* http://ipumich.temppublish.com/cgi-bin/print.cgi?Releases/2002/Mar02/chr031202a.

   Also, studies that show a balance in work hours within home and work are Rydenstam, K. (2002, October 15). *Time use among the Swedish population, changes in the 1990s.* Paper for the conference of the International Association for Time Use Research, Lisbon. http://pascal.iseg.utl.pt/~cisep/IATUR/Papers/rydestram87.PDF; Statistics Canada. (1995). Households' unpaid work: Measurement and valuation. *Studies in National Accounting.* Catalogue no. 13-603-MPE1995003; Stone, L., & Swan, S. (2000, March). The 1996 Census Unpaid Work Data Evaluation Study. Statistics Canada. http://www.statcan.ca:8096/bsolc/english/bsolc? catno=89-532-X.

10. For a discussion on improved sexual interactions when husbands help out around the house and for statistics on marital dissatisfaction following the birth of a child, see note 2 above.

11. See note 2 above.

12. See note 2 above.

Chapter Seven

1. Gur, R. C., Alsop, D., Glahn, D., Petty, R., Swanson, C. L., Maldjian, J. A., Turetsky, B. I., Detre, J. A., Gee, J., & Gur, R. E. (2000). An fMRI study of sex differences in regional activation to a verbal and a spatial task. *Brain and Language, 74,* 157–170.

2. Pease, A., & Pease, B. (2001). *Why men don't listen and women can't read maps: How we're different and what to do about it.* New York: Broadway.

Chapter Eight

1. Waite, L., Browning, D., Doherty, W., Gallagher, M., Luo, Y., & Stanley, S. (2002). *Does divorce make people happy? Findings from a study of unhappy marriages.* New York: Institute for American Values.

2. Gottman, J., & Silver, N. (1999). *The seven principles for making marriage work.* New York: Crown.

3. See note 2 above.

4. Austin, J. (2004, October 16). Vision of love, family and self. *Salinas Californian.* http://jabba.biztechsource.com/pipermail/ aernet/2004-October/000787.html.

5. Laurer, J. C., & Laurer, R. H. (2002). *The play solution: How to put the fun and excitement back into your relationship.* New York: McGraw-Hill.

Chapter Nine

1. McCarthy, B. (2004, July 11). *Rekindling sexual desire.* Paper presented at the eighth annual conference of the Coalition for Marriage, Family and Couples Education, Dallas, TX.

2. Christiansen, K. (2001). Behavioural effects of androgen in men and women. *Journal of Endocrinology, 170*(1), 39–48.
   Shifren, J. L., Braunstein, G. D., Simon, J. A., Casson, P. R., Buster, J. E., Redmond, G. P., Burki, R. E., Ginsburg, E. S., Rosen, R. C., Leiblum, S. R., Caramelli, K. E., & Mazer, N. A. (2000). Transdermal testosterone treatment in women with impaired sexual function after oophorectomy. *New England Journal of Medicine, 343,* 682–688.

3. Wilcox, A. J., et al. (2004, July 19). On the frequency of intercourse around ovulation: evidence for biological influences. *Human Reproduction, 19*(7), 1539–1543.

4. Ward, D. (2004, August 6). We had more sex in the 50s, says survey. *The Guardian*. www.guardian.co.uk/gender/story/0,11812,1277408,00.html.

5. Lister, P. (1999, November). What 5,000 couples do in private. *Redbook*, p. 146.

6. Day, E. (2004, February 29). Sex really is all in the mind for women. news.telegraph. www.telegraph.co.uk/news/main.jhtml?xml=/news/2004/02/29/wviag29.xml&sSheet=/portal/2004/02/29/ixportal.html.

7. Sex in America. (2002, July 13). *Leadership U*. www.leaderu.com/everystudent/sex/misc/stats.html.

8. Gottman, J., & Silver, N. (1999). *The seven principles for making marriage work*. New York: Crown.

9. Pease, A., & Pease, B. (2001). *Why men don't listen and women can't read maps: How we're different and what to do about it*. New York: Broadway.

10. See note 8 above.

11. McCarthy, B. (1999). Marital style and its effects on sexual desire and functioning. *Journal of Family Psychotherapy, 10*(3), 1–11.

12. Basson, R. (2002). Women's sexual desire—disordered or misunderstood? *Journal of Sex and Marital Therapy, 28*(Suppl. 1), 17–28.

13. McCarthy, B., & McCarthy, E. (2003). *Rekindling desire*. New York: Brunner-Routledge.

14. Moir, A., & Jessel, D. (1992). *Brain sex: The real difference between men and women*. New York: Delta.

Chapter Ten

1. Bartlett, E. (2003, June 10). *The life-span gender gap and the role of medical research*. Paper presented at the 1st annual Massachusetts Medical Society Symposium on Men's Health: An Emerging Field for the New Millennium, Waltham.

2. Kruger, D. J., & Nesse, R. M. (2004). Sexual selection and the male-female mortality ratio. *Evolutionary Psychology, 2,* 66–85.

3. Kessler, R. C., Berglund, P., Demler, O., Jin, R., Koretz, D., Merikangas, K. R., Rush, A. J., Walters, E. E., & Wang, P. S. (2003). The epidemiology of major depressive disorder: Results from the National Comorbidity Survey Replication (NCS-R). *Journal of the American Medical Association, 289,* 3095–3105.

4. Laumann, E., Gagnon, J. H., Michael, R. T., & Michaels, S. (1994). *The social organization of sexuality in the United States.* Chicago: University of Chicago Press.

About the Authors

Scott Haltzman, M.D., is clinical assistant professor of psychiatry and human behavior at Brown University, medical director of NRI Community Services, Distinguished Fellow of the American Psychiatric Association, and founder and editor of SecretsofMarriedMen.com. He graduated from Brown University with a degree in English and biology and went on to medical school at Brown. While he was completing his psychiatric fellowship and chief residency at Yale, he met his wife, Susan. He moved back to Rhode Island, where he counsels individuals and couples in his Barrington office and researches men and marriage on the Internet.

Theresa Foy DiGeronimo is an award-winning author of many successful books, including *How to Talk to Teens About Really Important Things* and other titles in the Jossey-Bass How to Talk series. She is an adjunct professor of English at the William Paterson University of New Jersey.